The GIRL who SAID GOODBYE

ลาเหีย

A Memoir of a Khmer Rouge Survivor

Heather Allen

Rebel
press

The Girl Who Said Goodbye
A Memoir of a Khmer Rouge Survivor

Published by Rebel Press
Austin, TX
www.RebelPress.com

ISBN: 978-1-64339-955-3

Printed in the United States of America

DEDICATION

This book is dedicated to all of the survivors of the Khmer Rouge and to those who lost their lives. You are not forgotten and have your own story to tell. I am also grateful to the following people: Aunt Chhiv Hong and Sok Yann, whose friendship is forever cherished. Sourn Leng, who brought me back to life by calling my name. Ko Pho, whose words of encouragement still speak to me today. He showed me the love of Christ before I met Him. My father, may his legacy live on forever. Ma Mouy, who loved me as her own, and Ma Houy, in whose sight we could do no wrong. Willis and Vera, who prayed for a lost girl. And to my niece Heather who brought my story alive. To Koann, who rescued me though she did not recognize me. My siblings Te, Loan, and Nary, whom I love dearly. My mother, YoKuy, who ran a successful business and raised her children alone. My three children and grandchildren, may you always remember and never forget. My husband, who is my best friend and the kindest person I know. And finally, the God of the Highest Universe and my Savior Jesus Christ. You were there from the beginning.

MAPS OF CAMBODIA

Village names added for reference

PROLOGUE

It is said that a thief comes in the night. This is true, but in my experience a thief can also appear in broad daylight, taking an entire country captive in a matter of hours. On April 17, 1975, in an orchestrated takeover, the Khmer Rouge took control of the capital city of Phnom Penh, Cambodia where I was living and attending university. Many educated intellectuals were sent to prisons or killed in the first phase. Days later, they evacuated the entire city, forcing the people to leave their homes, move to unfamiliar villages, and work in labor camps.

People from the small villages were responsible for taking in the "new" city people and overseeing their labor. All cities across Cambodia were evacuated during this time, putting everyone in the country at the mercy of the all-consuming Angkar. The leaders of the new government were secretly led by Saloth Sar, otherwise known as Pol Pot. After the reign of the Khmer Rouge, the death toll in Cambodia estimated at more than two million, with over twenty thousand mass graves discovered across the country. One third of the population of Cambodia was forever erased.

This memoir is my personal account of growing up in Cambodia, surviving the Khmer Rouge years, and living through the aftermath. Many names have been changed to protect identities. I will never know why I survived and my loved ones didn't. Some questions will never be answered.

My story can in no way even begin to cover the scope of the Khmer Rouge years, the complex history of Cambodia, the politics of the war, or the experience of survivors. This is my personal story, and the events are recalled to the best of my knowledge almost forty years after the fall of the Khmer Rouge.

CONTENTS

PART 2

The
GIRL
who
SAID
GOODBYE
ລາເຫີຍ

FAMILY TREE

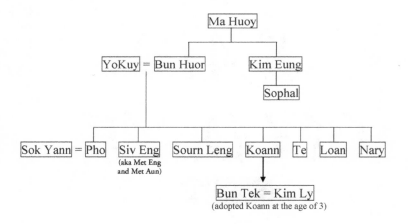

Grandma = Grandpa

YoKuy | Su | Be | Kee = La Nee | Kheat | Chhiv Hong | Elisa | Melaine

Ma Huoy

YoKuy = Bun Huor   Kim Eung

Sophal

Sok Yann = Pho | Siv Eng (aka Met Eng and Met Aun) | Sourn Leng | Koann | Te | Loan | Nary

Bun Tek = Kim Ly
(adopted Koann at the age of 3)

Pouk Chhay = Mai Neang   Ma Mouy

Little Aun | Sok Chea | Sok Kong

PART 1

"Three things cannot be long hidden: the sun,
the moon, and the truth."

– Buddha

THE SEND OFF: 1974

Battambang, Battambang Province

It was long, black, and looked ordinary. That was the point. It wasn't meant for a fashion statement. Mom was always hoping for the best and simultaneously planning for the worst. She knew that communication would be difficult because of the ongoing Civil War, and didn't want to send her two young daughters away to Phnom Penh empty handed. She also didn't trust giving us *Riel[1]* to put in the bank. It's not that she didn't trust us personally, but rather that she didn't trust the bank.

At our home in Battambang, before we left for university, Mom sewed belts with secret compartments to hide jewelry for my sister and me. They were made of black cloth and were meant to tie around our waists, hidden under our shirts. Before leaving for the start of the term, Mom double checked that we had packed them.

"Siv Eng and Sourn Leng, I hope you never need to use these, but you must have them just in case. Be careful with your gold and jewels and use them wisely. Protect these belts and always keep them by your side."

"Yes, Mom," we murmured in unison. We took the belts as instructed, tying them around our waists.

"And don't forget that your Uncle Kee and Aunt La Nee aren't far

---

[1]   Currency used in Cambodia.

away if you need them."

"Yes, Mom, we know," I said.

Uncle Kee was one of Mom's younger brothers who lived in Phnom Penh.

We were excited about the coming day and our move to the big city for university. My sister, Sourn Leng, was younger than me, but she graduated the same year. She was a smart girl with very slight features. I was small and thin, but Sourn Leng was even thinner. She was incredibly reserved but equally sweet. She didn't like to be around strangers or meet new people, so college would be a big adjustment for her.

"Please don't go," interrupted a small but mighty voice. I felt a tug on my arm. "I will miss you, *Je²* Eng. Can I come with you?"

Nary, my youngest sister, threw herself on the floor, begging us to stay. Tears followed, and the crying commenced. Little Nary had a set of healthy lungs. Who could have known that this would be our last goodbye for many years?

My mother, YoKuy, was wise and had a premonition about the war. She had a foreboding sense that things could become dangerous, but she wanted us to continue our education and move forward with our lives. She also wanted us to be prepared, just in case, which is why she sent the belts. Mom's forward thinking and excellent sewing skills would end up playing a role in our survival.

We couldn't drive to Phnom Penh because the roads weren't safe. They were blocked due to the ongoing Civil War. Cars could be driven within the cities, but long-distance travel by car was impossible. Communication between provinces was already stilted. Instead of driving, we flew on a small airplane and arrived safely in Phnom Penh. Even with her forward thinking, our mother could have never predicted what lay ahead for our family or our country. No one could have predicted the savage rule of the Angkar.

---

² An honorific used when addressing an older sister.

NEW ROOMMATES: 1974

Phnom Penh, Cambodia

Phnom Penh, the capital of Cambodia, was the largest and most progressive city in the country. I had travelled to the bustling city several times to visit family. Many of my mom's brothers lived there. When I visited, Mom's younger brother, Uncle Kheat, took us all around the city. He acted as our private tour guide, taking us to all the fancy shops. It was always a big treat to go shopping for new shoes and dresses as a young girl.

Phnom Penh wasn't the same city that I remembered as a child. We enjoyed our first year at college without any problems, but because of the war, we usually rode our motorcycles directly to classes and then straight home.

I was no longer a child living in a small village. I was a city girl. Sourn Leng and I were now students in Phnom Penh attending the University of Health Science. It was a big step to move away from our mother and younger siblings in Battambang, but it was worth it for the education. Not many students who passed high school were able to further their education at university. It was a great opportunity, and we were now independent young women living on our own.

Mom didn't send us away to school completely alone, though. There were five of us who lived together in our apartment. My sister and I joined my oldest brother, Pho, and his young wife, Sok Yann. They were recently married. Pho was a bright, handsome young man and had just finished his degree in electrical engineering. He had a promising career and had recently started a new job in the city. Sok Yann was a beautiful, soft-spoken girl. She was tall for a Cambodian and had a lighter skin color. Sok Yann's family was Chinese, and she spoke the language fluently. Pho and Sok Yann had been high school sweethearts and were still deeply in love.

Aunt Chhiv Hong was our fifth roommate. She was Mom's younger sister and happened to be the same age as Pho. Aunt Chhiv Hong was a city girl who was born and raised in Battambang without the experience of having lived in the country. Although, older, she was short and petite. She and I had a mutual love of all things fashion. Aunt Chhiv Hong was a pretty girl and looked like my mom, sharing her smile.

Our apartment was in one of Grandfather's buildings. He owned several properties in Phnom Penh and was a man of means. The first and second floors of our building were rented out, and we lived in the rooms on the third floor. I studied pharmacy along with my sister. It was my life-long dream to become a pharmacist like my dad. Aunt Chhiv Hong was a student of business with Sok Yann. We were all on our way to becoming productive, successful citizens of Cambodia.

We attended university less than a year when the trouble hit close to home. The Civil War was becoming more intense with each month, but the attacks remained outside of Phnom Penh. The city became crowded as the people who lived on the outskirts moved in droves to the capital for protection. There was no room for them to stay, and many slept in the streets. After a few weeks, even Phnom Penh was no longer safe. It, too, was attacked by artillery shells and explosives planted in public places. One day, the business district was hit. The secretive and deadly Khmer Rouge had an objective—to overthrow the seated government of Lon Nol. Khmer was the word for both our language and our people. Rouge meant red in French. Red was the color of communism.

Mom feared for our safety. She was anxious over the unrest in our country and worried about us being so far from home. I was primarily concerned about security but was also troubled about the possibility of missing a semester of classes. Mom was living in Battambang and running the pawn shop with my younger siblings. Our family was separated with no idea of what was to come.

"I wonder if your classes will resume with all the attacks?" asked Pho. "They hit the building where the professors live today."

"What should we do if we can't return to class this semester?" asked Sourn Leng. She was sitting at the kitchen table leafing through the pages of her chemistry book.

"I'm going to get some extra studying in," I said. I poured over a diagram in my pharmacy book, attempting to commit it to memory, but my mind was only on my family. Would we be able to return to Battambang before the fighting intensified.

"Let's listen to the radio," suggested Aunt Chhiv Hong. "Maybe there's something on the news." We were all stuck in the apartment together.

Sok Yann leaned over the counter, reaching for the cupboard. "We might as well eat some lunch," she said. She grabbed the rice bowls and began to fill a pot with water.

The university was closed and classes were cancelled because of the fighting between the Khmer Rouge and Lon Nol's government. When it was clear that the war was coming closer, I desired nothing more than to be teleported home. I longed to be standing in Mom's shop, on the red and white checkered floor, helping customers find just the right ring or necklace. I was safe there in my home, shielded from the world behind the shiny pawn shop counter. In Phnom Penh, we were living in a house of fractured glass that was on the verge of shattering.

LETTERS FROM MOM: MARCH 1975

Phnom Penh, Cambodia

Today, mothers send their college students gift cards, cash, cookies, and coffee mugs in brightly covered care packages. My mom sent us an urgent letter from Battambang. Most citizens in Cambodia did not have phones in their homes, and communication outside of the city could take several days by mail. The first letter arrived three weeks before the takeover.

"Look, a letter from Mom," I announced as I walked into the kitchen holding the envelope in my hand. I recognized Mom's handwriting and couldn't wait for news from home.

"Read it aloud so we can hear," said Pho.

Standing in our apartment kitchen, I opened the envelope and read the letter.

My Dear Children,

Pack your things and prepare to fly home as soon as possible so we can all be together. We will either be staying in Battambang or escaping over the border to Thailand. Be prepared and wait to hear from me for further direction. I want to keep you safe.

Love, Mom

I folded the letter and started to set it on the table, but Pho snatched it up to reread it himself.

"That sounds intense," said Sourn Leng.

"Yeah, is it really necessary to leave?" I asked. "Can't we just go to Battambang and wait this out at home?"

Pho interjected, "Siv Eng, Mom knows what she's doing. It sounds like things may not be safe in Battambang either."

We had a plan. Things were going to be just fine. We didn't really have much to pack. My sister and I threw together our clothes and some personal items. If we were forced to cross the border, it could be an extremely dangerous situation.

I was unable to send a letter in return to Mom. We were still preparing and packing to leave when the second message arrived.

"Another letter," I said as I walked through the door with the mail. This time, I directly handed the envelope to Pho.

"I wonder if we are to leave today," asked Sourn Leng.

Pho stood at the window as he opened the envelope and read aloud. The letter was franticly written, short and to the point.

> *Dear Children,*
>
> *Please remain at the apartment. There is a new plan. We will fly to you in Phnom Penh. I will bring your grandparents and the children. We will be safe in the city and will all be together. See you soon.*
>
> *Love, Mom*

Plan A was scratched, and Plan B was set in motion. Mom, like most of the people in Cambodia, thought Phnom Penh would be a safer location than the smaller cities or villages. Pho, Sok Yann, Aunt Chhiv Hong, Sourn Leng, and I remained in the apartment. We were happy that our family would be coming to us. My sister and I began preparing for guests.

"I can't wait to see Mom," Sourn Leng said.

"Me too," I replied. "I bet everyone looks different and has grown over the past year."

We were anticipating a joyful reunion and would endure together until things were more stable with our government.

I could picture the reunion in my head. Hugs for my little brothers, Te and Loan. Kisses for my mom, Nary, and grandparents. Good food and togetherness in a time of uncertainty.

"Maybe Mom will make some fresh curry," said Sourn Leng.

We happily prepared beds and checked the food supplies, completely naïve to what was ahead. Mom and the family planned to arrive at the airport any day.

Plan B never happened. The Khmer Rouge had their own plan. When the airport was destroyed by incoming explosives, the communist regime ruined my family's chance to reunite. Roads had been cut off months before. I was prevented from giving Mom a hug goodbye. I was unable to express to her and my siblings how much I loved them—not a phone call, not a letter, not a whisper.

DAY ONE, THE TAKEOVER: APRIL 17, 1975

Phnom Penh, Cambodia

"They're here. Look at the soldiers coming," said Pho. With those words, an eerie silence fell over our apartment. It was happening. It was real.

"What should we do?" Sourn Leng asked.

"Just stay here and lay low," said Pho.

"Let's turn out the lights," I suggested.

We waited in silence in our apartment, occasionally whispering a comment or concern.

"How many more soldiers are coming?" asked Aunt Chhiv Hong as she pulled back the curtain and looked out our third story window.

We looked on as the trucks and soldiers and more trucks and more soldiers entered our city, filling the roadways. It was quiet in our apartment, but there was a cacophony in the streets. Blaring announcements were projected from loudspeakers down below.

On April 17, 1975, the Khmer Rouge regime took over the capital city of Phnom Penh, along with the entire country of Cambodia. The five-year Civil War between the Lon Nol government and the Khmer Rouge had come to an end. I wasn't alarmed at the time. To me, they were just another communist government. I wasn't involved with politics and avoided them whenever possible.

"I hate politics," I said, "and detest fighting and war."

I walked aimlessly around the apartment not knowing what to do with myself.

"I hope this fighting is over quickly, and we can get on with our lives," said Sok Yann.

We were college students who were interested in our studies. We had lives to lead. I assumed that after the initial unrest, things would settle back down. I wanted desperately to check in with my family to make sure they were okay and resume my classes.

Even on the third floor, we could hear the Khmer Rouge soldiers shouting from below. Multiple armored personal carrier trucks were overflowing with soldiers. They filled the streets. There was a stridency in their voice. I stopped pacing the floor and rushed to the windows.

"Siv Eng, don't let them see you," instructed Pho. "Keep your head back."

The soldiers were everywhere and seemed to be reveling in their victory. Sourn Leng was standing behind me, peeking over my shoulder. She couldn't believe her eyes.

"Look at those people. They are jumping on the trucks with the soldiers."

We watched as some citizens of the city stepped onto the trucks alongside the soldiers to welcome them. There was shouting and the occasional smile. The soldiers victoriously raised up their hands in what appeared to be salutation. The mood was a reserved relief. At that time, everyone in the building, including the five of us, celebrated. We watched as others stepped out onto their balconies and cautiously joined the city of Phnom Penh in applauding the victory.

We supported Lon Nol and his republican government, but we were truly celebrating the end of the war and fighting. Khmer Rouge or Lon Nol, it made no difference to me who was in charge as long as the war was over. We didn't have any adults with us to explain the brevity of the situation.

The first day most people in the city appeared to be pleased about the Khmer Rouge overthrow. At first, we shared in a sense of liberation. Now that the fighting had ceased, things would be well for our country.

"Quick, *chap, chap*[3]. Get the broom," said Pho. I ran to the closet in the hall.

"I'll find a white shirt," said Sok Yann. She hastily searched through her drawers looking for anything white.

I watched as my brother tied a white t-shirt onto the end of our broom as a sign of peace and surrender. The girls and I stood on the balcony watching Pho. It was our first form of communication with the new government. Our first message to the Khmer Rouge: *Peace*. Everyone on the balconies waved their white flags. We cheered with our voices and waved our flag, sharing hesitant smiles of restraint with one another.

On the surface, it appeared to be a party, but the balcony celebration was short lived. Not everyone in the city was rejoicing. Unknown to us, many people who held government positions were being arrested or killed along with their wives and families. Lon Nol's soldiers were being murdered en masse all over the city. A message was heard from the loud speakers:

"Do not leave your home. I repeat. Stay in your home, and do not leave the city."

Pho stepped toward the window. "Keep the curtains closed," he warned, checking all the windows, "and keep the doors and windows closed and locked."

Pho was the only male figure with our party of five. It was his job to keep us safe, and he took it seriously. Sok Yann was looking in the cupboards taking stock of our food supplies.

"We have plenty of food and rice to last for several days," she said, attempting to reassure us.

"At least we are all together and weren't away at classes," I offered.

---

[3]   Hurry

We were trying our best to stay positive and not to bring any undue attention to our apartment rooms. Sourn Leng and I attempted to maintain normalcy by finding things to keep us busy in the apartment. Little did we know that the Khmer Rouge had big plans for our country and that this same scene was occurring simultaneously in cities all across Cambodia.

Pho owned an impressive radio from France. It sat on our side table in a place of distinction. He received it as a gift from a professor. The professor had given Pho the radio weeks earlier as he left the country for his home town in France. He begged Pho to leave with him and flee Cambodia. His warning carried a serious tone.

"Pho, your country is headed in a dangerous direction. Please, take your wife and get a plane ticket right away. Let's get out of here." Pho was torn from the dilemma of this opportunity. He discussed the idea with our mother in a series of letters.

"I know it would be a great opportunity for you," said YoKuy, "but your family is here."

Pho was married and had responsibilities as the oldest child of the family. This was the final, deciding factor that swayed him to remain in Cambodia. If he hadn't been so completely bonded to his family, he most certainly would have fled with his wife, and his life would have taken an altered path.

Foreigners and diplomats were fleeing the country in a mad scramble to get out while they could. The airport was a targeted and dangerous place. Days earlier, on April 12, the U.S. evacuated the American Embassy personnel, foreign journalists, and several Cambodians by helicopter in a field near the embassy. My roommates and I were unaware of this.

Later that evening in our apartment, Pho turned on the radio with thoughts of his friend, the professor. When the Khmer Rouge took over Phnom Penh, they also owned the airways. The radio announcer spoke convincingly and encouraged us to surrender to the Khmer Rouge.

"The war is over." The radio voice resonated in our apartment. "We have liberated the country. We will rebuild Cambodia. We have paid the price of victory in blood. Now we will start the cleansing of our country."

The message brought an icy chill to the room. From that day forward, April 17, 1975 was referred to as Day One, Year Zero. The capital city was under seize, and the country of Cambodia would never be the same.

DAY TWO, VISITORS: APRIL 18, 1975

Phnom Penh, Cambodia

Early the next morning, there was a knock at our door. I cautiously opened the door to find my Uncle Kee. His face was a broadcast of deep-seated worry. Uncle Kee was my mother's younger brother. He was a member of Parliament from 1972 – 1975 with Lon Nol's government. Uncle Kee delivered eight new people to our apartment on the second day of the Khmer Rouge takeover. He brought his wife, La Nee, their four small children, and La Nee's two teenage brothers and one teenage sister. That was a lot of people for our small apartment.

Uncle Kee's family owned their own home in Phnom Penh, but my uncle wisely feared for his life. He needed to flee and go into hiding until things settled down. He wanted to ensure his family and his wife's siblings would be safe. Uncle Kee didn't know what would happen with the takeover. No one knew. He didn't want his family to be alone or to be in association with him and his government position. Everyone assumed we would be safe if we were together. Everyone was wrong. Uncle Kee tightly embraced his family in an emotional display, not knowing when he would see them again, and left to go into hiding.

On Day Two, everything changed, and we dared not leave the apartment. Something was in the air, and Cambodia was in trouble. A dark, ominous cloud shadowed the country in the form of small boys wearing black and carrying weapons.

"Look at all the guns," I exclaimed. Pho joined me, looking out of a crack in the window.

"They are just boys. Some of them hardly look eleven or twelve years of age."

"How can they possibly be in charge?" asked my sister-in-law.

Some of the boys were the same age as our little brother. The Khmer Rouge soldiers wore a red checkered *krâma*[4] tied around their waist or neck. The same cheering soldiers from the day before now looked menacing and strange. They covered the streets like cockroaches. Their faces displayed a somber, serious mood, and we were beginning to see them for who they really were.

"Look over there. They have prisoners," said Aunt La Nee.

"They look to be Lon Nol's government workers and soldiers," said Aunt Chhiv Hong.

The silence was deafening, and our thoughts drifted to Uncle Kee. We were all standing near the window taking turns to peek below. We tried to make Aunt La Nee's family feel comfortable, sharing a small meal of rice and vegetables. We never stopped looking out the window, keeping an eye on the streets below. Some of the soldiers had victims in handcuffs and were walking them away at gunpoint. The atmosphere was transformed overnight. Chaos reigned as soldiers changed their tone and started shouting orders.

It became apparent that the new government did not consider us their people. We saw the cruelty of their actions and heard their harsh commands. Most of the citizens who were arrested were soldiers, policeman, and government representatives.

"This is terrible! I hope Uncle Kee is okay," I sighed.

"I'm sure he made it into hiding," replied Aunt La Nee, but her voice betrayed her worst fears.

"We should be safe because we are simply students with no connection to the government, right?" I asked.

---

4 A versatile scarf.

It was a rhetorical question and was left unanswered.

Later that day, it was announced that we would be moved out of our apartment. The Khmer Rouge soldiers shouted from the street along with repeating loudspeakers.

"We will keep you protected. We will ensure that no enemies are hiding weapons. We will search homes to keep the city safe," they said. "You will be evacuated for three days."

Three days. We were assured that we would return to our homes after they determined the city was secure. They were barking commands from their trucks in the street.

The soldiers ordered, "Pack up food and necessities for three days. America is planning to bomb the city of Phnom Penh. We want to keep you safe."

Three days. Safe. Return. These words were a common theme in their announcements. This was the first of many lies told to the Cambodian people. This same lie was repeated in all the larger cities across the country. We started to pack our things, but we weren't quite in a panic. In my innocent interpretation, it was a major inconvenience to be gone for three days, but it did not seem to be a life or death situation.

Aunt La Nee already had her things packed and ready to go as she had just arrived. We began sorting rations and randomly throwing clothing items in our bags. I wondered where we would sleep. I worried about missing my studies. I yearned for my mom and siblings and privately wished that I could tell my mom what was going on. If she were with us, things would be fine. Mom always knew what to do. I hoped that she was safe in our home in Battambang selling jewelry in our shop. I pictured her debating with a customer about the value of his ring. I imagined my siblings at school, seated at their desks and taking notes from the chalkboard. I believed it was only Phnom Penh experiencing this safety evacuation.

DAY THREE, THE EVACUATION: APRIL 19, 1975

Phnom Penh, Cambodia

How do you evacuate an entire city in one day? It was a recipe of lies. Fill the people with fear and pump them with promises. Add a pinch of deceit. Finally, spice it up with convincing weapons. On the third day, the bitter nightmare began. By late morning we were forced from the apartment into chaos and confusion accompanied by the sound of crying, shouting, and gunfire. There was a mad rush of packing.

"Did you get the rice?" asked Sok Yann, her speech frantic.

"Yes," Pho said as he secured our things to our bicycle, "and I have the pot, too."

"I packed some blankets," said Aunt Chhiv Hong.

I threw in an extra pair of clothes and also grabbed my scissors along with a small sewing kit. I usually kept one close by. I packed several other items into our suitcase. It had a combination code and would keep our things safe. Aunt La Nee was getting her children ready for travel and making sure everyone had eaten their breakfast.

Multiple babies were heard among the terrified families. When the soldiers heard the babies crying, they became enraged and threatened to kill us. They wanted order, and they wanted it immediately. The young soldiers continued to yell commands from the street.

"You shouldn't be in there. Get out now!"

We were still trying to figure out what to bring when we were hurriedly removed from our apartment at gunpoint. We had packed some items the day before and quickly grabbed other supplies that we might need.

We left most of our belongings behind. There were so many possessions that we could have taken, but why would we need them if we were coming back? Stepping out the door, I felt the black belt around my waist. It was secure and hidden under my clothes. A piece of my mom nestled by my side.

We followed the rush of people from the apartment down the stairs. With everyone leaving at the same time, a traffic jam ensued. As we made our way out of the building, a series of parents, crying babies, and possessions were squished into a small stairwell. We became a wind of evacuees blowing into the street. I never took my eyes off my brother and sister, but I stole one last glance at the motorcycles Mom bought for us. They were our prized possessions. Mine was green. I hoped to see it untouched when we returned.

We carried everything we could and joined thousands outside awaiting the next order. I stood there with my siblings and Aunt Chhiv Hong outside the apartment with our locked suitcase, food, bicycle, and a hidden belt. *What now,* I thought? Confused, worried, frightened, and angry: the faces of the crowd reflected my feelings exactly.

The soldiers positioned themselves on all sides. They were in front, behind, and beside us. We were surrounded. The soldiers were all dressed in black with red checkered *krâmas*. Some of them were such young boys. What would their mothers think? The Khmer Rouge regime had trained children to do their dirty work. All of them had guns. Every single one. The youngest ones were the worst. They had no understanding with babies and young children. They were like zombies filled with destruction and looking for any excuse to kill. They were controlled by power and hate.

"You don't listen to my order, I shoot you," they yelled.

As we were walking out of the city, thoughts were spiraling in my head. I thought about our apartment. If only I could stay there. I was sure the Khmer Rouge would probably ransack our place. Would anything be missing when I returned?

When everyone in the city was forced to leave their homes simultaneously, my four roommates and I left together with Aunt La Nee and her family. There were thirteen of us altogether. We also joined another family of eight. They were cousins from my mother's side of the family. They lived close by our apartment and ended up in the same area outside.

We couldn't talk much during the slow parade out of the city because we were constantly being watched. It was April, and the heat was oppressive. We had no shade or cover. The crowd was heavy laden and slow moving in the sweltering heat of the day. Some walked or pushed bicycles, some had ox carts, and others drove cars. The overpopulated city was evacuated in a matter of hours.

We didn't share our meals with Aunt La Nee's family or my mother's cousin's family along the road, but we travelled and marched as a group for days. The entire city didn't leave in the same direction. The soldiers with guns made the decisions. They separated us into groups to send us to different parts of the country. From there, the weapons pointed the way. My group was sent south on the Ta Khmau route.

As we were walking, we counted our provisions. We brought along a bicycle, a suitcase, a pot, eating utensils, a blanket, some rice, extra food, and clothes. Pho was smart and brought along cigarettes and tiger balm as well. We took just as much as we could carry with us. The blue bike proved useful as a carrier.

The Khmer Rouge didn't just vacate apartments. They emptied hospitals, schools, homes, and offices. Restaurants, theaters, and markets were cleared. Any building that contained life was void. The first wave of highly educated professionals and soldiers were killed immediately, others were taken as prisoners. We were among those spared. People carefully whispered among themselves.

"Did you hear they blew up the bank?" a man announced as we walked along.

"I hear that money is no longer needed because the Angkar will provide everything for us," said a woman with two young children.

"What is Angkar?" a tall man inquired.

"I've never heard of it," said another.

"This can't be true," said an elderly woman. "I'm keeping my money." She gripped her purse tightly. The highly populated, bustling city of Phnom Penh was little by little becoming a ghost town.

THE MARCH: APRIL 19, 1975

Phnom Penh, Cambodia

As we continued to walk, many families pushed the sick in their hospital beds or wheelchairs. It was a bizarre scene. I witnessed multiple sick people along the way, loved ones clinging to life and left to die alone by the side of the road. They were the living dead.

"*Ko*[5] Pho, look over there." I motioned to a woman who was laid out on a stretcher.

"Please, someone. Anyone," she pleaded. "Help, *jouy phong*.[6] I have no one."

Another older woman was imploring for assistance from strangers passing by. Some patients and stranded elderly were silent. Others used their voices to make their final pleas for mercy. Several were waiting for the relief of death. "Keep moving," said the soldiers with the guns. I no longer thought about my apartment or my classes but began to think about survival. What if it were my sick parent on the road? Where was Uncle Kee? I kept my thoughts to myself. We had to be careful with our words because the soldiers were everywhere. We didn't want to encourage unnecessary attention.

---

5   An honorific used when addressing an older brother.

6   Help

I locked eyes with Sourn Leng when we passed the first rotten corpses along the road. The smell was putrid. The skin discolored. They had been gone for days. It was a real, live horror film playing in slow motion. The gray color. The flies. The stench. The haunted faces of the dead looked on as we passed by. Were they ghosts foretelling our future?

Many families were forced at gunpoint to leave their sick or elderly loved ones behind. Some hospital patients dragged their own IVs behind, receiving their last drips of medicine. Rumor was that the Khmer Rouge soldiers immediately killed several doctors and nurses during the takeover. The patients who did not have family were also killed. If no one was coming to rescue them, they were of no use to the new government.

Visions of death and cries for help consumed my thoughts. The sounds of helplessness echoed our fear as we walked on.

Many wealthy home owners lived near the edge of town. Their beautiful properties lined the streets behind gates and trees. The stunning homes appeared to be empty, and we assumed that the residents had joined with the parade of Cambodians leaving Phnom Penh.

When night fell, we had nowhere to sleep.

"Let's make camp here," suggested Pho, taking a quick survey of the space near the road. "We have no place to go and need to rest."

"Okay, I'll get some wood for a fire," I said. I walked a few feet into the forest to gather supplies. Sourn Leng and Sok Yann began looking through our provisions.

"I'll prepare the rice," offered my sister in-law, Sok Yann. The five of us were forced to lie along the side of the road without shelter or protection. Many of the crowd had the same idea. Although we walked along the road with Aunt La Nee's family and my mother's cousin's family, we set up camp separately and ate our meals apart.

A few travelers ventured into the seemingly abandoned homes to sleep or to find food and supplies for the three-day journey. Instead, what they found when they entered the homes were murder scenes. The owners of the homes and their families were dead. Mothers, fathers, children, grandparents, and servants: they were all rotting corpses. House after house told the same story. Families were slaughtered in their own kitchens and living rooms.

"They were killed! All murdered," shouted a shocked man who came running out of a residence.

Despite the dead bodies, some people found pigs or chickens that were left behind and brought them along on leashes for future meals. The animals joined the wretched parade of people, marching along with the crowd.

I told myself I was on a long, nightmarish walk. I was naïve to believe it was simply a walk. I'm unsure of the point at which I recognized myself as a refugee. Looking back, I guess it was the day we left the apartment. I was a refugee in my own country and was oblivious to the fact. Where were we heading? We weren't in control and couldn't change our direction. Our tired feet ambled on in silence, and we were lost with our thoughts. *Are we there yet?* played over and over in my head like an eerie broken record. I later learned that approximately two million people left the city of Phnom Penh and were spread out in all directions that day.

During the march out of the city, my brother was the one who kept all of us together and obtained food for us by sneaking into some of the wealthy homes.

"Girls, look what I found. I think we can use this." Pho, who would never think of breaking and entering, was holding up a bag of stolen rice and mosquito nets.

I never asked him what else he saw in the house. I didn't want to know. The rice and nets proved to be useful in prolonging our lives. We never needed mosquito nets in Phnom Penh.

In one of the homes, Pho also found a thick, camouflage blanket that had obviously belonged to a soldier of Lon Nol's government. The blanket was perfect to lie on or to use as a cover. It would keep us both dry and warm while we traveled. It was a great resource. We couldn't believe our luck. Pho placed the blanket on the bicycle as we continued our march out of the city.

Many displaced travelers did not walk but drove their cars or motorcycles out of Phnom Penh. They drove as far as they could until the gas ran out. Soon, both lanes of the road became clogged with empty cars and motorcycles, void of both gas and drivers, lined up haphazardly one after another. The gas stations had been taken over days before. No gasoline for sale.

We had all our belongings packed on the blue bike. No gasoline required. It was genius that Pho had thought about bringing it from the apartment when we left in such a panic. Pho walked beside the bicycle the entire way, pushing our supplies and provisions. The four of us girls also carried everything we could. The heat was unbearable and became more intense with each mile. We were exhausted with the burden of our weighty loads and heavy hearts.

Three days came and went. Four days? Five days? I lost count. One day, a Khmer Rouge soldier saw us from a distance and approached. With authority, he commanded us to stop. In the heat of the day, we were stricken with cold fear. He pointed the gun at us, directing his questions at my brother.

"*Met*[7], were you a soldier with Lon Nol?"

We knew then that my brother could be killed because several of the dead bodies we saw lying on the ground were soldiers. The blanket had been our first mistake. A grave mistake.

"*Ott tay, ott tay*.[8] No, no, Met Bong, I wasn't a soldier. I just found this blanket along the road," said Pho.

"You shouldn't be seen with it. It's not good for you. I will keep it for you." Pho willingly handed the blanket over to the soldier.

The practical, useful blanket had associated us with the government of Lon Nol. The soldier spared our lives that day. He made a choice. He could have killed my brother in the street without question. We could have fallen right beside him or been taken to prison—guilty by association.

---

[7] A male form of address used by the Khmer Rouge.

[8] No, no.

Day after day, we were forced to walk along the road out of Phnom Penh with hundreds of city dwellers. Where were we headed? We were constantly watched by the Khmer Rouge guards. We cooked and ate and slept along the road whenever night fell. In the daylight, corpses were seen here and there along the path. We also observed more and more captives in handcuffs being marched away. As we walked, there were whispers. Teachers, engineers, artists, and musicians—killed. Doctors, monks, and persons of Chinese descent—assassinated. Government workers and French speaking people became despised overnight. The list was long, and we were among the scorned.

It was hot and dusty on the road. On numerous occasions, we found ourselves in a place where we couldn't find clean water to drink or use for cooking.

"We should have brought more water," Pho reflected. He was shaking his head in frustration.

Aunt Chhiv Hong looked in the rice bag. "And more rice," she said.

We tried not to complain. I continued to march along with my roommates. Aunt La Nee was close by and walked with her family. My cousin's family was not far away. It was challenging to stick together as a group. We moved along with the citizens of Phnom Penh: store owners, students, and professors; hospital patients, chefs, and bankers; mothers, children, fathers, cousins and babies. The old and young alike were marched along in a slow-moving, panicked exodus.

My thoughts often drifted to my mom and younger siblings during that long walk. *Where were they? How would they find us? What if they came to the apartment, and we were gone?* Ko Pho and Sourn Leng were entertaining similar conversations in their minds. There were no answers. A delta had opened, and the countryside was flooded with rivers of city people. My mother and siblings were flowing along a separate river out of Battambang. The river possessed a strong undercurrent and was taking casualties.

HIDDEN JEWELS:
APRIL 18, 1975

Battambang, Battambang Province

Confusion reigned in all the homes in Battambang after the city-wide meeting. There was no time for the households to meet and confer about what to do or how to make a solid plan. Each family was independent, and the Khmer Rouge had the upper hand with the element of surprise.

"Do we have enough gas?" YoKuy hoped the answer was yes. They might have a long drive ahead of them.

The maid had been sent home days before. With the impending evacuation of the city of Battambang, YoKuy prepared to take the car. Her parents and younger brother, Be, were coming to the house so that they could leave together as a group. Te was still young at the age of thirteen, but he was now the oldest child at home since Pho, Siv Eng, and Sourn Leng were away at university in Phnom Penh. He had important responsibilities with his father being gone. Te stood in the pawn shop and grabbed as many gold pieces and valuables as he could grasp. It was a whirlwind of activity with elbows flying and feet in motion. He didn't want to leave one scrap of gold for the communists.

YoKuy's mind was spinning with the force of a tornado.

"Te, put the jewels in your pockets and in the car," she instructed.

YoKuy also cleverly slid several jewels into the rice bag. "We will take this rice with us," she said. "We must hide everything in the house from looters."

YoKuy's mother in-law, Ma Huoy, was elderly. She lived with YoKuy and the children and sat on a chair in the kitchen quietly observing the commotion. Soon, YoKuy's parents, Grandma and Grandpa, arrived. They lived not far from YoKuy's home. They were a wealthy couple who owned several properties. They possessed loads of jewelry and valuables, yet they brought nothing with them for the evacuation. They fully trusted the Khmer Rouge.

"This rice bag is too heavy," exclaimed Grandma, as she examined the densely packed bag.

"You see, we may need more than three days of rice," said YoKuy, "and I have some gold and jewels hidden among the rice."

Grandma was visibly upset about bringing so much unnecessary rice, and she certainly didn't approve of hiding anything from the Khmer Rouge.

"YoKuy, didn't you hear about the meeting?" In a rising crescendo she shouted, "You must remove the jewels this very minute. You could put all of us in danger."

Earlier that day, YoKuy's father, her brother, Be, and her cousin, Bun Tek, were called to attend a city-wide community meeting. At the mandatory assembly, an announcement was made by the Khmer Rouge soldiers.

"Listen carefully, don't take anything with you because you will return in three days. The Khmer Rouge will be checking all residences for weapons, then you can return to your home. We are keeping you safe," they promised. "We won't even take one needle from your homes." Grandpa, Be, and Bun Tek left the meeting with these words hanging in the air.

YoKuy was wise to the truth and could smell the lies. The Khmer Rouge were not to be trusted. She and her husband had worked hard to build up their business one piece of jewelry at a time. She knew there was no way to pack up all that she owned. The pawn shop was very well stocked with an abundance of valuables and would be a treasure trove for looters. It was up to her and her young son, Te.

"There's no way we can hide the motorcycles or radios, but we *can* hide the jewelry," she said. "We will put some gold and jewels in the ground, on the roof, and on the top and bottom of the display cabinet," said YoKuy. Multiple hiding places were hastily created throughout the house and property.

"Mom! Mom! Uncle Be is here. Uncle Be can drive the car," said Te's little brother, Loan.

His ten-year old feet carried him through the house to spread the news. Things were getting chaotic, and the atmosphere was charged with a mixture of contention, anxiety, and secrecy. Be and Grandpa repeated the warnings from the town meeting like a broken record.

"YoKuy, what are you doing? If they see that you have jewels, watches, or gold, they will kill you. Te, you must stop now."

Be felt strongly that it wasn't worth the risk to bring any valuables along. He removed some of the hidden jewels and gold out of their covertly chosen places, setting them back on the shelves for display. When he wasn't looking, YoKuy and young Te cunningly returned the jewels to their concealed homes.

The row house was very large and divided into two sides. The front part of the house was for the business and the back rooms were the living space. An enormous and ornate wooden cabinet with glass doors ran the length of the shop, displaying the items for sale and separating the two areas. A beautiful, wooden, arch-shaped door allowed for entry between the pawn shop and the living quarters. Auspiciously, a small gap was present between the ceiling and the top of the cabinet. This space was only reachable with a tall ladder, providing an excellent location to quickly throw valuables. Who knew how many days until they could return? YoKuy and Te tossed several of the gold pieces and jewels into a bag and heaved it on top of the tall display cabinet. YoKuy hoped with all hope that the communists wouldn't look there. The same wooden display cabinet had intricate wood carving designs at the bottom, concealing another empty cavity between the floor and the base of the cabinet. The communists were going to have to search with a metal detector if they wanted to steal YoKuy's gold.

YoKuy hastily sewed a cloth belt for herself with hidden compartments to conceal jewelry. She tied it up and handed it to her son.

"Here, Te, take this to the car and put it in the rice bag for now." Te grabbed the belt and dutifully followed his mother's instructions.

As YoKuy clutched the most expensive pieces and shoved more jewels into the secret compartment below the cabinet, Grandpa intervened.

"*Ott tay, ott tay*! No, no! Stop, what you are doing? They promised not to take anything. They are only looking for weapons. Your treasures are safe."

YoKuy didn't listen. She respectfully disobeyed her father. In a mad rush, she discreetly grabbed several more pieces of gold and jewelry and continued to drop the valuables in numerous secluded areas. Ruby rings, sapphire necklaces, emerald earrings, diamonds, watches, bracelets, and gold pieces were stowed away until they could return to their prominent place on display in the cabinet.

YoKuy and Te stood near the back of their home looking for additional places. There was an extended space beyond the backyard where the family did some of the cooking. It was like an outdoor kitchen, and there was a watery ditch area below where the dirty laundry and dish water flowed away from the home.

"I have an idea," said YoKuy. Te watched as she prudently shoved jewels and gold in the bottom of an old wine bottle.

"Look here, Te. Take this to the ditch and push the bottle down into the muddy water." Te followed directions, leaving only the tip of the bottle visibly sticking out of the mud.

Both Te and YoKuy were making mental notes of their hastily made hiding places. Holes were dug in strategic places in the ground—at the corner of the house, near the tree, by the large rock. Nooks and crannies became top secret places of honor to protect the family jewels. The men who attended the town meeting never stopped with the warnings.

"*Ott tay, ott tay*! No, no! Don't take or hide any more gold." The urgency in Be's voice was dominant.

Te and YoKuy were as equally vigilant in their hiding practices as they were in their insubordination to the instructions. The house now held many secrets. If only the walls could talk. There were other valuables that were left there that day—family pictures on the walls and years of photo albums. The cherished letter from YoKuy's husband was left on a stand in the living room. Why would she bring the letter along if they would only be gone for three days?

Her eyes took one last sweep through the house, hoping that she didn't miss anything. If only she could hide her three eldest children in a safe place far from the greedy eyes of the Khmer Rouge. What would become of Pho, Siv Eng, and Sourn Leng? They weren't alone; they were with her daughter-in-law, Sok Yann, and her sister, Chhiv Hong. YoKuy had no choice but to take care of the children who were with her at that moment. There was nothing more she could do. After stashing all her valuables, she barely had time to pack.

Next door to YoKuy's home, Bun Tek was sick with worry about the Khmer Rouge. Bun Tek had lost so much weight in the previous weeks that he looked like a skeleton and could hardly fit into his clothes. Suspenders became a required accessory to hold up his sagging pants. His wife, Kim Ly, was YoKuy's cousin. She was also filled with concern about her husband and what would become of this mass evacuation.

Their adopted teenage daughter, Koann, watched the chaos unfold in her home. The young fifteen-year-old observed her parents running upstairs to a large safety deposit box. She was shocked at the amount of gold it contained. There was a sprinting race on the stairs. Back and forth, up and down. It took several trips for Bun Tek and Kim Ly to carry the gold downstairs where they frantically began weighing and measuring. They did not own much in diamonds and precious stones but possessed an abundance of pure gold. There was no time to properly weigh the gold on a jewelry scale, so Bun Tek threw piles of gold onto the large hanging meat scale. In place of raw chicken and bloody slabs of beef were piles of shiny, sparkling 24-karat gold. Young Koann looked on with disbelief at the proceedings in her home. Something was very wrong.

Bun Tek had also attended the men's meeting in the city of Battambang, absorbing the same absurd warnings as the men of the city. It was obvious they weren't given a choice. Like YoKuy, Bun Tek decided to take as much gold with him as possible and to hide the rest. He knew not to believe the Khmer Rouge promises. He and his wife, Kim Ly, brought along whatever they could carry and hid as much as possible, leaving the rest in the house for the Khmer Rouge.

An old friend from a nearby country village happened to be staying at the home of Bun Tek. He was escaping the war front in the countryside. This man was a close confidant and was trusted by Bun Tek. Koann silently watched as her father dismantled her bicycle and filled the hollow frame with hundreds of gold pieces. There were rings, bracelets, and necklaces. The value of the bike increased with every ounce.

Her father reassembled the bike and instructed his friend, "We are desperate. Please take this bike and keep it hidden from the Khmer Rouge. Take it with you to the countryside. When things settle down, I will visit your village to retrieve my bike and will reward you for your assistance."

The man knew that Bun Tek was in a rough place and agreed. He left that day on the heavy gold-filled bike heading to his village home. At that time, the Khmer Rouge allowed persons from villages to freely return to their homes. The city dwellers were not given the same option.

When YoKuy's brother, Be, reached his house, a few blocks away, the women of the house were busy hiding loads of diamonds and valuables behind a wall of the house. When the men returned from the meeting, they were in a state of panic.

"Quick, get all the diamonds out immediately. Our lives depend on it," insisted Be. "We must leave the diamonds in full view. Don't hide one ounce." He hoped to appease the officials with unquestioning obedience. "If the government finds out we took our diamonds, we will be killed for sure."

Be's family did not own much gold, but instead invested heavily in diamonds. They were in such a hurry, that one of the men injured his fingers as he was tearing into the wall to remove the hidden jewels. A large hole was left in the wall, a visual image of pandemonium. Be's family chose to believe the Khmer Rouge and did not take one single diamond with them when they were evacuated. It was only three days. They would be back soon.

ROAD TO NOWHERE:
APRIL 19, 1975

Battambang, Battambang Province

After hiding most of her jewels and packing many more to take with her, YoKuy and her relatives prepared to leave. She and her three youngest children (Te, Loan, and Nary) were not alone when the Khmer Rouge forced them to leave their home in Battambang. YoKuy left with her parents, her younger sisters (Elisa and Melaine), her mother in-law (Ma Huoy), Kim Ly and Bun Tek, and their adopted daughter, Koann. YoKuy's younger brother, Be, drove the car for YoKuy as she did not have a license. Like everyone else in the city, they thought they would only be gone for three days. They drove away from their homes under the watchful eyes of the Khmer Rouge until the cars could no longer maneuver the narrow roads on the off-beaten path. The cars were soon abandoned. The last link to modern civilization. From there, the family took what necessities they could carry and were marched on foot. They had no bicycle to help lighten their load and left behind many valuables in the car. YoKuy and her relatives walked along with hundreds of others through the jungle, not knowing where they were headed.

Their journey ended in a secluded small town in Banteay Meanchey Province. Day one, day two, and day three passed quickly. They were not returning home as promised. In the first few months, the families were shuffled around from village to village, but they were able to stick together, relying on the strength of their group.

NEW ARRIVALS: APRIL – MAY 1975

Prek Touch, Kandal Province

Kmien tgnay a:tit té mien taè *tngay chan*
(There are no Sundays; there are only Mondays)
– Khmer Rouge Saying

We marched at least ten days in the heat of the dry season.

"*Khnhom strektuk,*"[9] said Sourn Leng with a sticky tongue. We were so thirsty on the long march. It was unbearably hot and no water was available, so we took desperate measures.

"We have no choice," said Pho. "We must reach the water level."

I dug with my hands, as deep as possible, a hole the size of my head. The mud was thick and cloudy and stuck to my fingers. When I reached the water level, it was not clear but brown and filthy. *I wouldn't want to take a bath in that water,* I thought.

"Let the water stand so the silt will fall to the bottom," Pho told us. I could hardly wait; my thirst was impatient, begging for a drink. I scooped up the brown liquid. My thirst was quenched, but later I paid the price. The diarrhea set in soon afterwards.

---

⁹ I am thirsty.

We continued walking until we reached a small village south of Phnom Penh called Prek Touch. We were mentally and physically drained from the heat and the unknown. Each village family in Prek Touch was forced to open their home to one or two city families. The family assigned to us built a small hut and gave us corn to eat. Our bodies weren't used to digesting corn, so our stomachs had to adjust. Prek Touch did not have much rice because there weren't any fields nearby. Instead, they raised corn, tended gardens, and fished. The Khmer Rouge referred to the village people as "Mulethan," and our designated Mulethan family was good to us during our stay at Prek Touch.

"Where did they take Aunt La Nee and our other relatives?" inquired Aunt Chhiv Hong.

"I don't know," said Pho. He was spreading our mats on the floor for the night.

"I hope their family was able to stay together," I added.

I laid down on my mat. It was our first night in almost two weeks sleeping with a roof over our heads. We later learned that Aunt La Nee, her four children, and three teenage siblings were taken to a nearby village. The other family of eight who left the city with us were housed in a separate part of Prek Touch. I was so grateful that the original five of us were kept together and couldn't imagine being separated from my brother and sister. After our long journey out of Phnom Penh, it was obvious that we were not going back home for a while. We slept in a small hut with another family, and when we woke up, the labor began.

I woke up before the light was fully shining through the cracks in our hut.

"Sourn Leng, *kraok laeng*.[10] Time to get up," I said. "We have to leave."

She rolled over on her mat, not wanting to face the day.

"Let's get some water," I said. I poked my younger sister on the arm to get her on the move.

---

[10]   Wake up.

"Be safe girls," said Pho. He looked over his shoulder with a kind face. "And look out for each other, okay?"

We were all sent to work close to the village of Prek Touch for several hours during the day. The Khmer Rouge was all about efficiency. Hard work and skillful labor were highly valued. Overnight we had become a commodity. We were forced to complete agricultural tasks from working in fields to digging trenches. The work was all completed by hand. The Khmer Rouge preferred it that way.

It was obvious that we, the "new" city people, didn't have the same level of skill as the experienced villagers. Our labor in Prek Touch was not intense, and we were given breaks and plenty of free time in the afternoons to fish, climb trees for fruit, or collect food in the jungle to add to our portion of corn. We had to be careful because Prek Touch was filled with poisonous snakes. Once, a young boy was picking fish from a net and was bitten by a snake. He used a tourniquet on his arm, but he died on his way walking back to the village.

⚫

One day, when we were washing in a pond, we saw our Aunt La Nee.

"I'm so thankful to see your familiar faces," she said. "Are you okay?"

"We are okay and are still together," I replied. We inquired about her children and siblings.

"I'm only in the next village, and it is a twenty-minute walk from here," she said. "Please know that I'm here for you."

We said goodbye, and Aunt La Nee returned to her village. She was worried about her husband. At this point, the Khmer Rouge was overbearing and separated families, and we were hopeful the control wouldn't intensify. We still had some freedoms, like traveling to other villages with permission. We lived in Prek Touch for a total of three months.

At the end of the three-month period, the Mulethan began asking questions about our background and education. They wrote down the information we shared. It felt like an interrogation.

"Where are you from? Where did you attend school? What did your parents do for a living? Who is here with you? What were you doing in Phnom Penh?"

We were naïve and didn't know we could be killed for being educated. We told them we were students and gave up our true identities. When we told them that our family was from Battambang, we were informed that Battambang had also been evacuated and sent to work camps. The Mulethan families were instructed to keep records on everything. We were being watched.

That night, the moonlight slipped through the cracks of our hut as a slight breeze blew across the floor where I slept. I missed Mom during those three months in Prek Touch, particularly at night. I wished to be near her. In the absence of light, the stars let their presence be known. I viewed my own private chandelier on clear nights and frequently looked to the moon.

"Mom, are you there? Can you see me? I'm still here with Ko Pho. He's taking good care of us, and I'm looking out for Sourn Leng." There was no answer. "We are together, Mom, and missing you so much. Are you okay?" I conveyed my private messages to the moon in hopes that she received them and wondered if Mom was soaking in the same moonlight. I desperately needed to speak to her. She would know what to do.

•••••

One morning there was good news. We were told the purpose of all the questions was to return us to our hometown. We now had a new hope that the change in government, although initially traumatic and violent, would be short lived. We were somewhat optimistic that things would go back to normal after a brief time. This was a relief, and my faith was restored. Overflowing with the anticipation of seeing our family, I looked forward to working in the shop and sharing a delicious home-cooked meal together in the safety of our home.

We had a new plan. We would return home to Battambang. Hopefully, when things settled down, we could continue our studies at university in Phnom Pehn. I assumed this nightmare was about to come to an end and didn't see the magnitude of what was happening to my country. Many people were given the same impression and were misled with false hope. Our host family in Prek Touch was very kind to us, but I read an uneasiness in their faces and concern in their glances. There was something they wanted to say.

CALLING ALL CAMBODIANS: APRIL 1975

France and Italy

Even Cambodians living abroad were not safe from the far-reaching fingers of the deceptive Khmer Rouge. Within days of the takeover, they spread propaganda all over Europe asking Cambodians to return to their homeland and rebuild the society. Their invitation to hell was disguised as a harmless plea for help. Cambodians from Europe felt compelled to assist their country in rising to greatness. Those who decided to return were instructed to meet at the airport in Beijing, China. Several waves of people returned to Cambodia from Europe. Cambodians arrived from Italy, France, Czechoslovakia, East Germany, Thailand, and America. Many were never heard from again.

Two of YoKuy's brothers were living abroad in 1975. Su was in France attending medical school and specializing in oncology. Kheat was in Italy studying architecture. Kheat heard rumors that things were not stable in Cambodia. He didn't want to leave, but he took a chance and joined his brother. They accepted the invitation, bought their plane tickets, and met in Paris. Kheat was single, but Su brought along his wife and children. The return to Cambodia was highly organized. All Cambodians in France were instructed to leave from Paris by Air France. The flight to Beijing was uneventful.

Upon arrival at the airport in Beijing, they could sense that something was off. Officials took their passports, but they did not return them. Their group of Cambodian passengers were escorted separately from everyone else as if they were with a guided tour group. First, they were taken to meet a Cambodian representative. The passengers expected to see a man in a suit. Instead, the liaison was dressed in all black with a red *krâma*. He looked like a village farmer and had gold teeth. The passengers were shocked and wished to get a message to their Cambodian friends abroad that something was wrong, but there was no way to communicate. They were being watched. The eyes of the Angkar were inspecting their every move at the airport. There was no call to warn family, no opportunity to send a letter, and no way to back out. Next, the Cambodian passengers from Air France were taken directly to their connecting flight to Phnom Penh, Cambodia.

As they boarded the plane, the atmosphere was noticeably icy. The flight attendants were somber, avoiding eye contact like a disease. Friendly chatter was absent, and the eerie silence was deafening. Su and Kheat along with the other passengers knew they had made a dire mistake.

As the airplane circled over Phnom Penh, the two brothers looked out the window at the capital city. From the air, they noticed the empty roads. Scattered military vehicles were seen here and there. The largest city in the country of Cambodia appeared to be completely empty.

Once in Cambodia, they were greeted at the airport by more people dressed in black clothes and red *krâmas*. It did not feel like the Cambodia they remembered. They were driven through the eerily vacant city. No pedestrians, cars, or bicycles were seen crossing the road. Restaurants and shops were void of customers, and schools were emptied of students.

The Cambodians from abroad were taken to the University of Technology campus. Kheat and Su's flight was in the fourth wave of Cambodians who returned to their country. When they arrived, they saw what had happened to the previous groups. They, too, were being held at the University of Technology. The people were sickly, nothing but skin and bones. They had left the comfort of modern conveniences for a ticket to hell. Su and Kheat's group was initially given rice to eat, but they noticed that the other groups were given only *bâbâ*.[11] No words were exchanged; questions and friendly conversation were a thing of the past. They were kept there for several weeks.

The architects did not re-build the infrastructure. The highly educated doctors did not use their medical skills. There were no students for the educators to teach. Eventually all the Cambodians from abroad were sent to labor camps outside the city. The children were taken from their parents and sent to suffer alone. The Khmer Rouge feared the Cambodians who lived abroad. They knew that relatives abroad would sound an alarm if they never heard from their families in Cambodia. They were brought home to be imprisoned and kept under the many pineapple eyes of the Angkar.

---

[11]   A very thin soup made of rice and water with barely any rice in it.

SWIMMING WITH COCONUTS: 1961

Khla Kham Chhkae, Banteay Meanchey Province

"Can we swim, Dad?" I asked in my excited six-year-old voice. "Please, please?" Four little, bare feet were jumping up and down with expectation.

"Are you feeling brave today?" asked Dad in his calm, gentle manner.

"*Ja, ja!*[12]

Yes, yes, Daddy," we shouted in unison.

"You get the coconuts, Siv Eng, and Sourn Leng can get the ropes. Let's jump in before it starts raining."

Swimming lessons in the small village of Khla Kham Chhkae were not like lessons given in the suburbs. Our mother didn't drive us to the local Young Men's Christian Association for weekly sessions with a qualified instructor. There were no fresh towels or clean showers. Swimming was a life skill during the rainy season, from May to October, when our home was surrounded by water. All the homes in our village were built up high on stilts. It was like our own little Venice. The landscape transformed from season to season. In the dry season, from December to April, there were about fourteen steps down to the ground. During rainy season the water rose, leaving only a few steps to reach the water.

---

[12]   A word for "yes" only used by females.

Mom knew how to swim, but it was our father who taught us. Our world was a swimming pool for months at a time, and Dad was the designated lifeguard.

"I've got the coconuts, Dad." I held them up proudly.

As Dad peeled back the brown stringy fiber of the coconut skin, I inhaled deeply. Most people think of chlorine or sunscreen, but to me, a coconut smelled like swimming lessons. The smell reminds me of swimming to this day.

"Here's the rope," said Sourn Leng in her even younger, childlike voice, lifting it up above her head. I watched as Dad skillfully tied the coconuts together, leaving a foot of rope in between. He would lay us on our bellies across the rope with a floating coconut on either side.

"Kick your feet. Faster, faster. Don't stop."

We were proud of our progress.

"I've got it!" I said.

"Now move your arms and don't stop kicking. You can do it, Siv Eng."

I kicked my feet as fast as possible.

After several lessons, the day finally arrived for us.

"Time to take away the coconuts," said Dad. "Swim to me now." We were excited to cut loose the coconuts. As we swam toward him, he kept moving back, increasing our distance goal.

"It worked! It worked! I can swim!" Sourn Leng and I became swimmers one at a time.

My father was wise and made us practice swimming with one hand holding onto a boat. We heard stories of people who had lost their boat after falling out. We often had to maneuver around bushes and trees when traveling, and there was always a chance of our boat tipping.

My mother, YoKuy, was the oldest of eight children, but my father, Bun Huor, had only one sister. Before Mom and Dad were married, they were both raised in rice farming families not far from Khla Kham Chhkae. Their families lived close to each other growing up, and mom and dad were the product of an arranged marriage. This was a common practice in those days and was an important part of our culture. They grew to love each other with time, and it was a good match for them.

My parents were married at a young age in Mongkol Borei. Mom was sixteen years old, and Dad was twenty. They joined in the family rice business and had children soon after the marriage. Pho and I were born in Mongkol Borei. Mom and Dad's business involved hauling rice in bags of a hundred kilograms from the fields to the city. They hired drivers to transport the rice by truck or boat. Later, when we moved to Khla Kham Chhkae, dad continued the rice hauling business. Mom chose to stay home, taking care of us kids and starting her sewing business. My father's mother, Grandma Ma Huoy, was single and lived with my family. Her husband, my grandfather, had left her many years previously. She was like a second mom to us. In my culture, you take care of your parents. It is your honor and duty, and a mother lives with her son's family.

Pho was the oldest child. His legal name was Kean Pho, but all his younger siblings called him Ko Pho. Pho was very responsible and took his position as the oldest child seriously. He was also serious about making his younger sisters laugh. Pho was successful in finding ways to entertain his sibling audience, and his ornery side persistently teased his young Aunt Melaine until she cried. He loved school from the very first day and excelled in academics. He seemed to excel at everything he attempted.

I was the second oldest. My name is Siv Eng So. I was the eldest girl in my family, and my mother described me as opinionated and determined. I often kept an eye on my younger siblings, and they called me Je Eng. All younger siblings addressed older siblings in a respectful manner.

My next two younger sisters were named Sourn Leng and Koann. Sourn Leng was two years younger than me in age, but we attended the same grade in school. My mother wanted to keep us together and chose to hold me back a year and send Sourn Leng early. Like two ends of a slinky, we were never far apart. I was in charge of looking out for my younger sister like a mother bird and keeping her under my wing. Sourn Leng was the shy one. She was only outgoing when she was with her group of close friends and family. We shared the same classes and the same friend groups.

Koann was born next in line. She was a sweet little girl and was very pretty. Koann was born in the village of Khla Kham Chhkae. Adopted by family members at the young age of three, Koann no longer lived with our family. I loved it when she was able to come to our home to spend time with us.

My younger brother, Kean Te, was also born in the small country village of Khla Kham Chhkae. We called him Te for short, and soon after his birth, we moved to Battambang. The babies of our family, Loan and Nary, were born later, after the move. Most families in Cambodia had several children, and we weren't out of the norm. We also had multiple aunts, uncles, and cousins nearby and saw them on a regular basis. In my small world, family was everything.

THE LOKRU: 1962

Khla Kham Chhkae and Doun Chaeng,
Banteay Meanchey Province

In the small village of Khla Kham Chhkae, Mom, Dad, and Ma Huoy worried about us kids. We were continuously exposed to dangers. We didn't come home for lunch in the early years because our school was too far away. During the dry season, it was about a thirty-minute walk to our primary school in Doun Chaeng. During the wet season, we took a boat.

"Time for school, girls," said Mom. "Siv Eng, you need to get up and get ready."

"No, *ott tay*, I'm too tired this morning." My little body just wanted to sleep.

"Tired or not, you're going to school," prompted Mom in a determined voice. We all loaded up in the rowboat: Sourn Leng, our cousins, an older neighbor girl, and myself. No adult chaperoned us to school, so it was a new adventure every day.

Our boat never sank, but we were prepared if it came to that. I valued the trees that grew along the water. They played a role in saving our lives on many occasions. It was a small rowboat that we paddled to and from school. When a larger motor boat passed by, it left a strong wake leaving our rickety boat to fend for itself.

"Hurry. *Chap, chap* to the trees. The boat is coming," said the older neighbor girl. "Row harder, faster," she shouted. "Don't stop! Keep going." Oars were slapping the water in a frenzy of movement.

We made it to the trees in a rush of man power, or more specifically child power, pulling our boat to the side of the riverbank. Each of us held tightly to the branches of the trees as the water lapped in large waves against the side of our small boat.

"Don't let go. Another wave is coming," said the neighbor girl as she looked over her shoulder. We could hear the concern in her voice.

"It's a big one," echoed little Sourn Leng. She was the youngest one. Our boat was already rocking back and forth when, suddenly, I heard a hissing sound.

"What's that?" asked a cousin.

"Snake!" the older girl shouted. I saw the curled-up reptile in the branches and was instantly petrified. I knew of several people who died from poisonous snake bites.

"Faster, faster," I yelled. "*Chap, chap!*" We shot out of the tree like lightning. There would be no death by snake that day.

"What if it had landed on my head?" asked Sourn Leng.

"I would have jumped in the water," I replied.

••••●●●●••••

It was a very small, rural school, and our *Lokru*[13] was a Buddhist Monk. He wore a yellow robe and taught us our Abugida script. This was our Khmer alphasyllabary system for the official language of Cambodia.

"Students, *ses*,[14] please copy your script carefully," said the Lokru. We each sat at our desk and dutifully followed directions, writing our letters in pencil. All eyes were on the chalkboard.

Buddhist Monks wore orange robes because they were originally made from cloth that was dyed with turmeric. There were specific rules

---

[13]   Male teacher.

[14]   Students.

to be respected when interacting with a Monk. We, meaning the girls, couldn't touch a Monk—ever. It was a grave sin. I was always afraid that I would accidentally touch our Lokru.

Be careful Siv Eng. Don't touch him. Don't touch the Lokru. I rehearsed this advice to my five-year-old self over and over. I was especially nervous when he handed me a pencil. I had to be careful not to accidentally brush his hand with my fingers. I attended the primary school through my kindergarten year. I was always seated up front in the class and was a rule follower, attempting to show the utmost respect to our Lokru.

The children wrote with pencils, but the Lokru wrote with chalk. It was a precious commodity in our small rural classroom, where the chalk often went missing.

One day, the Lokru made an announcement.

"Today I will choose a student to be in charge of the chalk." He looked around the room judiciously. "You are in charge of the chalk now, Siv Eng. Don't lose it," said the Monk.

"Yes, Lokru," I replied in a courteous manner, nodding my head in understanding.

"Siv Eng, collect the chalk in this bag every day and keep it in the drawer in my desk. I am counting on you to be trustworthy with this task. Never forget."

Everyone knew that it was my responsibility. I was the "chosen one." I faithfully made sure that all the pieces were accounted for and tucked the precious white chalk in the drawer every night. A few days later, when we were learning our Cambodian alphabet, I got a bad case of the hiccups.

Hiccup.

"Take your pencils, class," said the Monk.

Hiccup. I covered my mouth and tried to swallow several times.

"We will start on the Abugida again."

Hiccup. I couldn't hide it anymore. At first, the Lokru pretended not to notice, then he changed his tone. He looked at me with piercing eyes as he addressed the class.

"I got it. I know who did it. I know who stole the chalk." Silence and anticipation filled the room. The young children, including me, were speechless.

"Lokru, who is it?" asked an older girl seated at the back of the room. The Monk looked at me with suspicion.

"It is you, Siv Eng. You stole the chalk." A rush of eyes were directed at my back with lazer focus. I could feel the penetrating stares surrounding me. Accusation charged the air.

"No, *ott tay*, Lokru. It's not me. I promise," I protested with a shaky voice.

The Monk's words became confident and stern. With increased volume he continued his tirade, "You cannot deny it in front of witnesses."

That was it. I couldn't take it anymore. A tear fell down my cheek, followed by another. My instinct was to flee the room. First there was a sniffle, and then the floodgates opened. I was outraged and humiliated. I had been so careful to always be respectful to my Lokru. He took a step forward.

"You can stop crying now, Siv Eng. Are you okay?"

"No, I'm not okay," I whimpered. "I did not take the chalk, I promise."

"Did the hiccups go away?" he asked with a smile. I looked at him in confusion.

"Yes, *ja*," I replied. "They are gone."

"Well class," he continued, "I guess it worked."

All the students began to laugh and giggle under their breath. Soon it was an uproar. My Lokru possessed a devious sense of humor and was my favorite Lokru in all my younger years.

A SECRET SHARED: JULY, 1975

Prek Touch, Kandal Province

"Virtue is persecuted more by the wicked
than it is loved by the good."
– Buddha

The night before we left Prek Touch, we shared our excitement with our host family.

"We are headed back home to Battambang," said Pho. "Thank you for your kindness. We can't wait to see our mom and siblings."

Our hosts discreetly looked over their shoulders to make sure no one was listening. The husband of the kind Mulethan family quietly whispered to us in hesitation.

"Good luck and take good care of yourself." There was an awkward pause. "You should know that you are not going to see your family. The soldiers are taking you to a village in the mountains far from here." He pressed in. "You must do everything they say without question. You are not going where they tell you."

The family didn't tell us any details but simply gave us a warning. Their parting words pierced as a dagger to our chest as our minds processed this devastating change of plans.

"Prepare yourself for the worst," he advised.

My stomach churned and the hair on my arms stood on end. How could things get any worse?

Even though they didn't share any details, our host family took a risk by saying anything contrary to the Angkar. They showed us mercy by dashing our false hopes and preparing us for a reality check. The family didn't have much, but they provided corn and vegetables so we would be equipped for the travel ahead. They warned us to use the mosquito nets to protect from malaria and were prepared to face the consequences if the Angkar got word of their treason. Compassion was illegal.

TRANSPORTATION: 1975

The next day we began our travel to an unknown village. I sluggishly climbed onto the ox cart.

"Hurry! *Chap, chap.* You're too slow. Get on the cart," shouted a soldier with a gun pointed my way. He was several years younger than me but challenged me with his piercing eyes. We were loaded on the cart along with our meager provisions. It was a long, bumpy, dust- filled ride, but we were not alone. Our fellow travelers were trepidatious, uneasy, and fearful of the unknown. I had more questions than answers.

"Ko Pho, where are we going?" I asked under my breath.

"No one knows," he whispered, shaking his head.

We were seated on the wooden cart with our backs leaning against the outer wall. The large oxen moved slowly, wagging their tails to ward off the flies. Their legs kicked up dust along the way. In the cart ahead of us was Aunt La Nee. She was clinging to her children, her teenage siblings by her side. The other family of eight was not far behind.

"How will Mom know where to find us?" asked Sourn Leng with a shaky voice.

My sister asked the question that we were all thinking. There was no answer. I gently held her hand in solidarity. They took us to a lake channel to wait for a ship. We were unloaded from the cart but were given no information. We stood there, looking down the channel, waiting for a glimpse of the ship. My roommates and I waited with hundreds of people by the beach side. The ship didn't arrive as promised, and we were forced to spend the night along the beach.

We slept there for three nights along the water. We were nomads with nowhere to call home. Our Mulethan family had been prudent to pack us provisions for the long journey. The soldiers gave us additional rations, and we shared our meals together. At least we had each other.

"Here it comes," said Pho a few days later as a large ship with two decks floated slowly toward our beach. Loading multitudes of tired, weary people was a nightmare.

"Line up single file," said the soldiers with the guns.

They herded us onto the boat like they were hauling pigs. We walked on a long, skinny, wobbly board from the beach to the ship. My brother pushed the bike on the plank. I was terrified he would lose his balance with the heavy load. We could have fallen at any time with no rescue. On the ship, we were packed like sardines shoved in a floating can. I sat still in a tiny ball, unable to stretch my legs.

When we were all aboard, the ship left the beach, headed to an unknown destination. I dreaded having to relieve myself. There were two restrooms on the entire boat. People shoved their way to get in line. Elbows were jabbed, arms were grabbed, and legs and feet were trampled. Civility was lost. It was left somewhere between the ox cart and the beach—or maybe it went missing along the road out of Phnom Penh.

We were trapped on the ship and stuck with our arms and legs touching strangers. Never touch a stranger, especially the bottom of their foot or leg. This was a number one Cambodian social rule. It was humiliating and demoralizing. The acrid smell of urine was suffocating and there was no way of escaping. If we had jumped, we risked getting shot in the back.

"How long have we been on this ship?" I asked. My eyes were closed to escape my surroundings, if only in my mind.

"Maybe two to three days," said Pho. Time was relative, blending nights and days together.

"Finally!" Aunt Chhiv Hong exclaimed when we arrived at Kampong Chhnang and were at last unloaded from the ship.

"Stay close by," directed Pho.

"Don't let me out of your sight," pleaded Sourn Leng as she moved closer to our brother.

"Maybe we are here," I suggested. "Maybe this is it." We were so sick of being hauled around and wanted so badly for our travels to be over.

Next came the jeeps.

"Get on the back and make room for others," demanded the soldiers. "Scoot over. Move it."

The five of us were loaded together onto an army jeep with several family groups. From the ox cart to the ship, from the ship to the jeep.

Near us was a woman. In one hand she held a big bowl for washing, and in the other she was holding her little baby in a wrap. Her husband helped her to get settled on the jeep and stepped down to get the rest of their possessions. As he turned around, the truck started to leave. Dust filled the air and our lungs as the jeep pulled away. The woman began screaming.

"Wait, Wait! Stop, my husband!" In seconds, the husband ran, reached up, and climbed onto the jeep. He barely had time to grab onto the rail and dared not let go for the duration of the trip. He almost fell out with every bump, his hysterical wife crying and screaming for most of the journey.

"Please, don't fall off," she shrieked, clutching her baby. "Hold on! Hold on!"

"Lady stop your yelling this second, or I will throw you and your baby off this jeep," said a heartless soldier.

It was a hectic jeep ride. As we hit pot holes, everyone shifted and lost their balance like marbles rolling around in a shaken box. Up and down, side to side, we were traveling at a dizzying speed.

"I don't know how long I can hold on," I said.

"You have to, Siv Eng," encouraged Pho. "You have no choice."

"How much longer?" asked Sourn Leng as she grasped tighter onto the railing. Her knuckles were turning purple from her grip.

Aunt Chhiv Hong placed a hand on her shoulder in a loving gesture. The soldiers drove like maniacs across the unforgiving terrain. Several exhausting hours later we arrived at a train station.

When we left Prek Touch, we were separated from Aunt La Nee's family, never to see them again. Another goodbye left unsaid. We went through many transfers but somehow, by God's mercy the five of us managed to stay together. So many families were separated at that time.

"Mom? Mom, where are you? Mom, come back," cried a little child who was holding a small stuffed animal outside the train station. She wore a pink dress and her frantic eyes looked all around. Tears were streaming down her face. Her hair a rag tag mess. Single children were seen here and there crying for their mothers. Fathers were heard looking for their sons.

"Rithy, Rithy. Where did you go?" A man grabbed me by the arm. "Have you seen my Rithy?" The Khmer Rouge did not acknowledge families. The Angkar was to be our only family.

The train had so many car boxes. They were lined up in succession on the tracks like long empty coffins waiting for occupants. We stepped up onto the train several at a time. The doors shut without apology, and we found ourselves in total darkness. It was impossible for our eyes to adjust. Each box was filled with people. Mothers, brothers, children, and elderly. Doctors, lawyers, craftsmen, and cooks. Once again, we had to stand for the entire trip. My legs shook like Jell-O.

We lost a piece of our humanity with every change in transportation. Traveling to an unknown destination was unsettling; traveling in the dark was unnerving.

"Are we heading west?" whispered my sister in-law, Sok Yann.

We yearned to stop in Battambang.

"Do you think Mom and Grandma are still near there?" Sourn Leng asked.

How I wished for a way to get a message to my mom.

JUNGLE WALK: 1975

Moung Roussei, Battambang Province

We arrived at the next destination, and the train doors were thrown open. The train was stopped along the tracks in the middle of nowhere at night.

"Get out. You—start walking," said a tall soldier holding tightly to his gun. "No resting; keep moving." One by one they forced each train car to empty and walk to various assigned villages in the middle of the jungle.

"Where are we?" a man asked.

We overheard a soldier's reply, "Near Moung Roussei."

When I exited the train, it was so dark I could hardly see my hands in front of my face. The night sky in the country was a new level of darkness compared to the city. It closed you in and touched your skin—a living, breathing, tangible thing. As I made my way through the nothingness, something warm and squishy moved between my toes.

"Ew! What's that?" asked Aunt Chhiv Hong.

The smell answered the obvious question. The warm substance was everywhere, like a steaming carpet on the ground. Several train cars had arrived before us, and the people had relieved themselves as they exited the train.

Lights seemed to appear out of nowhere. We made out six men with torches. They weren't dressed like soldiers, but it was clear they were in charge. We walked along without question on another march to an unknown destination despite our shaky legs and tired bones. I didn't understand why we weren't allowed to walk along the road. The forest was choked with ferns and underbrush. It was the darkest night, with no moonlight, and I felt claustrophobia sinking in with every step deeper into the trees. The only sound was that of our weary feet along the winding path. I thought for a second about running away, but we had nowhere to go. The air was steaming from the heat of the day. I saw my brother's and sister's forms in front of me. I had to be strong for my sister.

The five of us did our best to keep together and made sure that no one was left behind. My mother's cousin's family was on the same path. We were afraid to talk, but I whispered to my brother.

"I don't think I can walk any further. I'm so thirsty, *khnhom strektuk.*"

Pho encouraged me, "Just follow me, Siv Eng. Don't stop, whatever you do. We have to stay together." Sourn Leng trekked on in silence. We ambled on for what seemed like an eternity until we reached a village.

"We sleep here tonight," the leader said.

We slept in the village among the mosquitoes, the people from the train, and the villagers. At that point, I no longer cared. I was grateful for the overdue rest.

TRUCKS FILLED WITH HOPE: 1975

Work Camp and Phum Thmei,
Banteay Meanchey Province

After being shuffled around to several villages, YoKuy, her three children, and her extended family were eventually assigned to live in Phum Thmei. Bun Tek, Kim Ly, and Koann lived in the same village along with Grandma, Grandpa, and YoKuy's two teenage sisters, Melaine and Elisa. Be and his family lived in a separate village with Ma Huoy.

It just so happened that Bun Tek had relatives who lived in Phum Thmei. These relatives allowed YoKuy and her family to stay with them in their home instead of a hut. This was a blessing under the circumstances. Loan and Nary were sent away to child work camps for several months at a time. They endured alone without a mother or father to look after their needs. Melaine, Elisa, and Koann were also sent away to teenage girl labor camps. The Khmer Rouge specialized in the displacement and break-down of families. Te was taken to a separate teenage camp for boys, but on occasion he was able to return to Phum Thmei to see his mother. It was painful being separated from each other. YoKuy suffered the added fear of not knowing if she would see her three children and family members in Phnom Penh ever again.

Miles away from Phum Thmei, young Koann was working in a teenage girl labor camp. She was bent over under the stifling, hot sun, standing in a wet and mucky field. Lost in the monotony of working in the rice field, she occasionally stopped to scrape the leeches from her feet and ankles or to adjust her sun hat and *krâma*.

"Look there. Another truck on the highway," said Koann, pointing toward the road a short distance away.

"I hear those trucks bring people from Phnom Penh," said a fellow teenage girl.

"I wonder if my brothers and sisters are on that truck," said Koann. "I'm missing several family members from Phnom Penh."

"It's break time soon," said the young girl. "Let's run near the road to see if we can check it out."

"Yes, *ja*," Koann replied. "I have a good feeling about this."

"No talking," barked a Mulethan leader with a brash voice. "Keep working. No standing around."

"Never stop hoping, Koann," whispered her friend. Koann continued her work with a dim smile on her face. A residual hope was building in her heart.

During break, Koann and several of the girls walked over to the road. The road was filled with trucks, and the trucks were filled with people. The girls stood along the highway as they passed by, and an idea came to Koann. She slowly removed the *krâma* and straw hat from her head, revealing her identity to any onlookers who may be looking for family. The loads of people in the rear of the trucks sat covered in dust, staring into the fields. All the trucks were headed in the same direction—away from Phnom Penh.

A NEW HOME: 1975

Phum Ou Krabau, Battambang Province

After traveling by ox cart, ship, jeep, train, and foot, we were exhausted. We woke up in the village called Phum Ou Krabau in the commune of Moung. It was miles from the railroad in the town of Moung Roussei and deep in heart of the jungle. Little did I know that it would become our home for several years. We were not going to return, as promised, to our home in Battambang. We, along with all the citizens of cities in Cambodia, were treated as prisoners of war.

Groups of families were assigned to live together in huts in the village. Children ages seven to twelve were sent to child labor camps and separated from their parents. Like Prek Touch, there were two groups of people in Ou Krabau, the Mulethan villagers and us, the "new" city people.

Battambang, my hometown, was nearly an hour away by car. Even if I would have made it, my family was no longer there. We had lost all contact since the last letter from Mom saying that she was coming to Phnom Penh. I had no idea if my family and relatives were alive or in danger. By then, I knew that all the cities in Cambodia had been evacuated and sent to the country to labor camps. Once again that night, I found myself rolling over into the moonlight. It became a habit, a ceremony of sorts. I felt the imagined warmth of the light beam on my face. Was she looking at the moon? Was she far away? Was Mom thinking of me? I took comfort in the moonlight. It was there that my thoughts drifted to my childhood home.

BICYCLES, BULLETS, AND BRANCHES: 1963

Khla Kham Chhkae, Banteay Meanchey Province

There was no swimming in the dry season. At that time, the steps led from our elevated house all the way down to the ground. One of our favorite past times in the dry season was bike riding. As we pedaled, the dust flew and the heat rose. We used a bike for both pleasure and transportation. Even though it was way too big for us, my dad taught us how to ride on our neighbor's large, blue bike. My little legs could barely reach, but I didn't care. I was determined to ride. I learned standing up because it was the only way for my short, skinny legs to reach the pedals.

"My turn, my turn," said little Sourn Leng.

"No way, you went first yesterday," said the neighbor.

They were kind to share with us. Since there were so many of us riding the neighbor's bike, we had to wait our turn. Sometimes we waited all day for just one long ride. It was worth it.

We hoped Dad would get a bike for our family someday, and we knew that day had finally arrived when dad said, "Children, wait for me at the ferry. This week, I will bring home a treat for you. I promise that you will not be let down."

We arrived early at the river's edge and knew it had to be a bike. *What else could it be?* The waiting seemed like an eternity. Time moved slower that day, and the anticipation was unbearable.

"Who will get to ride it first?" asked Sourn Leng. We stood on the dock and saw a boat coming from far away.

"Do you think it's him?" I wondered aloud. The first boat floated by. No bike for us. The next ferry boat pulled into the dock.

"I see him. I see him. It's Dad. It's Dad!" The shouting and jumping commenced.

I held my breath. Our father didn't show up empty handed. The wrapping paper was still masking our surprise. We tore it off in a frenzy, and our bike was revealed. It was bright green, the color of grass and trees. We rode it on the dirt roads for hours without a break. It was my first time riding a bike sitting down. So, this is what it's supposed to feel like, I thought. That shiny, green bike never got a rest, and we were happy to share with our neighbors. Green became my favorite color that day.

Some of my best childhood memories were created in the village of Khla Kham Chhkae where we had the freedom to play and use our imagination. Little sister Koann was the baby of the family and stayed home with mother.

"Children, go play outside," said Mom. "Keep an eye out for your little sister, Siv Eng. You are in charge."

I was a big seven-year-old in charge of my younger sister. She was always under my wing. Sourn Leng followed behind me, matching my footsteps as we walked down the path to find our daily adventure. My favorite times were when Ko Pho came to visit. We missed him dearly while he was away. Pho stayed in Battambang with our grandparents because he had better study opportunities in the larger city. He only came back to our small village for holidays and summer break.

There was a river bank near our home made of a white, clay-like dough.

"Let's make some bullets," said Pho. "Scoop it up in your hand just like this. Now make it into a perfect round ball," he said.

We watched Ko Pho form the river mud into pebble sized balls. We made hundreds of them that day, shaping the white clay between our fingers. The bullets were the size of our big toe and perfectly round. We chatted while we let them dry in the sun.

"I saw some wild ducks down the river," I said. "Let's head there."

We followed the path and planned to use the hand-made bullets for our homemade sling shots. No one owned guns at that time. Ko Pho slowly pulled the sling shot back, holding it patiently. He often missed several times before making a kill. A surprised duck ultimately fell to the ground.

"I got one!" he shouted. We shot at wild ducks on the water and birds in the trees. Pho brought the birds home to Mom. He pulled the feathers out, but Mom had the maids prepare them for dinner.

<hr />

When I was older, I liked to get dressed up and wear lots of lipstick. I loved getting my hair done professionally at the salon and took pride in high fashion shopping trips. Thailand and Phnom Penh had an endless supply of beautiful clothes and fabrics with intricate designs.

No matter my age, deep inside was still the little girl who loved climbing trees. I climbed as good as any boy. My brother and I would search for tamarind, ampil toek, and mangos. The mango trees were too big to climb, so we beat at the branches with a long stick. My favorite fruit was the ampil toek. It had a softer texture, and the peeling curled up. The tamarind tree was larger than the ampil toek. Its fruit was delicious, too, but it had more of a sour taste.

Climbing was great physical exercise, but mostly we climbed for bragging rights. Pho learned to maneuver unbelievably high in the branches.

"Bet you can't climb up here," Pho boasted.

I loved a challenge and I didn't want my big brother to beat me, but Pho could do some things that I could not master. He climbed coconut trees and palm trees which were the most difficult of all. This was impressive, considering he had lost a toe from stepping in a camp fire at the age of two. There was no medical care available, and his toe fell off days later. Pho was forever seen wearing tennis shoes, never sandals. We all learned to climb trees, but Pho was by far the best climber. He was a brave and daring older brother.

MEDDLING, MEDIATION, AND MAIDS: 1964

Khla Kham Chhkae and Battambang,
Banteay Meanchey and Battambang Province

Things weren't explained to us as children. If we did something wrong, we got spanked by Mom. Dad never spanked us, but if we were remotely perceived to do something wrong, we were punished. A childish mistake was punished in the same way as a purposeful act with bad intentions. Ear twisting was another common practice when we were ornery. If we forgot something, we got a twisting. We often deserved it.

No one was required to give us a reason for our punishment, and our questions were ignored. My mother often reminded me that I was born a strong-willed child. She told me this with a mischievous smile. Maybe this character trait contributed to my future survival. Mom said I would frequently argue with her and demand an explanation for my punishments. I didn't care about cultural norms. I just needed adults to tell me the "why."

"Why did you spank me? I did nothing wrong." Whether I was right or wrong, I stood up for myself.

One day I was stepping out of the shower, and Grandma grabbed my arm.

"Siv Eng," she said in a piercing voice. "What have you done? No gossip in our family. Never carry words from one person to another. If I hear again that you do something like this, I will pull your mouth out to cover your ears."

I'd never been taken so off guard. Tears stung my eyes. I was innocent to gossip up until that point and had no idea of the power of words. A woman in our village had asked me a series of questions with the intention of getting information about another family. I was a young girl and simply answered the questions. From that day forward, I treaded carefully in conversation with adults. This was my first grown up adult issue as a young child. I still don't remember what I said, but apparently my words caused a problem.

We were raised in a very conservative family and were taught to never look down upon a person because of their appearance, race or social economic status. We were instructed to stand up for the underdogs in life. This belief was demonstrated by my parents in the kindness shown to neighbors and friends. They had a heart for people who were unfortunate but were very strict with high expectations for their children. The love we experienced in our home far outweighed any punishments, deserved or undeserved. We were taught to be independent, hard-working problem solvers and to show respect for those in authority.

----••••••----

I repeatedly stood up to my mother when I thought I was right and wouldn't back down. My persistent personality was probably reason I was chosen to deal with a neighborhood problem.

One day, after we had moved to Battambang, Loan got in a fight with a much older and bigger neighbor boy. Mom was busy working and sent me as the negotiator to the neighbor boy's home. I had no choice but to confront his mother about her son.

When she opened the door, I started right in.

"Your son was in a fight with my brother, Loan." My voice was shaking as I chose each word carefully. "You should know that he hit Loan."

I began to cry as I was standing up for my brother. It was an awkward moment. Confronting a bully and his mother was a hard thing for a young girl to do. In the end, the boy admitted to his wrongdoing, and his mother was furious. Back then, parents expected their children to apologize and take responsibility for their actions. As we walked away from their home, I swallowed the lump in my throat, but a sense of accomplishment was rising. There was much work ahead to improve my mediation skills, but that crash course may have shaped my future self.

⸺••●●••⸺

Our home was unceasingly busy with customers and children coming and going. Mother relied on the maids to help with daily chores, and they were another constant presence in my home. Many of our maids lived with us and were young girls close to my age. Kmao served us the longest. I addressed her by her first name, but my younger siblings addressed her as Bong Mao. This was a softer name that showed respect since they were younger. Many times, our maids stayed in our home until they got married. We were taught to treat them like one of the family, but they did not share meals with us at our table. This was cultural.

Mom had us work alongside the maids to complete daily chores. The older children and I assisted with cleaning, cooking, and laundry tasks. My parents wanted us to have more than a book education to ensure we would be able to run a household someday. Laziness was the greatest sin, and we weren't allowed to sit around. When I was older, I washed my own clothes. Everything was done by hand.

Sometimes, when our maids returned home for a holiday, they cried to Mother.

"Oh *Neak*,[15] please, let me stay here over holiday."

"We love having you with us, Kmao, but you need to go home to your family," said Mom.

"But I can help with the children and the cooking when you travel. I will miss you," pleaded Kmao.

"Your family misses you too, Kmao. The holiday will be over soon, and you will be back with us," promised Mom.

Some of our maids didn't have a home where they experienced the love of a family like ours. Mom enjoyed giving gifts to them on the holidays. She found any excuse to shower them with love and attention.

"Oh… Neak, this necklace is beautiful. How can I thank you?" Kmao asked.

"It's a gift for your new marriage," said mom with a loving smile. "I want you to have it to remember our family. We wish you the best in your new life. You have become part of our family." Mom took pride in giving them something special and unique. She had an eye for jewelry and bought only high-quality pieces that would increase in value.

The maids kept our home clean, but Dad was into the details. He was a kind and loving father who held to the belief that cleanliness was next to godliness. Dad was an extremely neat and tidy person. When we were young children, it was my father who taught us how to wash our hair properly and trim our nails. He was very concerned about our hygiene and how we presented ourselves in public.

Sitting on a small stool facing my dad, I saw his eyes filled with concentration.

"Relax. Sit still, Siv Eng. I don't want to cut your finger off. I'm just trimming your nails." I was terrible about sitting still.

When we came in for dinner, Dad completed the hand inspection.

---

[15]   An honorific used when addressing an older woman.

He turned my dimply childish hands over in his strong calloused hands and shook his head with a smile.

"I think you can do better, Siv Eng. Please go wash again. I will check thoroughly when you are finished."

He didn't work in an office, but in my memory, he was always perfectly clean. He never let the maids wash his clothes and took care of his own wardrobe. It's safe to say that he was a bit of a perfectionist. We didn't own a washing machine, yet he kept his garments pristine. With high standards for appearance, Dad consistently encouraged us to be our best at everything, no matter how small the task.

WORK CAMP LIFE: 1975

Ou Krabau, Battambang Province

Phum Ou Krabau had been our new home for several months. We were still roommates, but no longer college students living in our apartment in the city. The walls and roof of our hut were covered by the sbow weed, and the floor was made of bamboo. It was an elevated hut but was only five steps up from the ground. The floor was a light brown, and the walls were the color of straw. We had no cooking utensils but used an old can or whatever we could find to boil our water. We weren't supposed to eat anything in addition to our rations, but this rule was often broken. My meager possessions were reduced to one pair of scissors, one needle, a spoon, a plate, two shirts, two skirts, and a black hammock given to me by the Khmer Rouge. When rolled up, my hammock was the size of an umbrella, and I could easily carry it to and from the worksites.

Each *phum*[16] had a Chief who was in charge but under the control of the Khmer Rouge. There were only about thirteen families who lived in Ou Krabau. We were sent out from the village to various work sites during the day. The work camps were set up similarly all over the country.

The girls in my group were often assigned to clear open areas for farming or plant and harvest in the rice fields. I dreaded traveling to the

---

[16]   Village.

work sites knowing full well what lie ahead—grueling work from dawn to dusk with not enough food or rest.

We didn't always work with the same people. There were girl camps and boy camps. Children were consistently separated from parents. Many times, our work group joined laborers from other *phums*, allowing us to hear news from outside our small remote village.

When away from Ou Krabau, we lived in makeshift tents for weeks or months at a time. While there, we were away from our families. My group often slept on hammocks, which kept us off the ground at night.

I considered my new family unit to be Pho, Sourn Leng, Sok Yann, and Aunt Chhiv Hong. Many times, I didn't see them for several months at a time. I counted my blessings when Sourn Leng or Aunt Chhiv Hong were placed in my work group, but more often than not Aunt Chhiv Hong was sent to a separate camp. I slept best at night when my sister was by my side.

"I'm going to sleep now, Sourn Leng," I said.

"Me too, sister," Sourn Leng echoed.

It wasn't our culture to say "goodnight." The sound of her voice was music to my ears. Just hearing her steady breathing brought a comfort from home, a memory of our shared bedroom in Battambang.

If I closed my eyes, I could pretend I was there. My dark wooden desk and chair sat against the wall by the window waiting for tomorrow's homework. We each had our own *paa hum* blanket on our bed. Mine was bright red, and Sourn Leng's was a Kelly green. The *paa hum*[17] provided a light covering for the hot summer nights. A picture of a blooming flower was displayed on the wall alongside posters of gorgeous movie stars dressed in traditional Cambodian attire. We often cut out magazine pictures to decorate our walls, and family photos were enlarged to commemorate weddings and school pictures. At night, our door was supposed to be closed, but we left it cracked open, leaving no barrier between us and

---

[17] A special Cambodian blanket.

our family.

One night in middle school, I left the window open, and the rain blew into my room. My prized school notebook was left on my table, and I had no choice but to re-write everything from beginning to end. Our teacher consistently checked our notebook for neatness, and I took my penmanship very seriously. The rain smeared the ink on most of the pages. It's funny to think about how that event was the biggest nightmare of my entire educational career. I borrowed a notebook from my cousin, Chhiv Lee, and meticulously copied every letter on every page from beginning to end.

----••●●◆●●••----

Chhiv Lee was my best friend, and I missed her. I had no way of knowing that she was with my sister Koann that night in a separate work camp. Chhiv Lee attended classes with me at the University of Health Science in Phnom Penh and was studying in the same pharmacy program. Fate took her on a very different path when she flew home to Battambang for a family wedding only two weeks before the April 17 takeover. I never saw her again.

In Ou Krabau, timing was crucial to seeing my family. Sometimes when we arrived at our hut in Ou Krabau, my brother and Sok Yann had not yet returned from the married couples work site. Those were disappointing days; Sourn Leng and I were left alone to fend for ourselves. Other times, the Khmer Rouge required all workers to attend the re-education Angkar meetings at the same time. Those were precious days when Sourn Leng and I could see our brother and sister in-law. I would willingly sit and listen to the Khmer Rouge chants, proverbs, and lectures as long as I could sit with my family. To be near them brought life to my bones and refilled the void in my heart.

MEETINGS AND THE MULETHAN: 1975

Ou Krabau, Battambang Province

tâ :va : khmang prâ :chhang khmaoch
("He who protests is an enemy; he who opposes is a corpse.")
– Angkar Slogan

What was the Angkar, and why did it control everything? Why did it take all our possessions and maliciously separate parents from children? It was evident that "Angkar" was the most important word. It was to be our religion and food source. It served as our parent, brother, sister, ruler and provider. Angkar was our new everything. With clenched fists, we chanted along during the mandatory propaganda meetings, organized to brainwash us each night.

We soon learned the hierarchy of the new society. In the utopian philosophy of the Khmer Rouge, we were all considered equal. In reality, there were definitive, tiered social classes. It wasn't specifically taught in a formal lesson but was evident in the day to day interactions. There were several new words created by the Khmer Rouge to refer to people from the different social classes. Even our language was kidnapped and held captive. The new vocabulary, like a disease infected our everyday speech. If anything, it was a vocabulary lesson in *inequality*. The village meetings were filled with sayings, music, and slogans of the greatness of the Angkar. These sayings introduced the dismantling of knowledge, reason, and everything good. We were forced to repeat slogans and praises of the greatness of Angkar—or else.

The hierarchy was as follows:

1. Angkar: the all-knowing everything. The Angkar was an ideology.
2. Pol Pot and his officials: the decision makers and creators of Angkar.
3. Khmer Rouge soldiers: heartless robots who carried out the wishes of Pol Pot.
4. Chhlop: armed secret service agents also known as tattletales.
5. Village Chiefs: the leaders of the village, given special privileges related to rights, ownership, and food.
6. Mulethan: the village farmers who lived in the country before the takeover and were put in charge of the "new" people.
7. "New" or April 17 people: the city dwellers who were evacuated from their homes and forced into slave labor. This group was both the largest and the lowest on the totem pole.

The Mulethan village people were deemed by the Khmer Rouge to be the true Cambodians and the pure race. They were farmers and did not have an opportunity for formal education. Many of these peace-loving villages had been taken over by the Khmer Rouge years earlier and given an education in despising the city people. They were taught to hate us to the bone. Compassion and pity were often nowhere to be found when a laborer was suffering from illness, malnutrition, or over-work. When a worker was beaten beyond recognition, some of the cruel Mulethan would laugh. They were abetting the Khmer Rouge in cleaning up their country and purifying their race. A picture of xenophobia. For some, the hatred ran deep.

The Mulethan were used like puppets to control and guard us. Most of their children grew up to be Khmer Rouge soldiers or Chhlop. Many of them didn't have a choice. The Chhlop were the young spies for the Khmer Rouge. They were like pesky cockroaches lurking everywhere. They crouched behind bushes, under huts, and behind trees. The Chhlop seemed to appear out of nowhere. Though unseen, they were a strong presence, the eyes of the Angkar, always watching, never sleeping. Secrets were safe with no one, and it was difficult to determine who could be trusted. The Chhlop were listening, the Mulethan were watching, and even the city people were encouraged to rat out any behavior that was considered individualistic. Tattletales were rewarded. The soldiers didn't live in the villages. I never knew where they slept, but they visited the villages unannounced to make sure that the Mulethan were doing their jobs.

The Mulethan were treated much better than the new people, and the Khmer Rouge officials made big promises to them. They were assured that they would play an important role under the new regime. The Mulethan cultivated their own gardens and received adequate rice portions from the village Chief. They were also permitted to speak at the Angkar meetings.

The village people of Ou Krabau were now charged with the daunting task of overseeing the housing, feeding, and labor of us—the April 17 people. Overnight, they became guards, work leaders, and managers. They had quotas to make. The Mulethan no longer had to work for a living, yet they needed us to perform the labor for the new regime before our impending deaths. That was our only role in this new upside-down government.

The Khmer Rouge utopian society was no Robin Hood. They did not steal from the rich and give to the poor. They stole from the rich, took control of the poor, and killed both rich and poor alike. The Angkar hoarded all resources. Where did all the rice go? They certainly didn't feed it to us. Who ate all the vegetables growing in the community garden? It was obvious that some citizens were more *equal* than others. The Angkar did not eat the rice or bounty of the fields. The Angkar feasted on the death of families and the demise of joy. The belly of the Angkar was full while the workers were famished. Violence and hatred replaced kindness and compassion.

The Khmer Rouge planted weeds of suffering and persecution. It was passed on from Pol Pot's leadership and sent down the chain of command. They took over our school buildings meant to grow the mind, choking out any resemblance of wisdom. This seed of brutality did not bloom everywhere. The people of Cambodia planted their own seeds of humanity and compassion. They bloomed in the shadows and blossomed in the dark, void of water and nutrients. These seeds were taking root and sprouting unseen. They were evident within the walls of the family huts, in villages, and at work sites between complete strangers. Demonstrations of benevolence were growing in the midst of sorrow.

A handful of the Mulethan committed acts of covert compassion. They sympathized with our situation and saw us as people with families. They recognized that the Angkar ideology was a disease that was eradicating our people, our country, and our land. It was harming both the Mulethan and the city people alike. Many of the Mulethan wanted to help, but they felt trapped. They were actors in a theatre cast as the villains. If they didn't pretend to support the communists, they and their family would be tortured or killed. If the villagers were judged to be too "soft" with a laborer, they would suddenly disappear. Death by kindness.

TREE CLIMBING: 1975

Phum Ou Krabau, Battambang Province

In the first year living under the Khmer Rouge, we often climbed trees to get a taste of our favorite fruits.

"Let's go climbing this afternoon during our break," said Pho.

"Yes. *Ja, ja.* I want some tamarind today," I replied.

"I can taste it already," said Sourn Leng with a smile.

Our faces brightened with the anticipation of the tartness of the fruit. Sometimes I used a vine to reach the branches of the tamarind tree. The branches were tough and strong. Tamarind was my favorite tree to climb and my favorite fruit to eat during captivity. The sturdy branches would bend down when I walked on them, but they wouldn't break.

Hand over hand, I climbed to the top of the canopy. Pho and I both ascended high up in the trees to get to the fruit and inhale a breath of fresh air. We were far from the Angkar and closer to the moon and stars. We collected the fruit in our *krâmas* and dropped it down on the ground. My sister was not a confident climber but helped in other ways.

"Look out below, Sourn Leng," I called. She stood down below looking up at us in the towering branches. The fruit made a plopping sound as it hit the grass below.

"I got it." Sourn Leng watched for the fruit as it fell to the ground. It was a team effort.

Tamarind was abundant in Cambodia and grew wild in the jungle. I also craved the sweetness of the mango and guava, but these trees were heavily guarded and grown in orchards.

The tamarind fruit looks like an oversized peapod. When it's ripe, the skin turns brown and is easily cracked. Sometimes we would crack the pods and eat them in the jungle, but we always brought some home for later. It was a well-deserved reward for our hard work. It tasted tart like a lime or lemon, but compared to the rest of our diet, tamarind was like a candy.

Not everyone had climbing skills. Most people only ate the fruit from the lower branches where they could reach it from the ground. When the lower fruits were harvested, we were able to climb up high for a taste. Our days as children in Khla Kham Chhkae paid off.

"Siv Eng, you're moving too fast," Pho warned. "Please don't fall."

"I'm going to get to the fruit first if you don't hurry," I laughed. A smile was a rare and precious thing. I was proud of the fact that I could provide for our family and liked to move quickly in the tree to find the most efficient path to the ground. In my mind, we were back in Khla Kham Chhkae, racing for bragging rights.

In the early months of the Khmer Rouge rule, we could eat fruit from trees without getting in trouble. Soon, though, even the fruit growing in the highest branches belonged to the Angkar. The Angkar owned the trees and the fruit. The Angkar owned everything.

In the trees, the songs of the birds were heard loud and clear. It was music to our ears. The songs of Cambodia had been lost and abandoned. Oh to be a bird. Our country had become a cage, but the birds were free. If only their songs could tell of our plight. Would anyone listen?

My college roommates and I tried our best to adapt in the bizarre new world. A world where music, dancing, and movies were against the law. Medicine, education, religion, family meals and friendly conversations became illegal. Money, markets, home ownership, and even the wearing of glasses were banned. Personal possessions were strictly forbidden, as all worldly property belonged to the Angkar. Opinions were silenced, and soon everyone in the country was shut off from the rest of the world. Cambodia had become a sealed crypt.

Cambodians were known for their beautiful, colorful clothing, but even our vibrant fabrics were soon to be masked under the all-consuming shadow of the Angkar. Everything was turning black.

THE DEATH OF COLOR: 1975

Phum Ou Krabau, Battambang Province

After several months of living at Phum Ou Krabau, the strongest front-line laborers were given a gift. The soldiers supplied one piece of black fabric to each worker to make as a wrap-around skirt or pair of pants. Not everyone got the new fabric. I was not one of the chosen. I was too weak and could not keep up with the rigorous demands of working in the rice fields or digging ditches.

The Khmer Rouge wanted to put their best foot forward for observers who came to witness the greatness of our new country. High-ranking Khmer Rouge officials occasionally came to the fields to view our progress. The leaders wanted us to look well dressed and organized for their propaganda, front pages, and visiting officials. Sometimes officials from other countries like China came to observe the front-line workers. The Khmer Rouge was showing off its prized possessions in a country where possessions were against the law.

I didn't bring many clothes with me when fleeing the apartment. I had to wear the same two or three shirts and pants over and over again. The fashion of the day had very layered pant legs with an abundance of material and pleats. The bigger, the better. I remember proudly wearing them to school in Battambang along with my girlfriends. It was like a fashion show. The boys would tease us about our floppy pants, and we would defiantly roll our eyes. So immature. They said our pants were so big we could sweep the street with them. We ignored their critiques and wore them with our heads held high. What did boys know about fashion?

My favorite shirt was a white and red polka dotted blouse that had pleats in the front and fit loosely. It was the current style but looked somewhat like a maternity top. When I wore the blouse at Ou Krabau, a woman spoke to my Aunt Chhiv Hong.

Her voice was accusing. "Isn't your sister single? How is it that she is pregnant?"

I never wore that blouse again. I didn't want to stand out in any way, and I certainly didn't want to look pregnant and bring shame on my family.

After the first few months, everyone was ordered to dress in an all-black uniform. We were forced to emulate the same soldiers who were controlling us.

A Mulethan woman in our village was chosen to teach us how to transform our colorful wardrobe into a drab, dull uniform. "Watch and listen," she said. We observed as she took a fruit in her hands, broke it up and placed it in a bowl. She crushed the fruit with a mortar and pestle and then added water, making a thick paste. Next, she took a beautiful yellow *krâma* and swirled it around in the murky, dark liquid. The first soaking did not change the color significantly, but after waiting overnight, the *krâma* was a dingy, grey charcoal. When the process was repeated, the *krâma* turned black.

As a child, I remembered seeing people in Khla Kham Chhkae dying their clothes many colors using fruit and bark. I was no longer the observer. It was now my turn.

I learned to dye my clothes that day. It was the most absurd fashion lesson. We repeated this process in our huts with a few clothing items at a time over several days. It was a painstaking process with a gloomy end product.

A yellow blouse became black. An orange scarf was turned a dark shade of grey. A green skirt, shabby charcoal. If it was in their power, it seemed the Khmer Rouge would turn the vegetation and trees black. What would stop them from coloring the sky? Then they might feel more at home. Purple and blue shades didn't take long to dye. My polka dot blouse and trendy pants went into the pot. It was a dark transformation and very fitting to our circumstances. A dim cloud had covered our country and now it covered the clothes on our back. That same dark veil followed us wherever we went like the leeches in the rice fields and the lice in our hair.

LOCKS AND LEECHES: 1975

Phum Ou Krabau, Battambang Province

All of us had lice, but Aunt Chhiv Hong had the worst case. It was a real problem at her specific work camp. When the three of us girls tried to remove the lice, we found hundreds of them. Aunt Chhiv Hong had thick, beautiful, coffee colored locks, and eventually I had to shave her gorgeous head of hair. It was the only way to get rid of the lice.

Weeks later, a new order was given: "All women will cut their hair short immediately." Individualism was forbidden, and this was one more way for the Khmer Rouge to demand uniformity on a personal level. My hair was already short when the communists took over. I had cut it to a short trendy look before leaving for Phnom Penh. That was one less head of hair for the Khmer Rouge to change. Sourn Leng had long beautiful tresses, and it wasn't something that could be hidden. I used the same scissors that were always by my side. Aunt Chhiv Hong cried for my sister as her long locks fell to the ground. It felt as if I was stripping my sister of her dignity.

Sourn Leng was a beautiful, young seventeen-year-old girl with the world ahead of her. As her hair dropped to the ground, her life fell apart before her eyes, but her beauty didn't fade.

One day during the second year at Ou Krabau, the girls and I decided to go into the pond to find snails. They were packed with protein and considered a tasty treat. The pond snails were easily found floating at the surface. We had nothing to use to catch fish, but we could catch the snails by hand. The pond was mucky, but we were used to getting leeches in the rice fields. They were disgusting, but we simply scraped them off with a vine.

"Ouch!" screamed Aunt Chhiv Hong with a panicked look in her eye. I stopped my search for snails and ran to her. She rushed back to the shore to release the leech that was latched onto her toe. We couldn't believe our eyes. The leech was huge, bulging with a monstrous, greenish hue. Its skin was stretched, translucent and puffy. We were horrified at the ugly state of the creature. It began sucking her blood in the few seconds it took to latch on. It was up to us to remove the leech. We were screaming, and Aunt Chhiv Hong was scared to death. We stood there for a few seconds, too terrified to move. We didn't dare touch it by hand.

"Quick, *chap, chap*. Grab the lily pads," I commanded. We jumped back into the pond not thinking about what was lurking below the surface and each grabbed a handful of lilies.

"Put them here," I said. We improvised and used the lily leaves to drape over the body of the large leech. Even in an emergency we couldn't bear to touch the slimy creature. We pulled and squeezed to force the leech to back away. It was at least six inches in length and stretched even further as we pulled, like a Stretch Armstrong with fangs. We did not let go but fought for our Aunt Chhiv Hong.

The slimy monster eventually backed away from her foot, releasing its fangs. The moment we threw it onto the ground, it started to crawl away. It moved itself like an alien inchworm. We were not about to allow this scenario to happen again. We committed murder that day. Sourn Leng and I killed it with rocks and smashed it to pieces. It had preyed on its last victim. Aunt Chhiv Hong closed her eyes. She was too traumatized to help and couldn't bear to face her attacker. From that day on, we all thought twice before stepping into a murky pond.

CATCH AND RELEASE: 1976

A Work Camp Site Near Phum Ou Krabau,
Battambang Province

A Mulethan work leader approached our hut one morning.

"Get up Met *Neary*.[18] You will travel to another village today."

Sourn Leng, Aunt Chhiv Hong, and I were sent out together with our teenage group to a labor site outside of Ou Krabau. We trudged along the path as we left our village. Our task that day was to look for a kind of plant that was used to make shelters. Looking for sbow was better than digging ditches or planting rice in the wet soggy fields.

The village needed to build new huts and repair the existing huts. The sbow plant was a weed used to create the roof covering. Some sbow grew in the jungle and other sbow grew wild along the edges of fields. As we were searching, Sourn Leng and I walked along a mung bean field, and Aunt Chhiv Hong went another way. Mung beans were full of protein and could easily replace the nutrients we were missing.

There were a variety of wild plants growing along the road near the field. Sourn Leng and I collected a reasonable amount of sbow before the designated break time. When I had my back turned, Sourn Leng's taste buds called to her. She walked away from me along the mung bean field.

---

18   A female form of address used by the Khmer Rouge

A starving girl saw food at her feet. It was right there in the field inches away. Sustenance was within her grasp, and when no one was looking, she snuck a few mung beans. Barely a spoonful.

Unfortunately, a sneaky Chhlop had been spying from a distance. He was waiting in ambush for someone to pick just one bean.

"You, Met Neary, put it down. You are stealing from Angkar."

She was caught.

I was concentrating on picking sbow, and the next time I looked up to check on her, Sourn Leng was gone. She was nowhere to be seen. I stopped searching for sbow and began searching for my sister. It was a good thing that we frequently checked on each other. If I hadn't been close by when they took her away, I would have never found her. I eventually saw her standing with a young Chhlop and ran to them.

Every time a loved one was seen with a soldier or Chhlop, it was a problem. It could mean an arrest, a violent beating, or death. It could mean the last goodbye. My heart pounded with heavy, heaving beats. Fight won over flight. I decided to project my voice over the thumping in my chest.

"Excuse me, Met Bong. What did my sister do?"

"She's a thief. She stole mung beans from the Angkar," the Chhlop shouted. I had no weapon but my words.

"I'm so sorry, Met Bong," I apologized in the most convincing voice I could muster. "My sister is not a talker. Met Bong, will you please forgive her?" The drumming in my chest pushed me to be bolder and courage grew with each word. "Please have mercy. She couldn't resist, Met Bong. She's starving."

The Chhlop shook his head and motioned with his hand. He could have taken her away right then.

"Come with me. We will take this matter to the Chief," he said. He walked both of us back to the village of Ou Krabau to the hut of the high Chief.

Once again, I pleaded the case for my sister. "Please have mercy and let her go. You see, *Pouk*,[19] she was only hungry. It was only a few beans."

My sister's future was in the Chief's hands. He could have severely punished her or sent her to prison, but he didn't. The Chief showed mercy on us and sent us back to our post to search for more sbow weed. There was no doubt that we had escaped a very serious situation. We were never so thankful to return to a mindless task.

My actions that day were a combination of bravery and stupidity. She was my younger sister, and I needed to take care of her. She looked to me and our older brother, Ko Pho, like a mom and dad. Sourn Leng was a very smart girl but was not a strong communicator in troubled situations. My love for her did the negotiating that day.

---

[19]   Khmer word for father.

SEWING FOR SURVIVAL: 1976

Ou Krabau, Battambang Province

My mother made my clothes when I lived at home, but all my favorite pieces were left at the apartment. I liked to sew clothes for my little sister, Koann, for fun, but I didn't have any formal training. I had learned the basics of stitching in high school and was glad that I paid attention in home economics class. In Ou Krabau, I quickly learned the value of sewing. What had previously been a casual hobby became a survival skill.

Since I had no way of purchasing new fabric to make clothes, I often fashioned items out of whatever scraps I had and patched clothes for my brother and sister. There was no sewing machine available, so everything was sewn by hand. If I had an old skirt that I couldn't wear anymore, I cut it and shaped it into a shirt. Out of necessity, I learned to convert skirts to shirts, scarves, or whatever was needed. At that time, the girls wore big pant legs with quite a bit of fabric, and I made use of every square inch.

Who would have known that my love of sewing and fashion as a child would end up being such a valuable asset under communist rule? When the thread ran out, I improvised. Sometimes I had to separate a cloth into individual threads. It was a painstaking process, but this way I never ran out. I brought scissors and needles with me the day I left my apartment and didn't go anywhere without them.

THE SINGER: 1961

Khla Kham Chhkae, Banteay Meanchey Province

At an early age, when Dad was still in the rice business, I often watched Mom sew. She owned a Singer treadle sewing machine which didn't require electricity. She started the hand wheel and rocked both feet back and forth in a rhythm on the treadle, working late into the night under the light of the Mansong lantern. Mom was a popular seamstress in the area. Customers came by ox cart from several hours away to drop off their material so Mom could work her magic. She designed and created beautiful women's clothing with intricate designs. I was impressed with her quick fingers and the speedy motion of the sewing machine. The rapid movement was mesmerizing. Her feet, her hands, and the machine became one in a sewing dance. I wanted so much to sew like Mom. She was my idol.

"Siv Eng, what are you doing, silly girl?" I was spiraling around unaware. My little feet tripping over themselves.

"I'm spinning like the Singer, Mom. See?"

"Stop that now. You need to go help Grandma Ma Huoy prepare the mung bean cakes. She is making the dough into balls."

"Okay," I said running off to the kitchen.

I never minded helping Grandma Ma Huoy. She made so many kinds of sweet rice cakes, fried bananas, and cakes from cooked mung beans and pork. Most of the food went to the Buddhist temple for special celebrations at the New Year in April and at memorial services in September. I loved helping Ma Huoy prepare food in the kitchen, but I was most helpful with eating the cakes.

Mom was extremely busy with her sewing business. When the holidays came, she sewed late into the night. She also designed and created the clothing for our growing family. Stores didn't sell clothing, they sold material. Seamstresses were the designers who made the dresses, *krâmas*, skirts, shirts, and pants. In Thailand, pre-made clothing could be purchased, but not in Khla Kham Chhkae. There was typically a mountain of sewing projects kept in a basket next to the Singer. The piles of fabric patiently waited to be made into something beautiful.

Mom had a strong business acumen with a sharp mind. This was a skill she was born with. She never had the opportunity to receive a business education. When she was a child most parents didn't send their young girls to school at all. She was lucky to complete three years of elementary. When she was a child, the country was controlled by Thailand. Therefore, Mom spoke Khmer in the home and learned Thai at school. Right from the start, she was a star student. Her pet name by the teachers was the Golden Needle Student because she was so sharp. Mom learned how to do math on her own because she wasn't allowed to learn it at school.

I wanted to emulate Mom and her sewing genius. At an early age, my favorite hobby was creating sewing projects for myself. I felt at home with a needle and scissors in my hand, but I longed to work with Mom's Singer. This was strictly off limits to me.

"Come on, Koann, let's use the sewing machine today. I have an idea for a new skirt," I said.

My first attempt ended in a bloody, sewing disaster. I selected my material, readied the seam, and was feeling very important and grown up, sitting behind the Singer. I placed my feet on the treadle and got the wheel spinning, just like Mom.

"Ouch! Ouch! Help, *jouy phong*. Look what I did."

First came the pain, then the blood, followed immediately with fear of my beloved Mother. How did she make it look so easy? Five minutes in and the needle went right through my finger. I felt a throbbing, pulsing pain and blood dripped down my arm onto the floor.

"Siv Eng, look what you've done," Mom looked at me in resignation, shaking her head, while I quietly sucked in my sniffles. "You are too young to be on that machine and you know it." The sniffles grew to a soft moan. "I knew something like this would happen one day," said Mom. My disappointment in myself had built up to full blown sobs.

"So sorry, Mom. So sorry," I said through my tears.

I think I scared my little sister, Koann. I was a young girl and a budding seamstress. I never actually had a proper sewing lesson until high school at Eap Khut in Battambang. I managed to keep all my fingers from that day forward. A wise person once said, "A lesson learned the hard way is a lesson learned."

When I was older, I used the same Singer to create new fashion pieces. In my mind, they were masterpieces. I saved scrap material and patched them together to make blouses for myself. I often forced Koann to be my model. She was so little, and I had to coerce her to stand still when measuring.

"Quit being so wiggly. I want this to look perfect." I treated my baby sister as if she were a famous model ready to walk the runway.

"I'm bored. Break time?" asked Koann.

"No, *ott tay*," I said. "Not until it's done." She was so young and patient. Koann didn't know enough to protest, and she wore everything I made for her. A pretty little doll to dress up as I pleased.

THE TOOTH FAIRY: 1963

Khla Kham Chhkae, Banteay Meanchey Province

Dad was a stickler about our teeth. He may have been a dentist in another life. He refused to let our baby teeth remain in our mouth. We did not have time or money to spend on dental care. It was a long journey to the dentist, and there were several children in our home.

"It doesn't matter how beautiful you are if you don't have two rows of teeth. Hair and makeup won't help your smile." He was definitely worried about those teeth. "You don't want to be ugly, do you, Siv Eng?" he asked with a sly smile.

Dad watched over our teeth like they were valuable jewels and kept the tooth fairy working overtime. She probably camped out on the roof of our house, waiting in expectation. I felt strongly that since the teeth were in my mouth, I should have a say in when and how they fell out, but I was wrong. I was constantly afraid that Dad would find out about my loose tooth and try to pull it prematurely. I waited until I couldn't eat properly, masking the tooth until it was hanging by a thread.

"Just open your mouth and let me have a look, Siv Eng. I want to see if your permanent tooth is coming in straight." He was also a smooth talker. "Will you let me look if I promise not to touch your tooth?"

I knew I didn't have a choice.

"You promise, Dad?" He looked me in the eye and lied through his very own pearly whites.

"Yes, Siv Eng, I promise." He projected a stoic poker face. I slowly opened my mouth with blind trust, and my father proceeded to pull out my tooth with sleight of hand.

"Dad! How could you?" I cried.

Dad would smile and say, "Relax, I did you a favor. If I told you the truth, that tooth would still be there." I returned his smile. I knew he was right. He not only looked out for my health and safety, he looked out for my beautiful smile. Braces were unheard of. He reasoned that the teeth needed to be removed so the permanent ones would grow in straight. In the end, I rarely lost a baby tooth naturally. My dad took it upon himself to be our dentist in residence. Most kids today fear the dentist. I feared my father.

ACCUSATIONS: 1963

Khla Kham Chhkae, Banteay Meanchey Province

Dad was raised near Khla Kham Chhkae. Wherever we lived, people listened to him and valued his business sense and medical advice. Cambodians from other villages came to him with their problems, and he gave his opinion. He wasn't a village Chief by title, but he acted as a leader.

One of the local men of the village considered himself to be like the Chief of Khla Kham Chhkae. When my father moved there, this man was reasonably jealous. We were Buddhist, and he was of another religion. This man didn't care for my dad and envied the respect that he was shown. One morning, during the dry season, my sister and I were playing under the house.

"It's my turn," said Sourn Leng.

"But you went first yesterday," I said. "Let's play a different game. How about hide and seek?"

Little Sourn Leng looked up, staring over my shoulder as two strangers approached the house.

One of the men inquired, "Girls, is this the home of Bun Huor?"

I spoke up, "Yes, *ja,* my parents are upstairs."

It was early, and Dad was still wearing his silk sarong. Men usually wore sarongs in the home and then changed to pants when going in public. Something was wrong. I didn't like the tone of these men. My father walked slowly down the stairs under the house. His look warned us to be silent. The men spoke sternly.

"We need to search your home."

My dad, who was highly concerned with his appearance, was now standing in the equivalent of his pajamas in front of these men. Meanwhile, Mom was up in the house trying desperately to listen through the floorboards to the conversation below. The undercover policemen refused to let Dad go or to allow him to change into his pants.

"We need to take you in for questioning," said the taller policeman. The men climbed up the stairs, entering our home without welcome. They rummaged through our things, but it didn't look like they found anything. Mom ran down the steps, handing Dad extra clothes and a pair of pants.

My sister and I stood in fear, watching as our father was taken away and our mother was left crying. Mom was terrified and feared the worst. He was treated like a criminal. It was a long night of waiting and worrying.

Later, we discovered that the jealous villager had reported that my father had many weapons. In actuality, he never owned a gun or even knew how to use one.

"It's Dad! It's Dad!" said Sourn Leng.

"He's coming, Mom," I shouted. "They let him go." Mom ran down the steps to embrace our father. It was a sweet reunion. Dad was returned to our home because he was proven innocent. Before that day, I never thought about the possibility of losing him. We were never so relieved to see our father.

MEDICINE MAN: 1963

Khla Kham Chhkae, Banteay Meanchey Province

Years ago, before I was born and while my parents were newly married, Dad left to play some basketball. He liked the exercise and occasionally played with his friends.

"I'll be home for dinner," he said as he walked out the door.

"Okay," Mom shouted over the Singer sewing machine.

That day Dad had an unfortunate accident. He was unintentionally slammed down on his back during the game. Although they were playing rough, it was an honest mistake. That fall damaged his lung, and the injury continued to get worse. Years later, the lung injury still haunted him.

"Sorry, Siv Eng, I can't ride bike with you today. My lung is acting up."

I remember Dad occasionally mentioning the pain in his chest. It wasn't severe, but after the accident he had to be careful to limit his physical activity and protect his health. The injury to his lung remained a thorn in his side. It really bothered him because he valued health and wanted to be strong for his family.

Dad had access to medicine and was knowledgeable about how to administer shots. He purchased his supply of medicines from France. Ninety percent of the medications he administered were given intravenously rather than orally. He was a kind of medicine man for the village. When villagers had illnesses, he did his best to heal them. We were all proud of my father, and I looked up to him like a superhero.

"*Hea*[20] Huor, can you cure my boil?" asked a neighbor.

"My son has a cough," said a young mother. "Do you have medicine for that, *Hea* Huor?"

"Would you help me, *Hea* Huor? My baby won't stop crying."

The patients came every week, and my father addressed each issue with care.

The downside of Dad's medicine man status was the daily dose of whale oil. Dad wanted us to have strong bones and teeth and to grow up in the best of physical health. He couldn't attain it for himself, so he passed his passion for excellent health onto us. There were always vitamins to take and concoctions to drink.

"Come and get your medicine, children," Dad announced. It was as if our hearing was suddenly impaired. No one moved. We acted like we were very busy doing something important to avoid what was coming. The vitamins weren't so bad. If he would have stopped there, it would have been fine.

"This will make your bones strong," he promised. The nasty whale oil came in a bottle. It was milky and smelly, and Dad made us take it by teaspoon one at a time.

"It's good for you, Siv Eng." It was the dreaded moment of the day. I gagged a little every time it was handed to me, but Dad made sure we had our whale oil every day. He was painfully consistent and punctual, and never forgot. I would have given anything to get the whale oil in the form of a shot.

My father never studied proper pharmacy at university but was widely read on various medical journals and articles. In those days, people who had money could buy any medications without restrictions. Regulations and red tape did not exist. Our private pharmacy was kept in a special

---

20   A Chinese honorific that means "older brother."

cabinet in our home. Dad didn't store an abundance of all medicines but accumulated the necessities for emergencies. No prescriptions necessary. Dad knew a family member who was a doctor and learned much of his knowledge from him. My father was often paid in Riel and other times he was paid in produce. He did make money, but for him it was more about helping people.

One day, Dad left for Battambang on an errand. He frequently traveled out of town. Unfortunately, that same day my school friend's grandfather was bitten on the arm by a snake. The jungle was filled with poisonous snakes, and this happened occasionally. It came with the territory. The medicine man was gone, so he couldn't help the grandfather. The man was screaming in pain, and we could hear him from our home not far away. My friend's grandfather died from the venom within hours. It was such a tragic way to die. We all wished that Dad had been home that day. He could have saved the man. Dad always had a supply of anti-venom in his medicine cabinet.

FIRE BELLY: 1976

Ou Krabau, Battambang Province

"Without health, life is not life;
it is only a state of languor and suffering; an image of death."

– Buddha

First came the chills. My whole body shook violently no matter how many blankets were available. I was chilled to the bone. It started from my spine and moved out to my fingers and toes. My already thin body became an icy sheet. Sourn Leng sat on my shaking body on top of all the blankets in a failed attempt to keep me warm. Thirty minutes went by, then the hot flashes started. The burning heat phase lasted another half hour. Then the unforgiving cycle began again.

My first sickness was late in 1976, and I was tormented with Malaria. I became too ill to work. I was still in Phum Ou Krabau with Pho, Sok Yann, and Sourn Leng. Aunt Chhiv Hong was away at a work camp for the duration of my illness, but four of the five of us were still together.

When I experienced the high fever, everything around me looked pink, as if looking through a rosy lens. The grass was pink. The hut was pink. The sky was a rosy shade of mauve. Everything was pink. I became exhausted and passed out several times with fever. The blank darkness was my only reprieve from the pain. It was a never-ending cycle, alternating cold to hot, back and forth, two extremes of torture.

"She looks pale," said a far-off voice.

"She's so weak. Will she pull through?" asked another. My hearing was coming and going. A touch and go scenario.

"Get the blankets. The chills are setting in again," said a voice of concern.

"Do you think she will make it?" Sourn Leng murmured. I recognized my sister's voice but couldn't respond.

"We can't take her to the hospital," said Pho. He was soaking a scarf in cool water. "It's where the sick go to die. I hear they bury people who may still be alive."

"Don't let anyone take our sister away. There's no medicine or doctors there." Sok Yann gently placed a fresh rag on my forehead.

My sister Sourn Leng spoke up, "We must fight for her."

The malaria lasted three grueling months. The village Chief had pity on me and showed kindness. I was spared once again. He allowed me to recover in my hut and permitted my family to care for me. The Chief could have been in trouble for showing us an ounce of mercy. I was so blessed that my siblings were assigned to work near the village during the day and could care for me at night. I was wholly depleted of all energy as the fever and chills sucked the life out of me. It hurt to move even just a little. I found comfort in hearing their voices and knowing they were near. They assisted me with eating, bathing, and dressing whenever they were able. I will never forget their tender, loving care. Sleep was my refuge. Malaria was easily cured with medicine, but the Khmer Rouge, in their infinite wisdom, had destroyed all medications. I, the hopeful pharmacy student, did not have access to drugs.

"Ma, Ma, Mom. Come back, Mom. I see you." She was right there, beyond my reach. She looked so beautiful and was wearing a white robe. She looked like an angel and was at peace. I called out to her.

"Stay here. Don't leave," I whispered. "I miss you."

I alarmed Pho with my cries. When I woke, he questioned me.

"Siv Eng, did you see Mom in a dream?" I remained silent.

Even in my sickness, I wanted to protect Ko Pho. I wanted him to live with the hope that she was still alive. I didn't need a fortune teller to translate my vision. Was I to assume that my mother was dead? Maybe she was very ill at that time or was facing disease. Or perhaps she was there to bring me back?

Pho still had to leave every day for work, but he made my care his priority in the morning and every evening.

"She can't go another day," said my sister-in-law. "We have to give her a bath."

"How will we get her to the pond?" asked Sourn Leng.

"Let's put her arms around our necks and keep her propped up in the middle," said Sok Yann. "We will drag her if we must. We have no choice."

I was in such pain, but somehow, we made it to the pond. The bath was much needed. I wanted to stay there, soaking in the still water, not moving a muscle. I was fading in and out of consciousness, leaving Sok Yann and Sourn Leng to bring me back to the village on their own strength.

"She's losing consciousness," said Sok Yann. "I don't think we can make it all the way."

At that moment, I collapsed. I had taken my last step, and my sister panicked.

"What do we do? We can't leave her here," asked Sok Yann. Sourn Leng ran and got my brother.

"Ko Pho, come quick this minute, Siv Eng collapsed!" I was going downhill rapidly. My brother threw me on his back and headed in the direction of our hut. He was so strong, even in the face of starvation. He knew. Ko Pho could feel it. I was fading. I remember those moments vividly, as I whispered my last breath to my brother.

"Ko, Pho, I'm going to die." Death was one step behind my brother and reaching for my hand.

"Don't give up Siv Eng! Don't you leave me." I can still hear his voice breathing encouragement into my bones. He was so faithful. Pho was a living demonstration of selfless love. He had nothing to gain by caring for me, his sister. Every day, he built up a fire for me in the hut to last for hours. He brought branches to warm my body at night. Not a word of complaint.

Our village Chief happened to be new to Ou Krabau, and he was knowledgeable about how to treat Malaria. Everyone in the village brought their sick loved ones to the new Chief because he was a sort of medicine man like my father. When Pho asked him for help, the Chief decided on an old remedy to cure Malaria using the cotton from a Ko tree. The Ko tree is large with hundreds of long hard green pods filled with silk-like cotton. Many people used the cotton to stuff their pillows. The village Chief took the cotton and formed it into several tight balls, the size of a large pea. The Chief touched his thumb and pointer finger to the corners of my mouth to get a measure. He used this exact measurement to strategically place three Ko cotton balls in a triangle shape on my belly. Two more balls were placed on either side below my rib cage. Two more were centered on either side below my belly button. There was a total of seven cotton balls.

The new Chief asked my sister and brother to restrain my arms and legs while he set each cotton ball on fire with the end of an incense stick. They were left there to burn deep into the layers of my skin. I was restrained like a prisoner in chains, and the remedy felt more like a torture. The pain was searing, and I screamed out in agony. The entire village of Ou Krabau could hear my cries that night. I was left with seven scars on my belly from the burning treatment. More pain followed. Agonizing, non-stop throbbing and unbearable discomfort. The malaria was gone, but I was left in misery.

The healing process that followed was laborious. After the skin burned, it turned into an ulcer. I couldn't wear clothes or allow anything to touch my seven sores. Sok Yann and my sister picked out healthy green leaves from the jungle to place on my skin ulcers. It created a barrier, protecting my raw skin from my clothes. They found the smoothest leaves, but there were no medications available, no bandages, no nurses, and no doctors. Modern medicine as I knew it had disappeared.

Eventually, my family helped me to sit up, tolerate food, and walk with assistance. I had walked through the fire and returned from the dead, a resurrected girl. My family were the nurses, they were the doctors, and they were my medicine. My family was my cure. My brother searched the jungle for herbs and natural remedies. I got better day by day, little by little. Later, Pho and Sok Yann admitted that they never thought I would make it.

"You're back, little sister. It's a good thing you are a fighter," said Ko Pho with a smile.

I will never forget how he carried me back from the pond and rescued me from the grave.

SUGAR CLIMBER: 1976

Phum Ou Krabau, Battambang Province

He tried everything. It was my brother who kept us alive. Food was the medicine for starvation. The main source of food we needed at that time was salt and sugar. People today get sugar in all their food, and it's hard to avoid. Sugar fills the body with goodness and energy, and this fact goes unrealized until it is erased completely from the diet. When it was taken away, we understood how much our body needed it. It's true that you are what you eat. Our bodies reacted immediately to whatever we ate because we were so starved and emaciated. If we ingested just a taste of salt or sugar, we felt it instantly. It was a powerful force.

It was dangerous to collect sugar. The palm trees were everywhere, but we didn't have the proper tools for processing. People made sugar from the palm tree and the sweet juice that dripped from the flower cluster. Bamboo tubes were tied to the tree to collect the priceless nectar. They stored up the precious, dripping juice for days. When the bamboo tubes became full, they were emptied and moved on to the next tree. Sugar was made by cooking the juice until it reduced. The palm trees were so tall that bamboo branches were cut up and fashioned into makeshift ladders for climbing. The ladders went up as high as sixty feet to the top of the trees. When the palm trees stopped producing, the trees were abandoned, but the ladders were often left dangling.

When I was recovering from malaria, I could hardly eat or drink. One day my brother came home with blood on his shirt and chest. Sok Yann stood at the entrance of the hut staring at her husband.

"Pho, did someone hurt you? Are you okay?" He looked exhausted and yet strangely pleased. "What were you doing? Where have you been?"

It looked like he was clawed by an animal. My brother had climbed a very tall palm tree using an old abandoned ladder to collect the leftover sweet nectar at the top. He knew I needed the energy to recover. At the top of the tree, he carefully dipped his cup into the nectar and wrapped it up tightly. The ladder was an accident waiting to happen. On the way down, the ladder broke, and Pho plunged several feet in a split second. He caught himself with his arms, interrupting the death fall. With the ladder unavailable, Pho had to use the raw muscles in his legs and arms to shimmy the rest of the way down. The tree was unforgiving, tearing up his shirt and chest, but he didn't come home empty handed. He brought with him the sugary juice from the treetop for me. Pho proudly shared the sweetness, which gave me energy and helped save my life. It tasted like nectar from heaven. He risked the climb for me. If Pho had fallen, he surely would have died. Any injury would have made him useless to the Khmer Rouge.

My brother never once treated me like I was going to die. He refused to let death get a foothold and spoke life over me. He repeated the same words over and over.

"Siv Eng, I will not let you die. You will not die alone. I still have my watch and can trade for anything we need." He promised, "Siv Eng, we will leave this village together, and we will find Mom together. You have to live. Don't give up."

I will never forget his promises. I will never forget his care. His words and deeds demonstrated the true love of family. He was a young man, newly married with a young wife to care for, yet he looked out for me as if I was his own. Pho's unconditional love is what ultimately brought my healing.

DEATH BY HOSPITAL: 1976

Unknown Hospital in Battambang Province

Aunt Chhiv Hong lived and worked separately from us for several weeks and months at a time with a single woman's work group. We missed her terribly and hadn't seen her for several months. We had no way of checking on her.

Aunt Chhiv Hong was raised in the city and had not experienced life in the country as a child. She really struggled with living in the villages and laboring in the fields without any modern conveniences. My previous experience of living in Khla Kham Chhkae, even though it was brief, proved helpful to basic survival. I inadvertently gained a valuable knowledge of plants, natural medicines, and jungle street smarts. Even as a child, I remembered the names of medicinal plants, leaves, and bark that could be used for healing remedies. My young aunt didn't have this advantage.

One day, a woman from her camp showed up at our hut in the evening with news that Aunt Chhiv Hong had become gravely ill and died alone in the hospital. The news was sudden and alarming. If we had known she was sick, we would have brought her to our hut to care for her and nurse her back to health. My brother got permission from his work leader to leave the village and check on our Aunt. When Ko Pho reached the hospital, he was given her only possession: a blouse. When he arrived back at Ou Krabau, we knew it was true.

I loved my Aunt Chhiv Hong. She was my college roommate, my mother's sister, my family, and my friend. Aunt Chhiv Hong was a lovely person, full of intelligence and kindness. A year previous, she was studying business at university in Phnom Penh. Now, she was gone. With access to proper food and medicine, she would have lived a long, prosperous life. Pho reached into his bag and handed me her blue shirt. It was her favorite. The navy blue, sheer blouse had solid, opaque polka dots. The material was exquisite. I kept her blouse in my bag to always remember her. She had protected it from being dyed black and wore it only at night. I held the blouse in reverence knowing it was my last link to my beloved aunt.

How long had she been gone? We never saw her body or said goodbye. The hospital was more like a funeral home with clients lined up in beds waiting their turn. The possibility of survival was grave. The caretakers never got a break from burying the deceased. They stood, ready and waiting. Many times, they stole any clothing or valuables and buried the bodies before the family had a chance to ask questions or retrieve them. They buried the sick swiftly to make room for new patients. The cycle was ongoing.

When meeting people who were moved to our village or in talking with other teenagers at the work camp sites, I occasionally heard their stories. All the stories were the same.

"I am from the village of _____ near the city of _____. They killed my _____." Fill in the blank. It was like a Mad Libs puzzle with only dismal word choices. "I lost my _____. I don't know if _____ is still living." My heart ached for each story and every person. All narratives had the same theme, yet each chapter was unique. Every experience carried its own pain and heartache with the occasional, joy-filled reunion of finding a sibling or relative.

I was scarred by malaria, disfigured by starvation, and wounded by loss—yet I was proud of my scars. They became a reminder that I was a survivor. There is a certain beauty in a scar. No two look the same, and the skin of the scar is tougher and stronger than the skin it replaces. The seven visible scars on my belly were part of my healing process from the village Chief, but the scars on the inside were hidden, invisible and unseen. My scars could not grow without first experiencing the pain; nonetheless, they made me stronger. My invisible scar was the longing I felt for my family. I thought of them most nights, when the only sound was the wind blowing through the cracks of my hut. Were they suffering? Were they together? Were they thinking of me?

THE RICE THIEF: 1976

Phum Thmei, Banteay Meanchey Province

Te's family was separated. He worried about his younger brother and sisters living alone in the child labor camps. He wondered about his older brother and sisters who were living in Phnom Penh during the takeover. With his brother, Pho, gone, Te was now the oldest male in his family. He was allowed to leave his teenage work camp on occasion and return to Phum Thmei to check in with his mother, YoKuy. He wanted to take care of her and help provide for the family.

One night, when Te returned, he told YoKuy of his plan.

"Mom, I'm going to get some rice for our family, and tonight is the night because it's so dark. Don't worry, Mom. I've got to do this."

YoKuy did not want her 12 year old son to risk being arrested, but she also understood he was starving and needed the nourishment. The highly valued rice was held in a storage barn, but it was frequently stolen by ravenous villagers.

"Don't do it, Te. It's just not worth it," warned YoKuy.

"But Mom, I've made up my mind, and I need something to carry the rice," said Te. YoKuy reluctantly handed her son a cloth bag. They were all malnourished, and she could use the extra rice to feed the family.

The night was pitch-black, the clouds concealing the stars and moonlight. Te couldn't see more than a few feet in front of him, but he took each step with faith and determination to feed his family. His rice bag was empty, but his heart was filled with courage.

Te never returned home that night, and YoKuy's anxiety continued building. After a few hours, she knew he had been arrested.

"I told him not to go," she cried. "I knew he could be killed. Why didn't I stop him?" She was distraught with guilt and ran to Grandma's home to explain what happened. Grandma almost passed out with the news.

"YoKuy, of all nights. If only he would have alerted me first. A neighbor told me yesterday that the communists added additional guards to the food storage barn last night. Te picked the worst night for stealing.

"What have I done?" pleaded YoKuy. Regret lingered heavy in the air with the burden on her shoulders.

YoKuy and Grandma were helpless. How could they argue with the soldiers? If he was caught stealing, he would be sent to a communist prison or worse. Grandma, Grandpa, Bun Tek, Kim Ly, and YoKuy were the only family in the village. They all cried together, mourning the loss.

"How will we tell Koann, Loan, and Nary?" asked YoKuy. "They will be devastated." Bun Tek and Kim Ly did their best to comfort the others. No one slept that night.

It was a welcome shock to everyone the next afternoon when Te casually stepped inside the door. YoKuy was overjoyed. She ran to his side.

"Te, Te, my Te!" she said. "What happened, my son?"

Grandma's response was a bowl of tears. The reunited family couldn't wait to hear as Te relayed his story of the previous night.

He silently approached the storage barn. There were no guards to be seen through the thick darkness, and he thought it was his lucky day. Ironically, there was no door on the high security storage barn. Te soundlessly stepped over the threshold, watching and listening. As he stepped inside, his foot landed on the chest of a Chhlop, and two hands quickly grabbed his ankle. Te was caught. He was taken by bicycle to the elderly high village Chief to decide his fate. Te looked up at the Chief.

"Met, who sent you to steal?" asked the Chief with unquestioned authority.

"No one," said Te. "I went on my own. I was just hungry." His only defense was the truth.

"Next time you are hungry, don't steal food," said the Chief. "Come to me instead."

In this backward society, who would have thought that telling the truth was a good idea? Somehow, the high Chief had mercy. The other soldier put Te on the bicycle and brought him back to his home. It was a simple case. This Chief, like the Chief in Ou Krabau, had a kind heart and was filled with compassion. He chose to ignore the crime and see the person. Common sense was still alive, and Te was lucky to meet it that day. Most of the village Chiefs were good people. No one benefited from the rule of the Khmer Rouge.

SEEING PINK: 1976

Phum Ou Krabau, Battambang Province

cheu: saté'a:rom
("The sick are victims of their own imaginations.")
– Khmer Rouge Saying

We were so hungry. The suffering was unbearable. Instead of using the rice to feed the hungry mouths, the Angkar was feeding bullets to guns. My family overcame our hunger to help each other. If we found something, we shared it.

My sister, Sourn Leng, contracted malaria soon after I recovered. She became delirious on our way to a work camp, and the Mulethan leader sent us back to Ou Krabau. When I was caring for my sister, I was also starving, longing to take just one more bite. Many times, I was tempted, but I would save the morsels for Sourn Leng. I knew she needed the food more than me. My family had done the same for me when I was sick.

My brother and his wife, Sok Yann, were sent away for several weeks to a married labor camp. Aunt Chhiv Hong was gone, never to return. I was now the sole caretaker who stayed in the village to nurse my sister. Our Chief allowed me to work near Ou Krabau during this time, so I could help my sister when we had work breaks. My job was to carry rice stacks on my head from the field to storage.

In the first year that we were at Ou Krabau, we were still allowed a break time during the day. On breaks, I searched for the *mreas prov leaf*[21] that grew wild and plentiful. I added it to our broth and rice when possible. The leaf had a similar flavor to lemon grass or lime. We ate lots of it every day because it grew like a weed in the area around our village. Sourn Leng needed more than a bit of mreas prov. She needed protein packed fish.

One day when the break was announced, I found my friend, Met Touch.

"Let's go fishing today on our break," I said. "We have a longer break today, and I need to get some fish for my sister." The Mulethan people knew that if we didn't find additional food, we would starve and wouldn't be of any use to them. At that point, fishing on break wasn't yet illegal. The two of us walked down to the pond with fish on the brain.

I hated to leave my extremely ill sister in the hut alone, but I had no choice. There were no nets, so we used our *krâmas* to trap the fish, tossing them along the bank. The fish were soon flopping in the grass by the pond when, suddenly, the atmosphere changed.

"What is going on?" I asked.

My friend looked at me, confused.

"Do you see what I see?" I squinted my eyes trying to blink and clear the air. When I looked around, everything looked pink. I wasn't sick, I wasn't tired, but everything was pink. I looked at my friend, pink. I looked at the water, pink.

"What's wrong with me?" I asked. "Do I look weird or different to you?"

Met Touch looked at me funny.

"You look fine to me," she said, "and we need to get some more fish. Let's hurry." She returned to fishing as I stared at her, trying to make the pink go away. Her irritated expression soon changed to one of concern.

"What's wrong, Met Eng? Are you okay?"

---

[21] Holy basil.

It was like I had malaria again. An overwhelming sense of purpose slapped me in the face and opened my eyes. I suddenly saw clearly.

"My sister! It's Sourn Leng!" I started heading for the shore.

"I must get back to my sister now!" My friend looked confused. "Met Touch, my sister is calling me. Sourn Leng is in trouble. Get the fish and let's run! *Chap, chap.* Hurry!"

The two of us sprinted back to the village at lightning speed. I saw my sister's form as we came upon the edge of our three-sided hut. She raised her hand. Even from a distance, we could see that she was gasping for air. This is it, I thought. My sister is dying, and Ko Pho is gone.

I had witnessed so many people die in the previous year. I was familiar with death. I never saw its face but sensed its presence on our doorstep. I dropped the fish and ran to my sister. Her lips were pulling apart, and her breathing was very shallow. I grabbed her sunken shoulders and shook her as hard as I could, calling her name.

"Sourn Leng! Sourn Leng! Listen to me. I'm here. Don't leave. Please don't die on me!"

Her eyes were rolling back and her lips were pulling up. Silence.

"Get the spoons," I shouted. We took turns *coining*[22] her back, her arms and her chest to see if it would revive her. We used water to lubricate her skin, but it still turned bright red from the scraping. I kept talking to Sourn Leng just in case she could hear me. Met Touch and I continued the coining treatment for forty-five minutes to see if she would come back to us. She could no longer fight the malaria and starvation. Her body longed for release.

"Sourn Leng! Sourn Leng, I'm here. It's me. Please come back. Please come back." I continuously called out to her. Her eyes seemed to twitch. "I'm here," I whispered. "Can you hear me?"

We never stopped coining her, flipping her from front to back. Soon her eyes returned to normal and her breathing started up slowly.

My sister had narrowly escaped death. Since modern medicine wasn't

---

22   A healing practice also known as *gua sha.*

available, the coining method worked in Sourn Leng's case. It is an ancient practice believed to stimulate immune and anti-inflammatory responses that can last for several days. Coining is often used in cases with acute infectious illnesses.

"She's back," said Met Touch.

"Back from the dead," I echoed.

I laid the spoons down on the floor never taking an eye off my sister. We saw the life return to Sourn Leng. It was time for death to leave. Its presence an unwelcome guest.

"I knew she would make it, Met Touch. Thank you for helping to save my sister." I hugged my friend with a grateful heart. It was all I had to offer.

"I'm so glad I was here with you," she said.

Later the next day, Sourn Leng told me she was waiting for me to come back before letting go.

"I wanted to say goodbye," she said. "You were right on time. I kept calling for you to come home. I didn't want to die alone in the hut."

I knew that what she was saying was true. I felt it in my bones. She was fighting for life that day.

"If you would have come ten minutes later, I would have been gone," she said. "I couldn't bear the thought of you returning to the hut and finding my body," she admitted. She knew I wouldn't be able to handle it and didn't want me to spend my days at her grave in mourning.

Earlier that year when I was sick, I heard voices from far away calling my name. If I was alone, I wouldn't have endured. My sister and I had now taken turns calling each other back from the grave.

After that fateful day, I was thankful for the color pink. Pink flowers, pink dresses, pink watermelons, and a beautiful pink sky. I was thankful for my sister and our shared memories. Today when I see a pink sky, I think of her.

THE SUITCASE: 1977

Ou Krabau, Battambang Province

When I was a young girl, before the communists took over, Grandpa had travelled to China and brought home a suitcase with a combination lock. Sourn Leng and I packed the suitcase full of our favorite clothes and scarves when we left for university in Phnom Penh. The same suitcase followed us through our evacuation, march, and transfers to Ou Krabau. In the village, we stored it along with our other meager possessions in our hut while we were away at work camps. We always kept the lock secure and knew the combination. One day we illegally traded some jewelry and accumulated three pounds of rice. I placed the rice in the suitcase.

"Let's go, *chap laeng*,"[23] said Sourn Leng. Before I left, I double checked that the combination was locked. Normally, we kept our jewelry in the belts from Mom. That day, we hid the last of our rings and rice in the suitcase and left for work.

Sourn Leng was still sick, and I was in recovery from an ulcer on my left leg. Ulcers were common for workers in the rice field. We had to keep the infection in check or it could result in death. Since we couldn't work at the labor camp, we were assigned to work in the village garden with the elderly people.

---

[23] Let's go.

When we returned to our hut after a long day of work, we found our suitcase pried open. It was lying on the floor, and all of our rings and rice were gone. Not a grain was left. My sister was broken. She cried day and night.

"How could this happen? We are going to die." Over and over Sourn Leng repeated her woes. "That's it. We have nothing. What are we to do now?"

Pho was still away at a work camp with Sok Yann. I tried my best to encourage my younger sister to return from the depths of hopelessness.

"No, Sourn Leng, we will not die. You have to stop saying this. We will live on. We will do the best we can." I endeavored to fill our hut with hope that day since we couldn't fill up with rice.

In reality, I was equally as desperate and hopeless as Sourn Leng.

The new village Chief was kind. He took care of delivering and distributing rice to several surrounding villages. Pho assisted him with the management of the distribution of rice. The responsibility was enormous and gave us even more favor with the Chief. Because of Pho's honesty and hard work, our family gained his trust.

We were blessed. Most people in Ou Krabau died from disease and starvation rather than murder. For most of our time there, the succession of village Chiefs were kind to our family. The Khmer Rouge switched the Chiefs from village to village. It was another way to add to the confusion and create a disconnect.

Sourn Leng followed me on the path to the Chief's hut. It was illegal to have our own stash of rice and jewelry, but I took a chance by pleading our case.

"Please help us, Pouk. *Jouy phong*. When we got home today, our suitcase was pried open. How will we survive?"

This Chief took my case seriously. A Chinese man in our camp was a suspect. The Chief interrogated the young man, but he was found not guilty. Days later, I met a woman in the village who was wearing one of our rings.

"Who gave you this ring?" I asked.

"I traded for it with the Chinese man who lives in the hut at the edge of the village."

In the same breath, I went straight to the young man's hut to confront him. In a fury, I stomped into his hut unannounced.

"Where are our rings? What did you do with our rice? I thought you were our friend. How could you do this to us?" The young man stared right through me without a word of defense. "If you only would have asked, we would have shared with you."

He could not make eye contact and was suddenly very interested in looking down at his feet.

"We wouldn't have closed our eyes to your starvation," I said. "You gave us a death sentence and have put all of my family in jeopardy."

The man looked at me with a blank stare. He was considered our friend. He knew we also were of Chinese descent and inquired about our family. We had crossed paths in the past at different work sites. He had shared with me about his father's death, and I had mourned with him.

"You betrayed me. We are all suffering together, and you took advantage of me. I thought you were my friend," I yelled. Rage was swelling in my heart. "Do you want to take this to your grave?" I asked.

"Sorry," was his only defense.

He obviously felt shameful, and I felt awful. I was more upset about the missing jewels than I was about his actions. His starvation was so great that it drove him to steal from a friend. He was also suffering from an ulcer and began to weep. No one benefited from his thievery. He died soon after our conversation, and it was a horrible way to go. Death by a guilty conscious. Our jewelry and rice never found their way back to us.

TASTY TARANTULAS 1977

Ou Krabau, Battambang Province

"I've heard that tarantulas are tasty, and several of the Mulethan people have eaten them. Let's go look in the jungle and see if we can find some on our break," I said.

Soon, Sourn Leng and I were walking through the thick steamy jungle looking for holes in the ground. We had to look very closely. When a spider web-like silken sheet covered a hole, a tarantula was residing there. We found several holes, but none belonging to our dinner.

"Found one," Sourn Leng finally said.

The telltale spider web covered a large hole at our feet.

"I can do this," I said with a shaky voice, summoning courage. We knelt down and poured water in the hole to flush the arachnid from its hiding place. Immediately, a large tarantula scrambled out. Sourn Leng's screams could have stunned the tarantula to death.

"Siv Eng, please don't let it bite you!"

I caught the bristly, hairy spider with my bare hands and then quickly stabbed it on the back. I had to be careful not to touch the fangs. Standing in the jungle, with the precision of a surgeon, using a cloth, I pulled the venomous hollow fangs one at a time. We repeated this process until we had about three tarantulas.

Back at the hut, we grilled the tarantulas over a fire. We turned them on a stick so the hairs would burn off evenly. Once they were disintegrated, the barbeque began. We were only lucky enough to find a tarantula a few times in our years at Ou Krabau. Grilled tarantula was far from our mother's home cooked meals, but we delighted in the delicious delicacy that tasted like a cross between coconut and peanuts.

Ongkrong[24] were another tasty treat we searched for in the jungle. The nests were like huge balls on the branch of a tree, and they were difficult to find. We tied a basket to the end of a long pole and kept a bucket of water on the ground ready to go. We used the stick to poke a hole in the nest, and the ants poured out in droves, landing in the hanging basket. We quickly pulled the basket down and shook the pile of ants and eggs into the bucket of water. The eggs were a delicacy, and the ants were tangy and sour. We grilled them over a fire in a hot pot, and they made a crunchy treat. People in Ou Krabau often used them in sour soup.

---

[24] Red ants that live in the trees.

NO TURNING BACK: JULY 1977

Work Site Near Ou Krabau, Battambang Province

Sourn Leng and I were often sent out to the same site to work on similar tasks. One day we each worked separately all morning to build a damn for the rice field. It was a beautiful day, but the sun was shining with a searing heat.

"Sourn Leng," said a girl in her group. "I've heard there are some mung beans to the east across the railroad tracks. The soldiers won't be able to see us there. It's far enough away. I've heard that several girls have been finding mung beans on their break."

Sourn Leng's empty stomach did the talking. "Let's go over on our break today and get as many mung beans as possible. I'll see if my sister can join us too," said Sourn Leng. "Her camp isn't far from the railroad tracks."

You never know what your last conversation will be. Our last exchange was on break when my sister stopped at my work site. I was resting under a tree.

"Here," Sourn Leng handed over her tattered brown sandals. "Can you fix these for me? They have a broken strap." The sandals barely had any life to them, but with patience I could extend their wear for a few more weeks.

"Ok," I said. "I'll see if I can find time later this afternoon."

"I'm going with some girls to get some mung beans today," said Sourn Leng. "Want to come with us? It's near the railroad tracks and far enough away that no one will see us."

I was exhausted that day and chose some rest for my feet rather than sustenance in my belly.

"I'm going to stay here today, Sourn Leng. You go ahead with the girls. I hope you find lots of beans."

"Thanks, Siv Eng. I'll be back for the shoes later."

"Be safe, Sourn Leng."

"*Leahaey*,"[25] she echoed. "See you soon."

The railroad tracks were considered a border because it divided the two villages. It was illegal to cross a border without a permission form, and it was an easy excuse for soldiers to arrest unsuspecting girls.

On her break that day, she stepped across the railroad tracks with two other girls. She only took a handful of the beans. A little here and a little there. She had just begun to collect a few beans, when she was interrupted.

"You!" said a young voice with beady eyes. "Stop! Come over here this minute." A young Chhlop was waiting for them in ambush. He was very proud of himself. He took the girls to the Chief in the next village.

"Comrade, these three girls illegally crossed the border and were caught stealing mung beans," he said with self-righteous superiority.

"I see," said the Chief. "Girls, open your hands." As they unclenched their fists, several precious beans dropped to the ground, wasted. "These girls will come with me," the Chief declared.

I didn't worry about my sister's safety because she was with a group,

---

25   Goodbye.

and the tracks were far from penetrating eyes. She was only making a quick trip. The field had already been harvested, so the girls were simply gathering the leftover beans. Many teenage workers had previously crossed the tracks and found the beans without incident. It was a daily occurrence—but that day my sister and two of her peers were caught. They were accused of crossing the border and stealing from the Angkar. There was no turning back.

After the hour break ended, my sister did not return. The two girls didn't return either. When it was time to go back to work, I looked but couldn't find her anywhere. I was unaware that Sourn Leng had been officially arrested and was being held in a camp in Moung Roussei miles from Ou Krabau. This time, I couldn't negotiate her release.

Days went by, and I worried even more. I was alone without my sister at the work site. I couldn't even tell my brother. I eventually heard the story of Sourn Leng's arrest. A week later, the two girls who were arrested with her escaped and returned to the village of Ou Krabau. The first girl pretended that she needed the restroom and took the opportunity to run away. After she was gone, the guards announced that she had been caught and killed. This was an effective scare tactic that was frequently used. The second girl didn't believe them and took her chance for escape the next day. The girls found me and told me about Sourn Leng.

"She wouldn't leave with us," they reported.

"They are keeping her in Moung," the first girl said. "It's far from here."

"Why didn't she run?" I asked, but I already knew the answer.

"She was afraid of getting caught," said the second girl. "When girls would run away and escape the prison camp, the guards told us they were captured and killed for their disobedience. We didn't trust them and took the chance. Your sister feared for her life and chose to stay. She believed their lies." A handful of mungbeans and a railroad track kept her from her family.

I had hardly said goodbye.

COMMUNIST COMPUTATIONS 1977

Ou Krabau, Battambang Province

I thought of my sister every day but could do nothing to help her. My brother and sister-in-law were away at a married couple work camp, Aunt Chhiv Hong was gone, and I found myself alone. I continued with my daily work for the Angkar and ended up helping a new Mulethan leader. The man was previously a Khmer Rouge soldier and was now in charge of the laborers in the field. This new leader often asked me, a young girl, questions. He was responsible for overseeing rice production and had immense pressure from the Khmer Rouge to increase efficiency. The Khmer Rouge expected three times the production of rice with the new, unskilled, and ill-prepared labor force. It made no sense. In pre-Khmer Rouge days, the villagers grew crops for their own families and owned their own land. They were the agricultural specialists, not the city dwellers. The villagers never asked for this new lifestyle, and no one was prospering with Pol Pot's communists in charge.

Most Mulethan people did not have an opportunity for formal education, so our work leader couldn't figure the simple math to keep an updated inventory.

"Met Eng, have you ever been to school? Do you know arithmetic?" His question set off an alarm. Was this man fishing for information? Was he preparing to turn me in to authorities? I was in the habit of looking over my shoulder and not trusting anyone.

"Met Bong, I didn't really have much schooling." I lied.

"What did your parents do before the takeover?"

"Met Bong, my parents ran a small grocery store, and I helped out a bit." I told another little, white lie, yet he didn't stop with the questions.

"Met Eng, are you sure you don't know how to do math?" It occurred to me that maybe he wasn't trying to trick me. More likely, he was asking for help.

We started that same day, and I held my first private math lesson. I became a *Neakru*[26] that day. First, we started with writing the numerals, and then moved on to solving simple mathematical equations. I made sure the leader could check his answers. Paper and pencils were unavailable, so we drew the addition and subtraction problems with sticks. Dirt + stick = math lesson.

The man kept reminding me about his position.

"Met Eng, I'm still your boss."

"Yes, *ja*, Met Bong."

"I'm in charge here."

"Yes, *ja*, Met Bong. I understand."

"You will tell no one about this," he said.

We both took a chance. I was worried he would turn me in for having an education after I gave him the initial help. In this case, my risk paid off. I earned continued favor with this leader and his new wife, the village cook. He turned out to be a quick learner and an excellent student. After several lessons, he was able to maintain an up-to-date inventory.

---

[26]   A female teacher.

GARDENS, STONES, CHICKENS, AND HATS: 1977

Garden near Ou Krabau

After the ulcer healed, I slowly began to develop a boil on my upper left leg. Most of the girls in my village were sent to work in a rice field far away from Ou Krabau. My new Mulethan math student, who was also my group leader, knew I couldn't make the trip. He asked me to stay with the seven "garden girls" who worked near Ou Krabau.

The decision was made, and I was sent to the outskirts of the village to live with the seven girls and tend the vegetables. Most of the garden girls belonged to important Mulethan families and were given special privileges. My back became curved due to the excruciating pain of the boil, and I soon walked with a shuffle. At first glance, one would assume I was an old lady. I had to use a cane to walk and would sometimes crawl to get around faster.

The food in the garden was for the Chief, the Mulethan people, and the soldiers. It was owned by the Angkar. In our utopian society of equality, I was not allowed to eat a bite. In the garden, we didn't have to work in the mud, rain, or jungle. We did labor under the hot, steamy sun, but the rice field was grueling work compared to the garden. We tended the fruit and vegetable garden with great care, and I was glad to be one of the chosen.

The garden was lush and filled with cucumber, watermelon, beans, lettuce, and cabbage. Zucchini, tomato, squash, and pumpkin were plentiful. Most importantly, the garden contained mango trees. I nursed and harvested the bounty that I could not eat. I wanted to consume food, but instead starvation consumed me. If I wanted a taste, I had to sneak the vegetables. If anyone ate even a bite of the vegetables, it was considered stealing from Angkar. This was an unforgiveable, forbidden sin. If caught, the punishment would be a severe beating or death. Some of the good hearted Mulethan villagers acted like they didn't see me sneaking a taste of food here or there. I only snuck a few bites in all the months I worked there.

My boil was getting worse every day. When I was unable to walk, I sat on a wooden stool in the garden and scooted it down the row as I made progress. The girls brought me the basket, I filled it with vegetables and fruits, and then they took the basket to and from the communal kitchen.

As the boil on my leg continued to progress, I could no longer work in the garden but was given a new responsibility.

"Scat, get away. Psssst!" The chickens didn't listen; they were as hungry as me. I sat at the edge of my hut and threw another stone, missing again.

"Get away," I shouted. I tossed stone number forty-eight at just the right angle. This one hit a chicken, and it scurried away. "Ha, I got you."

The chickens were my only source for conversation during the day. They loved to eat our rice, but we worked too hard to share such a precious commodity with them. Let me be clear, the rice wasn't shared with me either.

My new job assignment was to scare away the pesky chickens and prevent them from eating the communal rice. I made a little game of hitting the chickens to entertain myself. It provided an added distraction from the unforgiving pain in my leg. The rice was laid out on tarps in a large area next to the hut and was left to dry in the sun. I could hardly move around. I couldn't collect the stones myself, so the Mulethan "garden girls" gathered them in a pile and left them by my side before they left for the garden.

The most tortuous activity at that time was going to the restroom. I could hardly lower myself down from the hut to relieve myself. The boil on my upper left leg hurt intensely when I moved even an inch. The pain took my breath away. I laid there hour after hour on the hammock of the hut throwing stones and making myself useful. Both the chickens and the pain were my constant companions. The days passed long and slow, and I often thought of my sister, my brother, and Sok Yann.

I eventually got bored sitting in the hut all day. On a whim, I started making hats out of palm leaves for the Khmer Rouge soldiers. The soldiers climbed the trees, cut the palm leaves, and laid them out in the sun to dry, then they brought them to me. I used my needle to sew the dried leaves. I produced one to two hats a day and created beauty amid boredom, even if it was for our enemies. I now had a hobby in captivity, and it kept me sane.

I decided on a polygon diamond shape for the crown of the hats, and it looked really attractive. If money existed, I could have made a good profit. The soldiers managed to collect colored yarn for me to weave into the hats, and I made intricate designs. Each hat was unique and was coveted by the soldiers. I don't know who took more pride in those hats, myself or the men who wore them. I soon developed a nickname. The soldiers called me The Hat Maker.

The soldiers and the Chief met me secretly to commission new hats.

"How many leaves do you need?"

"When will my hat be done?"

"Can you put some red yarn in mine?"

They didn't dare talk about it in public. Our conversations were covert. They had to be careful so that others didn't know who was receiving my next creation. I soon came to be known as the best hat maker in the village of Ou Krabau. Some people of the village didn't like it, thus the secrecy. They didn't want me to be successful and it wasn't safe for me to be noticed. Of course, I never received any payment or special favors for my beautiful hats, but I did get the satisfaction of creating them.

I could only make hats during the break times, between throwing stones and serving the Angkar. The boil was torture, but it was also a blessing in disguise. When I was alone making hats, my mind was so consumed with the task that I momentarily forgot about my situation. I could no longer climb to the tree canopy, so this became my new escape.

The hats served a purpose of protecting the soldiers from the sun, but they also became a status symbol in the village. I made them only for the Khmer Rouge soldiers and a few of the Mulethan men and women.

One of the "garden girls" had previously suffered a boil like mine and had recovered from the episode. I hoped to pull through like her. She showed mercy and empathized with me. I found her company a welcome distraction.

"Here," she said, "I found some mangos. I know you really like them. It will take your mind off the pain." She brought me fruit when I was in unspeakable agony. The ripe mango tasted like heaven and looked bright and cheery in our bleak, dark hut.

All the garden girls took turns bringing me stolen ripe mango and watermelon as a treat. They bravely demonstrated kindness in my darkest hours.

PORTIONS OF PRÂHOK: 1977

Ou Krabau, Battambang Province

The Mulethan work leader who oversaw the "garden girls" was recently married, and his new wife was the cook for Phum Ou Krabau. The cook was one of the most important jobs in the village. She was a beautiful, young woman with a perfectly clear complexion and dark, deep set eyes. Only the prominent people of the village could be in charge of the kitchen because it held the new gold standard—food. I was so sick that I couldn't even eat the few, lonely pieces of rice with *prâhok*[27] for my ration. I often saved my portion and shared it with the others. In the Khmer Rouge society, when you could no longer eat, you were considered the walking dead.

The cook had a blind mother who lived with her and her husband. She was an elderly woman and looked after me. She often saved and hid leftover rice. The woman was clever and waited until her son-in-law was asleep to make the delivery. One night there was an unexpected tapping on the wall of my hut.

"Who's there?" I asked with a weak and drowsy voice. A young boy stood at the entrance.

"It's only me," said the shy, young boy. I recognized him as the elderly

---

27   Fermented fish paste.

woman's son. The old blind woman had been blessed with this boy in her later years. Many people incorrectly assumed he was her grandson.

"I have rice for you," said the boy. He set the small offering next to my bed and left the hut. After that, the blind woman regularly sent her young son in the cover of darkness to bring me morsels of rice.

"Please tell your mother, 'Thank you. *Arkoun*.'" [28]

"Yes," he said as he stepped back out into the darkness. He was probably eight years old.

The Mulethan leader's family ate well. They were treated even better than the average people from the village because they were one step below the Chief in the hierarchy. When I was sick, the work leader's wife knew that I couldn't digest the prâhok that was in our rice broth, so she occasionally prepared fresh fish just for me. Once again, I was shown favor and kindness. These small acts of humanity, although illegal, helped prolong my life.

---

[28] Thank you.

FISHING WITH DAD: 1963

Khla Kham Chhkae, Banteay Meanchey Province

"Siv Eng, go with your father and catch some fish today."

Mom was always glad to have fresh fish for dinner. I followed my dad and walked in his footsteps down the path to the pond. I was a little girl with little feet, careful not to miss one step. I loved being outside, but the hours with Dad were even more precious.

Dad used his own fishing equipment. He had a very long fishing pole and an even longer fishing line. There was a large pond near our home in Khla Kham Chhkae. In the dry season, we stood by the edge of the pond. We didn't talk much but listened to the silence. I watched as he expertly cast the line and pulled the fish in by the string. The pole was shaped like a wishbone of a chicken at one end and had a smooth texture. There was no reel. Dad hooked the pole to his leg, so his hands were free to maneuver the line and handle the fish. When one would bite, Dad pulled hard on the line and swung the fish onto the bank.

"I got one," he said.

"Dinner!" I cheered. His smile was my catch of the day.

We caught multiple large fish. They were common in that pond. We took our catch home and ate fish for dinner, a reward for a hard day's work. The fish were delicious in soups and with rice, and my mother prepared them to perfection.

There was a different fishing strategy in the wet season. We rowed together across the rice field, stretched the net across in a large expanse, and attached it to the tall rice plants. Then we waited. The next day, we returned to the fish nets and caught the unlucky fish who swam into the trap. I watched as Dad took the fish one by one out of the net. He threw them in the boat. Just like at home, I had responsibilities. I was the rower, the big girl helping my father. I enjoyed tagging along. We kept water in the bottom of the boat to keep the fish fresh. Our boat was like a giant, floating bowl. It was alive, flopping around at our feet. We soaked up the quietness and the togetherness. I watched my dad in awe. He was my hero and a master fisherman. It was just one of his many talents.

NEW FAMILY, NEW HOME: 1964

Khla Kham Chhkae and Battambang

Aunt Kim Ly was Mom's first cousin. She and her husband, Uncle Bun Tek, were very close to our family. They were married but were unable to have children of their own. Bun Tek and Kim Ly were well respected members of our community and were financially affluent and stable. Several families knew about their situation and offered their son or daughter for adoption, but Bun Tek and Kim Ly had their eyes on only one family.

One day, while visiting our village, they approached my parents with a very serious appeal.

"Bun Huor and YoKuy, we come to you with a request. We want to speak with you about the possibility of adoption."

"Go on," said Bun Huor waiting for the inevitable.

"You have several children, and we have none. We long for a child of our own to love and nurture. Would you consider allowing us to adopt one of your children?"

A knowing glance was exchanged between Bun Huor and YoKuy. This was a common practice in Cambodia, and it was not unusual in a case where a couple was unable to have children. They discussed the possibility of adopting Sourn Leng or myself, but we were considered too old to adjust. My younger sister, Koann, loved Aunt Kim Ly and Uncle

Bun Tek, and they were smitten with her. Koann was a young, sweet, and very special girl. A somber agreement was made, and a young child's life was forever changed.

YoKuy did not want to go ahead with the adoption and was very torn about giving up her youngest daughter. She gave Koann to her cousin, Kim Ly, in love, so that she could also experience the joy of motherhood. The only reason that she agreed to the arrangement was because Bun Tek and Kim Ly promised to always live close by. YoKuy never wanted her precious daughter far from her sight.

When Koann turned three, she was unofficially adopted. No legal papers necessary, instead, a simple agreement was made between trusting adults. One day, little Koann had three older siblings and called YoKuy "Mom." The next day, she moved in with her Aunt Kim Ly and Uncle Bun Tek and was told to refer to her biological parents as "Aunt" and "Uncle." She addressed her new adopted mother as *Mai Om*[29] and to her new father as "Great Uncle." Little Koann, with her big searching eyes and innocent smile, didn't have anyone to call Mom and Dad from that day forward.

The day Koann left, YoKuy sent the maid with her so she would bring back word about how Koann was adjusting. The maid reported that Koann was filled with candy and sweets and that she was a happy girl. She was loved from day one and taken care of financially in all her heart's desires.

Koann did not understand what was happening to her. She transitioned from having a busy house with siblings and chaos to become a single child with doting parents. The word "adoption" was never used in her presence. She wouldn't know for sure until several years later that Bun Tek and Kim Ly were not her birth parents. Everything was kept hush hush. Kim Ly and Bun Tek loved her as their own and wanted to protect her.

---

[29]   Mother Aunt.

Soon after the life changing decision was made, YoKuy gave birth to baby Te. He brought joy to the family at a time of extreme sadness for his mother. YoKuy and Bun Huor knew that Koann would be well cared for and wanted to ensure that they could keep their daughter close by, so Bun Tek and Kim Ly agreed to purchase a lot next door and move with the family to the heart of Battambang.

It was decided. Our sister was adopted, and we were moving. From that day forward, Koann had a new family, yet she remained our sister. It was hard on my mother to give up Koann. Her baby was given up out of love, but her heart now had a missing piece.

Dad and Uncle Bun Tek purchased two lots in Battambang and built adjoining homes. Our homes were connected by an upstairs door. To me it was just a door. To young Koann, it separated two families, two homes, and two worlds. The door was a barrier between her and her siblings. My younger sister was occasionally allowed to pass through the door and play with us, but her new protective parents often called her back too soon.

"Koann, Koann. It's time to get ready for bed," said Kim Ly, calling her daughter back home. The sound of her voice was the ending of a fairy tale for the little one who had to walk back through the door. In my childlike brain, I thought my sister was lucky to be the only child and not have to share her possessions. She was a fortunate girl who could have whatever she wanted. Ko Pho, Sourn Leng, and I were busy with school and with our lives. We didn't think about how she must have missed having a big family and living in our home. Baby Te did not grow up with Koann under the same roof.

On the other side of the door, Koann heard our friendly banter—Pho's joking, the sisters' giggling, the shouting and fighting typical of the chaos in a young family. It was like a one-way observation mirror, and yet we were unaware of being watched. Koann often peeked through a hole in the wall of the stairs when she heard us. Her tears were left unnoticed. She occasionally snuck through the door and into our bedroom at night. Sourn Leng and I would chat with her and tell her stories. Sometimes, Pho would join in, making jokes and getting laughs.

When Koann was older and more mature, she occasionally brought her inquiries to her parents. "*Mai Om*, am I adopted?"

This question was persistently evaded and denied by Kim Ly and Bun Tek. After the adoption and the move to Battambang, most evenings were spent with the two families sitting casually on the bamboo chairs on the front corridor of the house. The parents talked together about the day's events and made plans for the next. The weather in the early evening was much cooler, allowing them to relax and catch a breeze. Koann often sat on her father's lap. She was Bun Tek's pride and joy.

Grandma Ma Huoy gently patted Koann's head. "Your parents love you so much they will carry you until your feet hit the floor." This was a common Cambodian saying. As Koann grew, many relatives and elders teased her about how lucky she was to be so loved.

⋯••●●●●••⋯

I was about eight years old when we moved to Battambang. It was much larger than our village in Khla Kham Chhkae. We were officially city people, and we had a new neighbor. She was there the first day we moved in, and she still stands unmoved today. We called her *yeay dool kan dav srov doek* (The Lady with the Rice Stack).

She was always present, watching over us and keeping an eye on our shop. The Lady never moved and held a stack of rice balanced perfectly on her head. She stood unaffected by the weather at the top of the steps on a pedestal.

My parents opened a new business with the move. Dad continued to be a medicine man, but only for our family. They owned and operated a pawn shop called So Kuy Huor in Battambang in front of The Lady with the Rice Stack statue. The shop opened around the time my newest little brother, Loan, was born.

It's best to think of a large train car when visualizing our home. Our long brick building was a row house. In the front was the business with the red and white checkered floor. A large wooden display cabinet ran the length of the wall, reaching just short of the ceiling. It created a wall separating our living space from the shop. The space for my parents' office was in a back room. The dining room and kitchen areas were also on the first floor behind the shop, and a stairwell behind the wall led up to the bedrooms and living rooms. I lived there approximately ten years before leaving for university.

We lived comfortably in the middle class of Battambang. Te was glad to finally have a little brother. Loan became the latest addition to our family, and a few years later we all adored our new baby sister, Nary.

Our family car was parked in the house at night time. Yes, inside the house. We didn't have a garage. In the daytime, we parked the car on the street so our customers could have room to walk around in the shop. At So Kuy Huor, things would get stolen if we weren't careful. We were always on the lookout to protect our inventory. Many relatives on Mom's side of the family were also in the pawn shop business. There was room for lots of shops in the lively city of Battambang.

Pho helped out at the pawn shop, but he also had a business on the side. Pho was an entrepreneur at a young age and rented a table to set up in the back room. He excelled in the subjects of math and physics, and students regularly came to our home for tutoring. He saw an average of ten students throughout the week. Ko Pho was on his way to becoming something great. On the side, he sold cigarettes and tiger balm. Pho had both street smarts and people skills. He always wanted to have children and would make a great dad someday, just like my father.

In our high school years, Sourn Leng and I both worked at So Kuy Huor. We spent several hours walking the red and white checkered floor helping customers from behind the counter. We didn't greet with a "hello" but rather with a smile.

"*Ming*,[30] how can I help you? Are you looking to sell or buy?" I asked.

"Let me show you the beautiful ring we just got in yesterday. What size do you wear?" I was assertive with customers who weren't so friendly and could sweet talk them when necessary. Sourn Leng wore her feelings on her sleeve and didn't enjoy answering customers' questions. She preferred to keep to herself.

In Battambang, we had a TV and refrigerator, but no washing machine for our clothes. We didn't get a TV until I was in high school. Most families didn't own one, but we were lucky. There were about four Cambodian channels to choose from. We watched advertisements, a few Cambodian movies, and previews for new movies.

Scheduled programs were only aired at certain times. At night, when the shop was closed and homework was done, we enjoyed watching TV in the shop. It was like our living room. The door to the shop had a picture window, and people could see inside. Customers sometimes stood outside of our shop on the street to watch TV through our window at night. The reception was terrible, and we consistently wrestled with the antenna.

In Battambang, we couldn't ride our bikes during the day because of all the traffic. My siblings and I waited until evening to use the sidewalk where it was safer. We were frequently seen playing directly in front of the store. We rode our bikes and played games out front every evening.

"I did it. I made it over," said Sourn Leng.

Koann watched us play and joined in when possible.

"Let's raise it again. I bet she can't jump this high," I said.

We played a game where we jumped over a rope and then raised it a little higher each turn. It was like limbo in reverse. We never got tired of that game. I remember the day Mom approached me and told me not to play in front of the house anymore.

"Siv Eng," she scolded, "you are done. You're too old to be seen

---

[30]   An honorific used when addressing an older woman who is not a relative.

playing out front. You are becoming a lady and are no longer a little girl."

This was news to me. I never thought about appearances and wasn't self-conscious. I loved playing with my younger siblings, neighbors, and cousins. That was the end of my childhood. I was the second oldest child and the oldest girl in my family. It was time to grow up and act like a lady.

BICYCLE + BROTHER = LOVE: 1977

Garden Near Ou Krabau, Battambang Province

"Neither fire nor wind,
birth nor death can erase our good deeds."
– Buddha

"It's turning different colors," I said. "It's bursting again."

The boil on my upper left thigh eventually erupted, and the poison was released from its prison. At first, I had immediate relief, then the infection set in. The boil was the size of a golf ball and would leave a large ugly scar. I don't know what caused it to develop, but it was dreadful. It was a common medical ailment in those years. I knew others who had survived with a boil, but many villagers died from the lack of treatment. A boil was another simple infection that medicine could cure within days or weeks.

I missed my sister every day, every hour and every second. She was forever in my thoughts. I yearned to crawl into my comfortable bed in Battambang in our shared bedroom. In reality, I was lying on my hammock in a tent with the seven "garden girls." I hadn't eaten anything in days. Both the agony in my heart and the pain in my leg were acute, preventing sleep. The boil was drained but left me with a high fever.

"Ooh."

The breeze was blowing through our open tent.

"Mm."

A deep moaning sound could not be contained. It oozed out of me, speaking the language of suffering and pain. Our team leader heard the groaning and questioned the girls around us.

"What's that sound? Who is that?" She was annoyed and didn't know someone was sick. One of the girls spoke up.

"Met Bong, I think it's Met Eng." The leader came looking for me. Her eyes perceived my suffering in the moonlight. She gently placed her hand on my forehead.

"Oh no, Met Eng. You are very ill."

"Ooh," was my only reply.

"Met Eng, you can't stay here. Tomorrow morning I'm going to send you to the hospital." Her words were a prescription for death. I heard the words through my pain, and my spirit and body were jolted awake.

It took all my strength to beg for my life.

"Met Bong, if you have compassion, please don't send me to the hospital. Take me to the village. I have a brother."

I knew the real reason they didn't want me to stay at the work site. I'd seen it before. The group leader wanted to avoid the dreaded task of burying my body. The next morning a young boy was sent to my brother's work camp to retrieve him. My Mulethan work leader knew I wouldn't make it and sent me to die with my brother in peace. In the midst of my pain, I took comfort in knowing I wasn't going to die in the hospital.

The next day, my brother arrived at my work camp.

"Siv Eng," he whispered, "don't worry. I'm going to take care of you."

He had with him the same blue bicycle that we brought with us when leaving the Phnom Penh apartment. Pho lifted my thin limp body onto the bicycle. I did my best to sit on the seat with his assistance. He supported me, holding me upright so I wouldn't tip over. If anyone would have observed us that day, they would have seen a simple math equation. A bicycle + a brother = love. Ko Pho walked beside and pushed me on the blue bicycle back to his hut on the other side of Phum Ou Krabau.

I was skinny and weak. It was a long ride back to the hut in the village. For the second time, I thought that my brother was taking me to my deathbed, but he had a different plan. He gently set my frail body down on the floor mat. He had nothing to gain by helping me. His sacrifice was my lifeline.

Normally, the group leaders did not allow their strong workers to stay back in the village and care for the sick. They didn't want to waste a perfectly good day of labor for the Angkar, especially from a solid, strong worker like my brother. It was better for the Angkar if sick people were sent to the hospital where they belonged. The Khmer Rouge mantra was drilled in our brains at the propaganda meetings, "If we lose you, we lose nothing." I was nothing to the Angkar, but I was everything to my brother.

Again, Pho and Sok Yann had to take care of me after working all day. I knew they were mentally and physically drained, and one day I overheard an argument. Our hut was very small with absolutely no privacy. My sister in-law expressed her concern.

"Pho, if we continue to care for Siv Eng and give her our extra portions, we could die from exhaustion ourselves." Pho did not reply. Sok Yann took a stand. "There's no need to keep fighting because she is going to die anyway."

This broke my heart, and the words stung with the intensity of the infection in my leg.

My sister in-law was a wonderful girl. She was faithful to my family and loved my brother to the very end. Sok Yann took such good care of me when I was sick. I knew her love for me ran deep, but her worry for her husband had a greater depth. Pho was caring for all of us and carried the additional burden of Sourn Leng's absence. We all depended on one man, her husband. He was so young and owned such mature responsibilities.

"Pho, your daily physical labor is so intense," she continued. "How can you keep going like this?"

I was silent, not daring to breathe. I knew she was right. It was so draining for my brother to work all day and then come home and take risks for me like climbing the trees for fruit or stealing corn.

Sok Yann pleaded, "I'm concerned about you, Pho."

My brother never said a word. The silence was deafening. I was occupying the small hut and assaulted with the obtrusive, awkward quiet. I heard my brother raise his voice. It was the only time I remember him speaking in that tone. Pho's words cut through the thick air like a sharp knife.

"Sok Yann, she is my sister. Anyone can be my wife, but not anyone can be my sister. You can't change your family." More silence followed. "Don't ever bring this up again. Do you understand?"

I laid there in the stillness, feeling the weight of the conversation embrace me. I felt nothing but honor for my brother. Pho stood by me in life or death.

I felt terrible that he said those words to my sister in-law. She was his wife. She was looking out for her husband and attempting to protect him. Sok Yann was in a desperate situation. I do not doubt that she loved me and truly believed I wouldn't make it. Pho saved all our lives and would have done the same for her. His words meant the world to me. When given the choice, he fought for life. He fought for me, his sister. After that argument, I held onto life, determined to persevere. I endured for Ko Pho.

A LUCKY CATCH AND A
SUSPICIOUS NEIGHBOR: 1978

Ou Krabau, Battambang Province

After miraculously recovering from the boil and the infection that almost killed me, I was able to return to my work in the rice fields. I completed all my daily chores like the other teenage girls. One day on break, I was starving and desperate to catch a fish.

There was a slight wind and a stillness over the water. We didn't own any fishing poles, so catching fish by hand was my only option. The pond was more like a swamp with lots of leeches and floating lilies. I tied my pant legs as tight as possible, almost cutting off my circulation. My fear of the leeches rivalled my hunger. With every step, my feet dug into the murky, muddy bottom, the slime squashing between my toes. Within minutes, the fat leeches clamped their fangs into my skinny ankles, but my tourniquet pant legs prevented them from crawling up my leg. I knew from others that leeches preferred to hide in dark places. No thank you.

I had developed a technique for finding small fish. My toes inched into the pond step after muddy step, the water rising up to my chest. I waited and stood as still as possible, scooping my hand under a floating lily. Normally, when I lifted my scooped hands, I would find very tiny fish jumping around. I caught them and tucked them in my *krâma* for dinner.

This day was different. When I attempted my usual scooping method and lifted my hands, I found myself looking in the eyes of a snake. We were so close, it could have bitten me in the face. It was curled up resting there in my hands. The snake looked short, fat, and delicious. It was black and white with a stripe across it's back and about a foot and a half in length. In the past, I would have run away in fear. This day, my first instinct was to kill and eat it.

The snake was sluggish, so I reacted first. I grabbed it by the tail and slammed it on the top of the water back and forth until I was sure it was dead. I killed it with my bare hands, put my dinner in my *krâma*, took it home, and skinned it. This was the first snake I ever caught or killed, and it held a surprise for me. She was a female, and her belly was full of eggs—a pregnant mommy. Not only did I eat a fat snake for dinner, I also ate several eggs. I had a good meal but ate alone in silence. Ko Pho and Sok Yann were away at the married work camp, and Sourn Leng was still being held in Moung. If they had been in Ou Krabau, I would have been honored to share with them.

The food supplied by the Angkar was never enough. At that time, they gave us one small scoop of cooked rice per day. The supply of rice fluctuated over the years, but we never got more than one scoop a day. In our village, people ate with their group in their hut. At the work site, we ate together in a large group. When possible, we added greens that we found in the jungle. This increased our nutrients and helped to fill our stomachs. We were not restricted from finding extra fish, fruits, or vegetation growing wild, but we could only search on our break time. We were supposed to bring our extra fish, snails, or greens to the community kitchen to share, but we never did. As time passed, our rice portions were cut severely, and we were careful to hide any extra food. If the Mulethan saw our fish or greens, they might try to steal it. We could be accused of stealing food even if we found it on our break.

Death was a sad but common occurrence in Ou Krabau. Every time a person died, the Chief ordered the villagers to take the body and bury it in the jungle outside the village. Most people in Ou Krabau died from disease and starvation. Many of the graves in the jungle were shallow, unmarked, and randomly placed. It wasn't uncommon to accidentally step on a grave without knowing. This was a forbidden practice in our culture.

One of the work families in our village consisted of a mother, father, and several children. We personally knew the father. Their hut was located close to ours, and this man worked alongside my brother at the adult work camp. Disease hit their family, and the first of his children died. The father watched the men carry his loved one away, and then offered to help bury his own child. Our hearts went out to him.

Unknown to the villagers, he waited patiently until the grave diggers left, secretly exhumed the body of his child, and ate the brain and the liver. There was no point in eating the muscle because there was no meat on the bones. The brain and liver were known to contain great amounts of fat.

A week later another one of his children was struck with disease.

"Please call me back to camp when our son is near death," the man said to his wife. "I want to pay my last respects." He headed out the door for the assigned labor camp site. His second child died soon after. Again, the man offered to follow the grave diggers and help bury his child.

After the death of the third child, the husband's behavior became suspicious to his wife. Something about his actions weren't quite right. The woman was distraught and mourning the loss of her son, but she was even more disturbed with her suspicions. She could no longer contain her wariness and alerted the Mulethan authorities to her worst fear. That evening, the villagers took the corpse to the jungle to bury the body. They dug a grave and buried her son. Her heart was broken.

Later that evening, her husband took a walk into the jungle. We saw him walk right by our hut with a sickle and a long scarf. I stood in the hut, and Pho called out to him.

"Excuse me, Met Bong, where are you going?" The man kept walking as he looked up at us.

"I need to collect some supplies from the jungle."

Several hours later, the man casually passed our hut on his way back to the village.

"Pho, look at his scarf," I whispered. "What does he have in there?" The scarf was tied up to the sickle.

"Look," whispered Pho, "there are branches tied around the scarf."

"That's weird," I said. "It's like camouflage. He's trying to hide something."

The scarf was obviously dripping and wet. We had our suspicions.

My brother boldly asked, "Met Bong, what's in the scarf?"

"Nothing," said the man casually.

The man returned to his hut, but two Chhlop soldiers were watching him under close surveillance that evening. They saw him go back into the jungle. They watched as he dug up the body, removed the brain and the liver, and washed them in the pond. He then returned to his hut hiding the organs in his scarf. The Chhlop caught the man and arrested him soon after he passed our hut. They found the organs in his scarf. Three Chhlop walked the man into the jungle, and they used his own sickle to kill him in the early evening before dark. He was buried in the jungle near his children. The soldiers never used their guns to kill us. It was said we weren't worth the bullets. Pho and I were thankful that our neighbor was dead. We were horrified when we learned that this man, in the hut next to ours, had consumed his children. Even the Angkar did not allow cannibalism.

We often heard gossip from other villages at the work sites. In a village near Ou Krabau lived an older Chinese woman. When her son died, the people became suspicious because she never asked for help to bury her son's body. She piled up dirt and planted sweet potatoes on the grave she dug near her hut. When the authorities became suspicious, they searched her hut and found meat preserves with fingers and human bones. The Khmer soldiers killed her immediately without hesitation.

In another village near Ou Krabau, I made friends with a girl at a work camp. Her name was Met Pha, and she was a teenager like me.

"Met Pha, why haven't I seen you very often? Where have you been?" She looked anxious.

"I needed to stay in my village and care for my sick, young brother."

"I'm so sorry he is ill," I said.

Met Pha confessed that at night she was exhausted but didn't dare sleep. She was worried that her grandmother would cut off her brother's leg in the night. Her grandma said he was going to die anyway, and it was good meat. This poor girl was worried about her brother all the time. The grandma was suffering from starvation and malaria and seemed to be losing her mind. In extreme cases, hunger can drive a person to do unfathomable things.

THIEVES IN THE NIGHT: 1978

Ou Krabau, Battambang Province

During the four years we lived in Ou Krabau, we thought about food every day, all the time. We had to steal to survive, and it became a valuable skill. We were starving, but if we were caught with even a kernel of corn, we were stealing from the Angkar. The penalty was death. There were fields filled with pumpkins, mung beans, rice, and corn. We were surrounded by bounty and plenty but could not eat a single bite. Instead, our hard work and resources were being traded for guns and ammunition.

Pho repeatedly risked his own safety for us by securing and stealing food. One night I was feeling particularly brave and volunteered to go with him. Pho vehemently resisted the idea.

"Siv Eng," he argued. "It's extremely dangerous to steal from the Khmer Rouge."

I gave my brother a dirty look that he couldn't miss in the dark.

"You aren't smart like me," he warned. "I'm afraid you might get caught."

The night we left it was pitch-black. The perfect night for a thief. No moon, no stars. Before moving to Ou Krabau, I had never experienced such darkness. There were always lights in the city, in the store fronts and streets. Even in Khla Kham Chhkae there were lamps in the windows of homes. In Ou Krabau, I couldn't see more than a few feet ahead. I stayed near Pho. If he was out of my reach, he was out of my sight, and I feared losing him in the dark.

We each had a long black *krâma* and laid them around our necks, letting the ends dangle at our sides. We then tied up each end into the shape of a bowl. This was perfect for stashing our pumpkins. Our hands were free to hunt for the largest pumpkins. As we walked together in the field, Pho found a large tree for a landmark.

"Come back to this tree, Siv Eng. Remember the shape of it and stay nearby. Whatever you do, don't get lost."

We picked pumpkins in the dark for about thirty minutes. When we finished picking, we ran back to the village where Sok Yann was waiting for us in the hut.

"Show me how many you got," said Pho.

I was ashamed. I had only a few small pumpkins, and my brother had several large ones. He looked at me, shaking his head.

"You silly girl. Why did you waste your time on the little baby pumpkins?" My face turned bright red, a mixture of anger and embarrassment.

"Ko Pho, don't *even* criticize my technique." I raised my voice. "I wasn't casually shopping for vegetables at the market. I was stealing in the night from the Angkar."

Pho smiled, then we busted out in a fit of subdued laughter. That night, the three of us had a good laugh and ate some pumpkins. It was one of the few nights I recall laughing.

——••◆••——

Several weeks after the pumpkin stealing incident, Pho ran into our hut huffing and puffing.

"Siv Eng, Sok Yann, you won't believe what I just got away with," Pho was clearly out of breath.

"What happened?" asked Sok Yann. "We were so worried about you."

The night before, my brother was feeling heroic. Pho had mustered the courage to sneak into the storage room near the communist kitchen.

"Ko Pho, are you crazy?" I asked. "You had the audacity to go into the kitchen?"

Sok Yann was shocked. "You could have been killed. Why did you risk it?"

"I was so hungry," said Pho. "I thought I could get away with it."

I was secretly impressed.

We heard that a Mulethan woman was always on guard and slept right in front of the rice stacks. Rice was priceless. We weren't getting any at that time, only the leftover dust. Money was a thing of the past, long forgotten and discarded without thought. Stealing and illegal bartering were the new currency. The rice storage was located right beside the kitchen. I don't know how he figured out where the guards slept, but Pho had street smarts. Once again, he chose a perfectly dark sky. He hid himself like a shadow in the dark. Only invisible thieves lived to tell their story.

Pho deftly stepped into the kitchen. He was so close to his target and almost ready to head back to the safety of the hut. As Pho reached into the rice bag, his hand brushed another hand.

He was completely startled and caught off-guard. It was a shocking surprise to both of them. Pho wasn't alone. It just so happened that another thief had the same idea on the same night as my brother. They were both in complete darkness, surrounded by obscurity. Neither thief had been aware of the other's presence. As their hands retreated, grains of rice dropped on the floor, making the faintest sound. Someone might as well have blown a bullhorn. The sound of the rice woke the guard.

She screamed out in a piercing shriek. "Thief! Thief!"

Everyone in the camp woke up.

Amid the chaos, Pho thought quickly. The thief ran one way, and Pho ran the other way.

The head guard loudly demanded, "We must catch one of them.

Someone will pay!"

The guards followed the other thief. They hunted and captured him without mercy. Always the protector, my brother ran toward another village, so he wouldn't be suspected. In the morning, the news spread that the soldiers caught a kitchen thief.

Several villagers heard the soldiers questioning him. "Who was the other one? Tell me now." The thief was silent. He honestly had no idea it was my brother.

When Pho went back to the kitchen and saw the thief, both relief and guilt overwhelmed him. The thief was on display for all to see. He was beaten brutally. Nobody knew what happened to him after he was tied up in the kitchen. He was never seen again.

After all the drama and risk taking, the other thief paid the ultimate price, and neither thief received a grain of rice in payment for their bravery.

FALLING HAIR: 1978

Ou Krabau, Battambang Province

Hunger had a taste. My mouth was filled with a spoonful of rice, but all I tasted was misfortune. The flavor was bitter.

As the years passed, stealing became a way of life. Everyone stole food, but not everyone got caught. One day, a girl in our village was unlucky. She was working in the rice field and, like every day, was thinking of her next meal. We were all wasting away to nothing. It was only a few grains of rice. Just a morsel. The Chhlop came out of nowhere and pointed.

"Met Neary, I saw what you did," he said. "Don't deny it." The solid, strong arms of the well-fed Chhlop restrained the girl's scrawny, feeble body. The grains of rice fell from her hand as a soldier grabbed her by the arm.

"Are you watching?" asked the soldier. "This is what happens to girls who steal from the Angkar." He held a large knife in his hands. The hair fell to the ground at her feet in clumps.

We struggled to avert our glances, looking down at our feet and the murky earth. Her beautiful crown of dark hair had vanished, revealing a dry, bald scalp. The unfortunate girl was used as an example to all of us. The punishment was successful, bringing waves of humiliation. Her scalp was exposed, and she was shrouded with shame, yet her stomach remained empty. The bald head was meant to send a message to all witnesses that the victim was untrustworthy. An outward symbol of an inward flaw. Now the girl would be watched with more scrutiny.

The head was sacred in Cambodian culture. The most revered part of the body. No one was to touch a person's head or hair. It could have been me or my sister. It was painful to see her suffer and be publicly disgraced in such a way. She took a risk and paid the price—but it could have been much worse.

Another punishment for stealing was suffocation. If someone was accused of stealing, the Khmer Rouge placed a plastic bag over the victim's head and kept it there until the person was asphyxiated. Before death, the bag was briefly removed, and the process was started over again. I don't know what was worse, watching it happen or experiencing it first-hand.

MICE MORSELS AND RICE DUST: 1978

Ou Krabau, Battambang Province

I had no more jewelry or gold because our suitcase was stolen, but Pho still had a few rings and pure gold chains. Only gold was valued in the very end. Even diamonds and rubies did not retain their worth. By year three, pure gold was scarce. At times, the rice was gone, and we could only trade for rice dust, sweet potatoes, or mung beans. Bartering was illegal, but Pho's jewelry kept us alive. Mother's wisdom was enduring as some pieces from the pawn shop were still with us.

Medicine, sewing needles, fabric, and cigarettes were sought after articles. They could also be traded for rice or needed items. Tiger balm, a popular healing salve from China, was also in high demand by the Mulethan. Since all medicine was destroyed by the Angkar, people possessing items to trade did not starve.

Back in Phnom Penh, Pho had a side business in addition to his electrical engineering job. He bought medicines and cigarettes in bulk at Battambang and then sold them to friends and acquaintances in Phnom Penh for profit. The day we left the apartment, Pho wisely brought along his stash of cigarettes and several jars of tiger balm. This side business was critical in boosting our ability to barter for much needed food.

I can do this, I thought. I was ready to eat my first mouse.

When describing food, the words sweet, bitter, savory, and sour come to mind. Mouse was certainly more savory than starvation. We ate mice not because they were tasty but because they were critical to survival. The protein was a necessity. Everyone was trying to catch them, and soon the mice were in limited quantity. Mice: an endangered species. Instead of bartering for rice, we now used our gold to barter for mice because they had increased in value.

My brother had also been able to save some expensive watches that he traded for mouse meat. What would Mom, the pawn shop owner, think of that trade? If only she knew when she sent us away with the belt of jewelry. You couldn't trade just anything for food. If a gold ring was offered for a trade, it needed to be 24-karat gold. At times, only pure gold could be bartered for rice. Nothing less. A big, flashy diamond ring could be traded for one cup of salt. Over time, supply and demand took over, and then a diamond could no longer be traded for salt. This was a harsh lesson in economics. The value of bartering and trading fluctuated from week to week, relative to the amount of rice available.

Mice were the foulest thing we ever ate. They were even worse than the bugs and worms. The thought of it was worse than the actual taste. We knew that mice feasted on the dead.

One day, when I was alone on break at a work camp, I found a nest of mice and ate the babies. I cooked them over a fire as if making a feast. I somehow felt better about eating them. I convinced myself they were cleaner than the larger mice because they hadn't left their nest or consumed any garbage.

Things went from bad to worse. At times, when food sources were completely depleted, we could trade for rice dust only. Rice dust was a fine powder that came from the rice skin. Before the Khmer Rouge reign, rice dust was mixed into the feed for pigs. It was now the new gold standard. We had become lower than the pigs, but we were grateful for the rice dust to add to our ration of water. The Cambodian people had their own saying: *The footprint is human, but the shit is a pig.*

We longed for the days when Sourn Leng was with us and Aunt Chhiv Hong was still living. In our hut at night we spoke of Mom's homemade dishes. Hot curry soup was one of my favorites, and I savored every bite. *Mi cala* was another frequent meal consisting of a steamed rice noodle served with shrimp, hard boiled eggs, salty daikon, and cucumber. The noodles soaked up the tasty soy sauce, fresh lime juice, sugar, and sweet and sour sauce making the dish even more savory. What I wouldn't have given for a just a taste. After dinner, Mom often made a mung bean dumpling dessert called *Banh Ja'Neuk*. It consisted of mung bean paste wrapped with sweet rice dough in a coconut ginger sauce. My mouth watered just thinking about it.

I had become a hollow frame of my former self. Reduced to a shell of the girl who swam among floating coconuts with her Dad and climbed tall trees. The girl who rode her new bike with the neighbors and watched her mother sew. The child who was miraculously cured from the hiccups and almost lost her finger to the sewing machine. I was young with an old soul, a girl who missed her parents.

DEATH BY TELEGRAM: 1967

Battambang, Battambang Province

One day in 1967, my father left Battambang for the Capital city of Phnom Penh. It was a day like any other. He frequently took business trips to the city to make purchases and visit family members who lived there. Dad told Mom that he was going to buy a motorcycle for Pho and that, while there, he was going to have a medical checkup. Pho needed the motorcycle to drive to and from school and would need it when he moved to Phnom Penh for university. What Dad didn't tell my mother was that he was also having a surgery to fix his bad lung. He didn't want my family to worry about him, so he scheduled the surgery in secret. The only person who knew was Mom's younger brother, Uncle Su.

Before leaving for Phnom Penh, my father's doctor reported that his lung was almost healed from the residual basketball injury. Dad didn't want to be *almost* healed, he wanted the injured part of his lung to be completely removed. The doctor in Phnom Penh was a highly respected surgeon, a university medical professor, and a friend to my uncle. It was a simple procedure. The doctor was going to remove part of three ribs to reach the lung. The damaged tissue was the size of a dime.

Sitting in his hospital bed before surgery, Dad wrote a letter to Mom so that she would know that he was okay. He sent the letter in person with an aunt, who was in Phnom Penh and happened to be traveling to Battambang the next day. The surgery was successful, and he was on his way to recovery.

My father died the next day following surgery. In his last words, he told Uncle Su, "Take care of YoKuy and the children." I'm sure he thought of each of us. Uncle Su stayed with Dad as he took his last breath.

Back home, Pho went to the train station to wait for Dad and bring him home from his trip. He was excited about seeing the motorcycle. Pho waited and waited, but Dad never arrived on the train. There wasn't a phone for Uncle Su to reach us. Pho went again to the train station the next day. Instead of my Dad, he saw my aunt. That's when she gave him the letter.

In the letter, Dad explained that he had lung surgery and would be recovering for a week. Mom was overheard talking to herself as she packed her things to travel to Phnom Penh.

"Why didn't he tell me? Why did he hide it? He can't recover on his own. I need to be there to nurse him back to health." Mom was so upset that Dad didn't tell her what was going on. She wanted to take a taxi straight to Phnom Penh, but taxis were known to be in frequent car accidents.

"Do not take the taxi, YoKuy," warned Grandpa. "They are far too dangerous. You need to wait for the train and leave tomorrow. It's best to be safe."

The next day, Mom was preparing to head to the train station, but some of my Grandma's neighbors received a telegram announcing my father's tragic death. Grandma sent her maid to our house on a bicycle with the telegram. We were all home that day.

"Mom, there's a telegram for you," said Pho. "I think it's important."

Mom saw the news with her very own eyes. She was filled with disbelief. It couldn't be real.

"Mom, are you okay? What does it say?" asked Sourn Leng.

My parents had been married nineteen years at the time of his death. Dad died in Phnom Penh in the hospital, but my family had to bring his body to Battambang for a proper burial. My uncles received permission from a hospital official to transport my father's body to Battambang in their car. When they arrived at the hospital, my uncles dressed Dad in his street clothes. They sat my father up in the back of the car, put sunglasses on him, and then drove his body to Battambang. It was Dad's last car ride.

I will never forget the day he arrived in Battambang. The car pulled up to the Buddhist Temple. All of us children ran to the car. I watched as Mom hurriedly opened the door and threw herself on Dad. It was such a shock and was so hard to accept. The last time Mom saw him, he was in seemingly perfect health. Only days before, he was on his way to buy the newest model of a Honda motorcycle.

His body was kept at the Buddhist temple for one week before the funeral. All of my siblings, including Koann, wore special white clothes. We slept at the temple in a room near the casket for one week until the day of the funeral service, which was held in the Chinese custom. I dreamed of my dad as I slept at the temple, knowing he was nearby. I sensed that he was watching over us. I saw what looked like his sarong walking by. He wasn't ready to leave us.

I attended the funeral ceremony with my mother and six siblings at the Buddhist Temple, and all of our extended family were there to honor my father. Neighbors, customers, family, and friends attended the funeral to show their respects. Dad was placed in a proper casket and dressed in white. I saw him lying there, still and lifeless, and was overcome with grief. Grief for my mother, my siblings, and myself. My father was gone. He wouldn't pull anymore teeth. He wouldn't ask me about my school work or check my hands before dinner. No more swimming lessons. No more medicine or whale juice. He wouldn't give me another shot. There was no warning, and our goodbyes were unspoken. I was overcome with unmeasurable sadness that day. Sorrow and shock shook me to the core. Mother forever treasured the last letter from my dad. It contained his last words. She kept it up until the day that the Khmer Rouge kicked her out of her home. It was stored in the stand where Dad kept his perfectly pressed clothes.

We will never read the letter again.

AKuy My Love,

I am having a surgery in Phnom Penh. I will be home in one week. It's not a major surgery, and I don't want you to worry about me. The doctor will remove the unhealthy part of my lung. Sorry I didn't talk to you about this first. Please, don't worry. I will come back a healthy man and be home in a week. I will see you at the train station. We have been married for 19 years, and I want to be a strong and healthy husband for my bride and my family.

Love,

Your Husband Bun Huor

Koann had a revelation at the funeral. All of Bun Huor's children sat in the proper place in front of the casket in birth order from oldest to youngest. The ceremonial food was placed each day in front of each child for their father: roast chicken, roast pig, rice, fruit, tea and wine. All seven children were wearing the special white ceremonial clothing. Koann sat with them, all her brothers and sisters, wearing white and mourning the death of her true father. She was only seven at the time, but her suspicions were flooding inside as the tears welled in her eyes. She went to Bun Tek and Kim Ly with the same question she had been asking for years.

"See? I'm wearing white like Bun Huor's children. I am his daughter. I knew I was adopted." Her parents looked to each other for mutual support, once again denying the adoption. They feared that Koann would choose her siblings and birth family over them. They loved her deeply and couldn't handle the pain of losing her.

"You are wrong, Koann. It's simple. One of YoKuy's and Bun Huor's children died, and you are taking their place for the ceremony." Koann knew this was not the truth. How could they blatantly lie to her? Even the guests were asking questions. They knew the truth.

"Who do you love more, Koann, your father, Bun Huor, or your father, Bun Tek?" They asked the questions in public for all to hear. These were unbelievable questions to ask a seven-year-old girl.

"I love them both the same," said the little girl whose head was spinning and heart was breaking.

⸻•••●•••⸻

The death of my father caused us all to grow up overnight. It was the first real stain of sorrow and grief on our happy, innocent lives. My brother, Ko Pho, immediately took on the role of our family leader and all of the responsibilities it entailed.

"Pho, you are young, but you are now the man of the house," said Mom.

I was the oldest daughter and took the main responsibility of helping Mom with the kids. Sourn Leng and I were in sixth grade when Dad passed away, Koann was seven, and Te was five. My youngest brother, Loan, was a toddler, and my baby sister, Nary, was only one year old. They never had the chance to really know Dad like the rest of us. They were robbed of their own memories of our father.

The first year after Dad's death, my heart consistently pounded. Mom felt like Dad left for a business trip and never came back. For a long time, we all looked for him to come home from that trip. Grief takes a toll on the mind, soul, and body. I often saw Mom weeping and mourning when she thought no one was watching. Everyone loved my dad. People from Battambang and nearby villages frequently stopped by to inquire about him. Every inquiry caused my mom to reopen the wound and relive the pain. Mom had several children to care for and was only thirty-three years old.

Ko Pho was seventeen, and Mom leaned on him to help her manage the household. Pho was there for her. He was there for all of us. Our hearts ached when we saw Mom cry. The very walls in our house seemed melancholy without him; our home was grieving the lack of his presence. Sorrow took residence and dwelled with us for a season. I dreaded coming home from school because I would find my mom drying her tears, alone. I had nothing to offer to heal her pain. None of Dad's medicines could bring comfort to my mother's anguish. She needed the very thing that she could not have. She missed her best friend.

GOOD ADVICE AND GRANDMA MA HUOY: 1968

Battambang, Battambang Province

After Dad died, Mom did what she never wanted to do—she raised us by herself. Thankfully, she had the support of loving grandparents who lived not far away. My father's mother, Ma Huoy, continued to live with us. That was the Cambodian way.

When Ma Huoy heard the rain and the thunder, she talked about her beloved son. For her, the rain was a connection to him.

"I never expected to bury my son. It's not supposed to happen like this," she said.

We listened respectfully not knowing what to say. Mom was completely lost without Dad. Grandma Ma Huoy worried that Mom would remarry. She didn't want us to have a step-dad who couldn't possibly live up to her son's tender, loving care.

When we were younger, Mom often spanked us when we deserved it. Ma Huoy was protective of her grandchildren and would take us away so we didn't get spanked again. When we got in trouble, she begged us to be good.

"Don't do that again, okay? I try to help you not get spanked." With a gentle touch on the head, she looked into our eyes. "I can't bear for this to happen again. Please mind your mother."

Ma Huoy was always on our side, taking our defense. I think we were perfect little angels in her eyes. We had her fooled. Mom knew better, and we couldn't fool her.

Ma Huoy lived with us and cared for us daily. She was in charge of giving the younger children baths and was part of the fabric of our family. She loved Mom as her own daughter, and the feeling was mutual. Ma Huoy was by Mom's side right up to the day when the communists took over.

--••••●●●•••--

"You are now in charge of your family finances. It is your sole responsibility," said Grandpa. YoKuy's father knew it was time to have a serious conversation.

"It's overwhelming. I just don't know if I can make it alone with young children."

"YoKuy, you are a wise woman with strong business and financial skills. You will make it. I have no doubt."

There was skepticism in her eyes.

"You can run the Pawn Shop on your own with help from the kids." Grandpa was full of encouraging words. He really believed his daughter would make it with her ingenuity and business sense.

"Well, I have no choice now," said YoKuy.

"I strongly advise you to store up gold and jewels to secure your future and the future of your children," said Grandpa. "Do not rely on the Riel."

YoKuy took a sip of her hot tea as she absorbed this information. They were sitting at the table only a few weeks after the death of her husband.

"Gold is the future and is more stable than money," said Grandpa.

YoKuy heeded the counsel. She already had a good stock of jewels and gold with the pawn shop and decided to no longer store up cash. This piece of advice from her father ended up saving lives in the years to come.

Mom took over running So Kuy Huor Pawn Shop on her own with help from the three oldest children. Pho, Sourn Leng, and I worked most days after school and on the weekends when we were old enough. My responsibility primarily consisted of selling merchandise in the store. We sold a few clothing items, and the shop had various jewelry pieces for sale. We specialized in gold, diamonds, rubies, jade, all precious stones, necklaces, rings, and earrings. We also had radios, Omega watches, bicycles, and motorcycles in our inventory. Customers could find a little bit of everything at So Kuy Huor. The shop sold 24-karat and 18-karat gold only, nothing less. Deals were made in cash or bartered.

It was very busy, and the business flourished. Our business was good for the family and good for the economy. We had a neighbor who couldn't believe how successful our shop was. She was outwardly jealous and accused Mother of using witchcraft to boost her sales. Mom giggled out loud at this suggestion. She was crafty, but not with that kind of craft.

WATCHING THE
WATCH MAKER: 1970

Battambang, Battambang Province

Even though our whole world was turned upside down when Dad died, daily life continued. On a typical week day, we rode to school on bicycles or Honda PC50 motorcycles in the morning. I had a green motorcycle, and Sourn Leng had a red one. Ko Pho had the larger motorcycle that Dad had bought for him before he died. This was very different than taking the boat to school in Khla Kham Chhkae. We attended morning classes and then drove home for lunch. The maid made us lunch when we were home, and then we were off on our bikes to head back to school for our afternoon session. In the evening, we worked on our homework in our bedroom or helped in the shop. Many nights, Mom worked late at the Pawn Shop. On those nights, I was responsible for checking my younger siblings' homework and putting them to bed.

My mother took our schooling very seriously, but Te didn't share her love for school. He liked the freedom of his spending money and the autonomy of making his own decisions. He was an independent thinker and got in trouble with Mom a lot.

"Te, did you get your homework done yet?"

"No, Mom, I'll do it later," said Te.

"You have to get your schoolwork done before you go with your friends."

Te was known for taking on challenges and being curious. He was smart and mechanically minded. He liked to take things apart and put them back together. The more challenging the better. The traditional school setting was not for Te. Mom shared my father's concern about Te's education. She wanted him to graduate high school and go on to university.

Te often worried Mom, but Grandma Ma Huoy was an optimist.

"Don't worry about him, YoKuy. Te is ornery just like his dad was at his age. He will turn out just fine."

Mom could only hope that Ma Houy's predictions were true.

One day, Te decided to skip school and go to a local watch store. He was fascinated with the watch repairman's skill. Te returned to the repairman again the next day and had an idea. He would pay the watch repairman to teach him the trade, so he could quit school. A few days later, when no one was looking, Te adeptly unlocked the jewelry case with the key and slipped a ring in his pocket. Te was an entrepreneur. He traded the ring in exchange for his watch work education. The watch repairman agreed to teach the basic mechanics, and Te quickly learned the names of all the components and how to fix them. While Te was watching the watch worker fix the watches, a relative was watching him.

----•••●•••----

As luck would have it, one of Mom's cousins took a *remok*[31] to the city that day. Mom's cousin saw Te at the shop and decided to act.

She drove back to the So Kuy Huor Pawn Shop and reported her observation to Mother.

"YoKuy, I saw Te at the watch shop in town today."

"You saw someone who looked like Te," said YoKuy. "I know for sure my son is at school."

---

[31] A bike with a carriage that pulls passenger from behind.

"I'm confident I'm not mistaken. It was Te for sure," our relative insisted.

Who does she think she is? Mom thought, yet her confidence was wavering.

Te came walking home from school that day just like any normal day.

"Te, what have you been up to?" asked a more than curious mother.

"What do you mean? I was at school."

"Te, you cannot lie to me. I have a witness."

"But Mom, I'm learning to repair watches. It is a valuable skill that I can't learn at school." Te continued with his defense strategy, "This way, I will be able to fix the watches in the shop for you."

Mom ignored Te's excuses and continued the interrogation.

"What did you give to that man?" Te hesitated and shook his head. "Nothing."

Mom threatened again. "No more stories. Tell me now, Te."

"I admit it. I gave him one of your rings." Mom was furious. She marched Te to the watch store that same day, demanding her ring be returned.

"That ring is stolen property, and you took it from a child. He's not even eighteen."

The repairman knew that Mom was serious.

"So sorry, it won't happen again," he said.

Te's embarrassment was spilling over and his frustration was rising.

"But Mom, I wasn't finished with my training. I need to go back."

Te was only trying to fix watches to make money. He was always looking for an opportunity to learn new skills. Although he had visited the watch shop only a few days, he was a fast learner and understood mechanics naturally. Mom's concern about missing school trumped Te's desire to learn about watches, and he never returned to that watch shop again.

BRAINWASHING: 1978

Ou Krabau, Battambang Province

dae min toan ké kâng padévoat kèn
("He who does not move forward fast enough will be crushed by
the wheel of history.")
– Khmer Rouge Saying

When I was left alone at Ou Krabau, my brother often stopped by my camp to check on me and give me reassurance. Pho did his best to lighten my spirits.

"Please don't cry, Siv Eng. It's not good for you."

"I know, but I miss Sourn Leng so much." Every time I thought of my sister, it was a physical, sharp pain of grief that took my breath away.

"She misses us too, Siv Eng."

The Khmer Rouge continued to hold mandatory meetings. There, they proclaimed the greatness of the Angkar, the government, and the revolution leaders. Their theory was that if they destroyed all technology, schools, books, medicine, art, religion, and progress, then started our country over from nothing, we would be a pure society. They were proud that we pulled ancient plows instead of using modern machines. I went from studying pharmacy in a brightly lit city to an ancient times existence in an obscure farming village.

Sometimes in the meetings, a worker would be punished publicly for committing a crime. All eyes witnessed the brutality, and all minds were thinking in unison, "This could be my brother or sister. This could be me." The soldiers often made examples of us using fear rather than weapons. The Angkar philosophy embodied the collapse of reason, morality, and all that was good. Certain phrases were repeated over and over: "*tuk min châmnénch, dâ:k chenh kâ; min kha:t*" (No gain in keeping, no loss in weeding out). Translation—you are nothing.

The history of our new civilization was described as a great wheel of revolution always in motion. "You must hold onto the wheel," they preached. It was clear that if we didn't hold we would be crushed. Many people lost their lives because they couldn't hold on to "the wheel."

GHOST SECRETS: 1978

Phum Ou Krabau, Battambang Province

Instead of planting seeds in the ground to feed the masses, the Khmer Rouge planted corpses. There was death by disease, death by starvation, and death by despair. There was also death by murder.

I would have rather died from starvation than take a chance of being imprisoned like my sister. I was extremely cautious, always on guard. Only one time did I venture to a field with my brother to steal pumpkins. Another time, I was brave enough to steal from a guarded corn field.

One night at a work camp, I was talking with my friend Met Mum.

"The rain is really coming down hard tonight," she observed.

"Yes, *ja*, and it's so dark outside," I agreed. "This is the best time to get corn from the field."

"I'm sure the Chhlop won't chase anyone down in the storm tonight." My friend spoke as if trying to convince herself.

"I want to go with you, Met Mum."

"Are you sure? It's so dangerous," she asked.

I was feeling brave. "Tonight is the night for some corn in my bowl," I asserted.

The corn was ripe and ready for picking. The ears were full size, and I could taste them already. The rain continued to pour buckets of water on the earth as the lightning flashed. We left together, leaving muddy footprints that were immediately washed away. We tried to stay close, so we could find our way back. I soon found myself wandering around in the field picking ears of corn.

Suddenly, I had a funny feeling, like I was standing on higher ground. When the lightening flashed, I saw the post marker on a grave. I was standing among the dead. This was taboo in my culture. My body trembled at the thought of what I had done. My feet ran back to the village so fast I barely left any footprints. I was terrified of the ghosts in those graves. The shallow graves were right there in the field, and the corn grew among corpses. They were probably family members from a nearby village.

Through the fear and racing in the storm, I never let go of the corn in my hands. The Chhlop didn't catch us, but the ghosts knew we had a little extra corn for dinner that night.

A PALM READING: 1978

Moung and Ou Krabau, Battambang Province

bae châng ruh nou daoy sérey ângka:
tuk dey aoy nou muey dom
("If you wish to live exactly as you please,
the Angkar will put aside a small piece of land for you.")
– Khmer Rouge Saying

Every day that she was gone, I thought of my sister. I didn't know for
sure if she was still in prison or even alive. I dreamed of her returning to
Ou Krabau in good health and envisioned her walking up the path to
our hut. The aching in my heart was intolerable. I continued to look to
the moon and send messages to my mom, and every night I rehearsed
childhood memories of my family and younger siblings to keep them
alive, if only in my imagination.

I had a feeling that more changes were coming to our country.
Cambodia was on a rapid, downward spiral. I was on break in my hut
when an old woman cautiously approached. I had seen her in our village
before and knew she lived in Ou Krabau.

"This is for you," she said as she handed me a large dried palm leaf.
The woman turned and walked away.

I carefully unrolled the leaf.

Dear Ones,

I'm being held in Moung Roussei. I'm okay, but my health isn't good. Please don't forget me. I am all alone here.

Your sister,

SL.

The old woman was on assignment from our Chief to gather vegetables outside our village near Moung. My sister was being held there at a labor site nearby and recognized the elderly woman from Ou Krabau. Sourn Leng quickly wrote the message on the leaf and covertly handed it to the woman.

"Give this to the family of Pho in Ou Krabau," she said.

The palm letter was written in pencil. How on earth did Sourn Leng get access to a pencil? I read and re-read the message, touching the words with my fingertips. To me the leaf was like a newly discovered sacred text. The power of Sourn Leng's words spoke volumes to me from the palm leaf, spurring my courage. I was overcome with determination. I was going to find my sister. I knew she needed me. It's funny how grit and resolve can stomp out the fear of reality.

Since her arrest, we wanted to bring our sister back to Ou Krabau. She had been gone for a year and a half. Pho was waiting for an official stamped permission form to bring her home properly. We waited and waited, yet the formal approval never arrived. When we received the palm leaf letter, I was done waiting. The intensity of the loss of my sister was burning stronger every day.

⋯•••●•••⋯

I wanted to go to Moung to be with my sister but traveling to another village without stamped permission was a death sentence. Some people moved from village to village with made-up stories, stating phony reasons that they needed to stay the night. These runaway nomads kept moving west in order to reach the Thailand border. They went to the village Chief claiming they were from the next village and were looking for a family member. Another popular excuse was that they were at a work camp and got lost. After a night or two, they would escape and tell the same story to the next village. Some people escaped alone. Others moved in small groups. When caught, they died brutally in the hands of the Khmer Rouge soldiers. We heard the stories, and they all ended the same. The escapees had no weapons, no food, and no shelter. They were brave nomads on the dangerous road to freedom.

One of Mom's cousins planned to escape across the border to Thailand. He was with a group of three or four young men. They left their wives behind with the intention of getting help for Cambodia and coming back to rescue their families. Mulethan people from a village nearby saw them leave and reported it to the soldiers. They were hunted like prized prey. When caught, their stomachs were cut open while they were still alive. Weeds and grasses were stuffed in their abdomen, and they were left as an example for witnesses to see what happened to runaways. We didn't know about my family member at the time, but those kinds of stories fed our fear and prevented us from attempting to rescue Sourn Leng.

A CHANCE MEETING:
SEPTEMBER, 1978

A Work Camp and Phum Ou Krabau, Battambang Province

Days after I received the palm leaf letter, I was back at a work camp a few miles from our village, digging a ditch for irrigation canals. I sat down for a much-needed break next to a girl my age.

"You live in Ou Krabau," I said. "What's your name?"

"Met Mao," she replied.

"I'm Met Eng."

"Who is here with you?" the girl inquired.

"I'm alone," I admitted. "My sister is being held in Moung Roussei." The girl looked surprised.

"I'm alone, too. I believe my sister is confined in the same camp as your sister."

"Really?" I said. "I want to go there someday. I miss Sourn Leng so much."

"I desperately want to find my sister too," Met Mao echoed.

We continued to sit and talk as we ate our measly meal. During the break, we decided we were going to rescue our sisters. We planned to escape and go together to Moung, but first we had to run away from our work camp and return to Ou Krabau to alert our families about our plan.

It was a dangerous and brave mission and proved to be life changing. I would have never undertaken this mission alone, but my new friend spurred me to finally take action.

After work that day, I ate very little rice, saving some in my *krâma* for the next day. We made a promise to meet in the morning.

If anyone was watching, two plucky girls could be seen in the early morning light running away from camp. We feared that a Chhlop or soldier would find us, but it was a chance we were willing to take. It was a long walk back to Ou Krabau.

Ahead of us, the outline of our village home came into view.

"You go to your brother, and I'll meet with my mother," said Met Mao.

"Okay," I agreed. We parted ways for the evening.

Pho looked shocked. "Siv Eng, why are you here?" he snapped when I stepped into the hut. "What have you done? You are supposed to be at your work site."

"I'm leaving tomorrow to find Sourn Leng," I asserted. "I have to see her. She can't be alone any longer."

"But Siv Eng, she's far away in Moung," he said. "You are making a big mistake, and you shouldn't have come here in the first place. If you will just wait, I have a feeling that the Chief will give me permission to go and get Sourn Leng."

We both knew the inevitable was about to happen. Since I had run away from the work camp, I couldn't go back, and I was no longer safe in Ou Krabau. I had already missed the time when I needed to report to my work leader and was now considered a missing person.

"I can't afford to let anything happen to you. Why did you do this?" Ko Pho scolded me harshly. He reprimanded me like a father, like my father. He spoke the language of love and concern.

"Ko Pho, I met a girl who also has a sister held in Moung. We are going to find our sisters together. I won't be alone. It was meant to be. If we are caught, we will say that we are lost orphans, and will ask to join the work camp in Moung."

My brother stared at me, shaking his head in resignation. His wife, Sok Yann, was also in the hut, listening to our dilemma. Her raised eyebrows displayed her unease. The ball was already rolling, and life or death choices had been made.

My brother spoke bluntly.

"There's more than a fifty percent chance that you will get arrested if you don't have a stamp."

"I'm willing to take that chance," I asserted.

"Siv Eng, please don't go tomorrow. Wait for the official permission, and we will get Sourn Leng legally with the blessing of the Chief."

"What if they never give us permission?" I shouted. "I can't wait one more day."

The soldiers were tightening up their security. In the past, we could travel to a nearby village with a hand-written note. The new rule required an official seal with tight security. Authorization could only be granted by the village Chief or a soldier.

"I see there is no changing your mind," Pho said as he prepared a fake letter for me. "No matter what they say, you must insist that your team leader gave you this document."

I knew I could be tortured for carrying false papers. The gravity of the situation quickened my pulse and turned my stomach. I embraced Sok Yann, and she handed me a precious gift—a wood potato from her secret garden behind the hut. She only had a few, and it was a sacrifice. I embraced my brother before stepping out the door. I paused there in his arms, if only for a fleeting moment. Even though he was skinny and starved, he was strong. He possessed an inner strength. Ko Pho's selfless love surrounded me and filled me for the journey ahead.

"Khnohm Leahaey, Ko Pho."

"God be with you, Siv Eng. Leahaey."

PART 2

"There are only two mistakes one can make along the road to truth; not going all the way, and not starting."
– Buddha

A WHISPER IN THE NIGHT: SEPTEMBER 1978

Moung, Battambang Province

Met Mao and I left for Ou Krabau together, setting off on a journey to search for our sisters. We were already missing in action. Instead of heading west to the safety of Thailand, we headed to Moung. If caught, we would be arrested. It was just before sunrise, and the darkness was our shroud. We chose to cross the rice field to get to the train tracks, but the water was deep, making it difficult to walk. It was wet season, and the mud was like a suction cup, restraining our feet and sticking between our toes. Excitement was surging, our footprints bearing witness to our secret journey. We wandered around looking for the railroad. The tracks would be our guide. In the darkness, we lost our direction, and when morning light arrived, we realized our mistake.

"Look behind you, Met Eng. I can still make out the village," said Met Mao. There was a shiver of fear in her voice.

"We didn't make it far enough," I agreed.

"What if someone sees us standing here in the field?" asked Met Mao.

As we walked to higher ground in the light of dawn, we found the tracks and followed the railroad. I was exhausted and hungry yet gained momentum as I trudged along. The anticipation of seeing Sourn Leng in person gave me strength; a magnet was drawing me to Moung.

We walked along the tracks with caution. As we made progress, we saw two men approaching from the other direction. We could easily recognize a soldier from a distance. Guns were a sure sign of trouble. These men didn't alarm us because they weren't armed. The men walked closer, shouting at us.

"Met Neary, where are you going?" said the one on the right.

I spoke up addressing him with confidence. "We are going to Moung to visit our sisters."

It was the truth. I had no reason to lie. The man did not approve of my answer.

"You have no family," he said. "You have no sisters. Angkar is your family now."

Again, the unnecessary reminder. At this point we knew they were soldiers.

He continued his tirade, "Do you have permission to be here? Where is your official stamp?"

I handed over the pseudo document crafted by my brother. The soldiers were puppets for the Khmer Rouge. I was an actor reading the script and predicted the next line.

"Who wrote this?" he asked with an annoyed tone.

"Our group leader gave it to me." The lie came easy.

"Girls, are you trying to run away?"

"Met Bong, we didn't *run* away," I said. "We were just *walking*."

My sharp words cut through the steamy afternoon air. The soldier thought I was being sarcastic, and I instantly regretted my comment. He assumed I was mocking his intelligence. Maybe I was, but I immediately apologized.

"I'm so sorry, Met Bong," I pleaded looking down and nodding my head in submission. "We were just *walking* on our way to Moung."

"You have a smart mouth, Met Neary." he said.

"Met Bong, please. If we were running away, we would have hidden from you when we saw you coming."

I was a bit sassy that day. My mind was consumed with my mission. This soldier was an obstacle in my path and a distraction from my agenda. He seemed to calm down, but my sense of fear was escalating. I realized that I was fighting for my life. My young friend did not say a word during the exchange. Met Mao stood behind me, counting on me to negotiate for both our lives.

"Hand over your bags."

They found nothing suspicious because we had nothing to hide. My bag held my wood potato, a plate, spoon and one skirt. Of course, I also had my scissors, thread, and needle.

"Follow me," the soldier said. We were taken together by the railroad tracks, just short of our destination. The soldiers did not treat us as prisoners or put us in handcuffs. It could have been so much worse.

We were walked about three miles further to Moung Roussei, to a holding place at a soldier station. It was previously a beautiful home. The house was tall and spacious with a stairway and an open balcony.

We were arrested for crossing the border to another village without stamped permission. My brother was correct. The letter he made for us didn't pass as official. Nothing was explained to us, and we had no idea what lie ahead.

One side of the upper balcony was open, and the other side had a small door leading to an enclosed room. Six male prisoners were locked on the other side of the door every night. These men were transported to a work camp in the daytime hours. As we slept there the first night, I thought of Sourn Leng.

"I'm here, sister. I'm so close to you. Can you hear me? I got your letter and have come for you. Maybe they will take me to your camp, and I can work by your side." I was still plotting to escape and join her. She wasn't far away.

We were kept at the holding station for one week in the stunning home. The house was far above the standards of our humble hut in

Ou Krabau which had a rickety floor and cracked walls. It's funny how you can appreciate things like fine architecture and design while simultaneously experiencing extreme angst. There was one other woman who was also being held at the house before we arrived. During the day, we helped her with the cooking and chores in the kitchen. I ate actual rice that week and was fed well by Khmer Rouge standards. I thought of Ko Pho and Sok Yann consuming only water and a few grains of rice after a long day's work.

There were seven guards who resided at the house-turned-soldier-station. I avoided looking at their faces and wouldn't have recognized them in a line up if my life depended on it. They remained nameless yet held my life in their hands. The three of us women slept on mats in the open area to the right of the balcony. I was afraid to use the outdoor bathroom at night because we were warned that we would be shot without question. I couldn't believe we weren't raped or beaten, two young girls and a woman living in a house filled with men.

On the seventh day, in the pitch-black evening around ten o'clock, we heard the sound of a loud vehicle approaching. We were almost asleep when it stopped in front of the house. The engine sounded like a large army utility truck. The three of us sat up on our mats and saw flashlights below. Footsteps were advancing toward the stairs. We couldn't see clearly and were terrified; the hair on my arms stood on end. Whoever it was, they turned their flashlights off, and we quickly laid back down. We sensed their strides coming closer with each step. The guards from the house were talking on the patio to new soldiers from the truck. Their voices were calm and relaxed. We were terrified while they were making casual small talk. Keys were rattled as they opened the door to the prisoners' room next door. The six male prisoners were brought out of the room. We froze, pretending to sleep. The soldiers handcuffed the men one by one, marching the bound prisoners down the stairs and taking them outside to the truck.

"What is happening?" whispered Met Mao. She grabbed my hand

in the dark, desperate for comfort.

"I don't know," I breathed.

"Where are they taking them?" murmured the woman.

"Shhh," I warned. "Someone's coming."

A hushed silence travelled through the air.

The flashlights ascended the stairs and were soon shining in our faces. We were blinded by the sheer brightness. The soldiers shouted their instructions.

"Met Neary, pack up your things. We will load on the truck."

We thought the worst. We were marched down the stairs and found ourselves standing behind the truck. Met Mao, the woman, and I hugged each other. We knew we were likely riding to our death. I had heard of many people over the years who were taken away by truck never to return.

We cried in the darkness, our tears fell wasted and unseen. They did not handcuff us like the men. I was the very last one in line. Before I stepped on the truck, one of the soldiers kindly whispered in my ear.

"Met Neary, don't be afraid. Everything will be okay." His voice was barely audible. "They are taking you to a prison, I promise," he whispered. His was the only soldier face I saw that week. I looked into his eyes and sensed kindness peeking through the darkness. "Do whatever they ask of you, only then you will be safe," he said.

Those were the same words that were often spoken before people were taken to their death. The Khmer Rouge preferred compliant victims. On the truck, I tied my *krâma* up tightly around my neck. The truck was open in the back, the wind blowing dirt in our faces. They drove fast as if chasing the night. I found myself traveling away from my brother in Ou Krabau and away from my sister in Moung. My mission was unraveling at lightning speed.

ALIAS: OCTOBER 1978

Poithisat Prison, Pursat Province

It was still nighttime when we arrived hours later. The truck did indeed drive through the gates of a prison. Maybe the soldier was telling the truth. Needless to say, my worst fears were coming true. I never knew what happened to the other lady or the six men. I never saw them again. They may have been held somewhere else in the prison compound, which consisted of several buildings. Met Mao and I were taken to the teenage building in the prison, but it became apparent that every cell was full. There was not room for both of us. Once again, I was separated from a friend.

"You, Met Neary, go in there," a guard said to a terrified Met Mao. She was shoved into the cell with the young teenage girls, clearly an unwelcome guest. I walked on, following the prison guard and leaving my only friend behind.

"You, this cell." He pointed to my new dwelling with his gun. I looked intently at the faces of the middle-aged prisoners. My new roommates looked me over and seemed to approve.

After a few days, I saw that my friend was still alive. When we were digging in the field near the prison, I saw Met Mao with another teenage group. I wanted to run to her, but we weren't allowed to talk to anyone while working. Conversation was strictly prohibited. We caught eyes and shared the collective relief of being alive. It was a small victory, and I clung to it tightly. Her small wave and warm smile became a final farewell. *Khnohm leahaey.*

In the end, I was lucky to be placed in the cell with the older middle-aged group. The prisoners in my room were more mature and compassionate than the short-tempered, single, teenage girls. Many of my roommates were widows, their murdered husbands had been high ranking officials with Lon Nol's government. They became my new family. There was only one man living in our cell of fourteen women. He was with his wife and their little boy. Every morning the husband worked in the men's group, and the women were sent to a separate camp. I worked with the teenage girls.

The man in our cell had been caught stealing rice for his pregnant wife. The Angkar punished his "high" crime with a prison sentence. I began my new life as a prisoner and quickly learned the rhythm of the daily routine. Thoughts of my brother, sister, and Sok Yann were always on my mind. Did Pho and Sok Yann assume I was killed or arrested? Was there a possibility of escape? No one knew of my whereabouts. I later learned that I had been taken to Poithisat Prison in the Pursat Province.

"Name?" demanded the guard.

My instincts were alerted. I needed to protect my identity. I needed an alias.

"Aun," I lied. I looked down avoiding eye contact.

"Where are you from, Met Aun?"

"I lived in a small village near Mongkol Borei by a rice field," I said. Persons from a small village were treated significantly better compared to those from a larger city like Battambang. What they didn't know wouldn't hurt me.

"What did your parents do?" he asked.

"They worked in the rice field," I replied. I exchanged the truth for little white lies in a game of survival.

"Where is your family, Met Aun?"

"They are dead, Met Bong."

As I said the words, I felt that I was betraying my family, but technically this was not a lie. I had not heard from my mother or siblings since Mom's letter was sent to our apartment in April of 1975. I had no idea if they were still alive or taken by disease or starvation. My dream of seeing my mother in white robes frequently replayed in my mind. The guards took my word about my history and moved on. I had passed my first test in prison.

The Khmer Rouge possessed a deep hatred for the Chinese. I traded my Chinese name, Siv Eng, for the new name, Aun. It was imperative to remain anonymous. I looked Chinese with my lighter skin tone and facial features. Though born in Cambodia, my mother and father were of Chinese descent. We considered ourselves Cambodian by culture and nationality with a mixture of Chinese traditions. "Aun" referred to something petite and small. It was a sweet Cambodian name for a girl and was very common. A wallflower was the safest disguise.

MANY HELMETS, ONE POTATO: OCTOBER 1978

Poithisat Prison, Pursat Province

Every day was the same. We started work at 5:00 a.m. with a whistle. In the morning, they threw open the door to our cell. Some days, we cleared fields for cultivation. Other days, we worked in the rice fields. Many days we dug holes and canals and carried the dirt away. We may have also helped to dig what would later become a mass grave near the prison. On those days, we were digging into our future. There was a fence located behind the property, and we were never allowed to go beyond the secured area. We did not officially know what was there, but we had our suspicions. Many years later, mass graves were discovered directly behind the prison building where I slept. When my fellow prisoners' names were called, they needn't travel far to their final destination. How convenient for the Khmer Rouge.

I worked with the teenage girls during the day. Some prisoners noticed that I was physically weak and could barely hold my own. When digging the canals, an assembly line was created to remove the dirt. One person stood in the hole digging up the earth with a hoe. The next person lifted the large, heavy basket filled with dirt. The rest of the prisoners stood in a row, passing the weighty basket down the line and away from the hole. Jobs were assigned each day, and one unlucky person was selected to stand in the hole and lift up the heavy basket. One day a Khmer Rouge girl who was a fellow prisoner stood up for me.

"Why do you always put Met Aun in that spot?" she asked a leader. That day, I was moved to an easier task and was forever grateful to the girl.

Another job in prison was to carry fertilizer on our heads from place to place. The baskets were heavy, and it was a nearly an impossible task given our lack of strength. One day, an announcement was made.

"Attention. We will be using a boat today. Who can row?" the guard asked. "Step forward now." I hesitated. Was this a good thing? Could this improve my status or get me killed? I slowly stepped forward.

"Met Bong, I can row."

I stepped onto the boat with one prisoner, one Khmer guard, and a load of fertilizer. I deftly rowed around obstacles on the river. I felt at home. We went back and forth that day up and down the river to move the fertilizer.

"Met Aun, where did you learn to row?" asked the guard. Not everyone had boating skills, and that made me a stand out.

"Met Bong, I lived in Khla Kham Chhkae and rowed a boat to school," I said. I was careful not to mention Battambang or So Kuy Huor Pawn Shop. Khla Kham Chhkae was a safe place to discuss.

"You have excellent rowing skills, and we may need you to row in the future." That was my first and only communist compliment in prison.

"Yes, Met Bong." I looked down at the water and placed my oar in the eddy, creating a swirling motion. The clouds were reflected in the water, making me think of days spent with my father. Those memories were still alive, flowing just under the surface.

The landscape around the prison was pebbled with helmets. They were everywhere. Every evening, when I settled in for the night, I set a helmet up on three stones near my bed mat. We used the helmets to relieve ourselves. It made for instant indoor plumbing. We only went outside at night when absolutely necessary. It was a dangerous plight because we could be shot by a soldier. The numerous helmets were a tangible witness to the ominous death of Lon Nol's soldiers. I tried to repress my true thoughts. Who wore this helmet? What was his story?

One evening we were settling in for the night when a soldier opened our door and shoved a woman onto the floor of our cell.

"This will be your new home," he said. She fell hard on the bare floor and landed with a thud. Her body was limp, and her black head scarf was soaked in matted blood.

"Maybe now you will stop stealing," the soldier continued.

The blood from her head stained the floor of our cell. Our door was slammed shut, and the soldier's footsteps faded as he walked away. Another prisoner and I knelt down and bent over the poor woman.

"What is your name?" I asked.

"Met Pheap." Her voice was raspy as she tried to catch her breath.

Met Pheap lay still on the floor and slept for a few hours while recovering from the head trauma. We soon learned that her husband was a communist Chief for the Khmer Rouge. He was recently killed because of some disagreement, and she was sent to prison because of her association with him. Even the communists weren't safe from the communists. She had previously been held in another building but was moved to our prison unit because of stealing.

That evening Met Pheap went out under the guise of using the restroom and was caught pulling a wood potato from the ground. The soldiers kicked her so hard that she flew several feet away. When they were finished with their brutal punishment, she wasn't even recognizable.

This young woman, Met Pheap, became a friend of mine. She was recovering from a beating and at the same time mourning the loss of her husband. I tried my best to encourage her, given the circumstances. For some reason I was drawn to her. I overheard gossip that she had a reputation for stealing and was sent to our cell to be reformed. Apparently, the prisoners in our room were known for being well behaved.

My roommates never had much to say to each other due to hours of hard labor. We were let out of our room for work only. After a long day of labor, the soldiers allowed us to jump into the river to clean ourselves and our clothes. I looked forward to these late afternoon baths in the river. It was the only highlight of our daily prison routine.

One day when I was working in an irrigation canal, a girl named Met Pat asked to relieve herself. She was taking too much time, and a guard was sent to check on her.

When she came back, the guard called out. "Met Pat, bring your scarf with the fruit for all to see."

He beat her severely. A Khmer Rouge object lesson. I never stole a bite of fruit, a potato, or a single grain of rice when I was in prison. Soon after, Met Pat's name was called. When the guards randomly called a prisoners' name, they were taken away never to return.

A HAIRY SITUATION: 1978

Poithisat Prison, Pursat Province

We were away at work one day when a woman in our cell gave birth. It was a miracle when a baby was born alive during the Khmer Rouge years. When we returned from work, Met Pok was staying warm on the bed with her baby. A small fire was burning underneath her bed. In Cambodia, it was customary that a family member would build a small fire for several days after delivery. Her bed was set against a wall under a boarded-up window. I usually slept on the floor on my old hammock next to a prisoner named Met Chan and her two small children. We slept near Met Pok's bed. That night after we ate our *bâbâ*, Met Pok made a request.

"Won't you come to sleep on the bed with me, Met Chan? I don't like to sleep alone, and I need to keep warm."

I thought it was weird that she asked people to sleep with her. She was an adult and yet didn't feel comfortable sleeping alone. Met Chan promptly gave an excuse.

"I can't sleep on the bed because my children may need me in the night but Met Aun can. Why don't you ask her?"

Why did she have to bring up my name? I was reluctant to sleep with Met Pok. I was fine on the floor, but had pity on Met Pok as she had just given birth. I sat on the bed beside her and started to lay down.

"Please, Met Aun, sleep over there on that side," said Met Pok.

I obediently climbed over to the side of the bed against the wall. I didn't have a preference and wanted to appease.

I couldn't sleep that night. After a few hours, I felt something pushing on my chest. It was heavy and bearing down on me. At first, I couldn't distinguish what it was. A hand? I readjusted and moved a bit, and it went away. I looked around; everyone was sleeping. I took comfort in the random snoring patterns and tried to fall asleep. I laid there in the eerie darkness, wishing for rest or at least the welcoming light of morning. Again, I felt the same dark presence pressing on my chest. This was not my imagination. Who or what could it be? I shrugged it off and turned over.

As I attempted to fall asleep a third time, I saw the shape of a hand in the light from the fire. It was attached to an enormous, hairy arm. My sixth sense kicked in, and my heart beat as if it would burst from my chest. An evil presence was trying to kill me. I was being suffocated, the pressure on my chest increasing with every passing moment.

I came to my senses and sat up in bed. With a trembling body and shaking hands, I quietly crawled onto the bare floor to resume my usual sleeping place. Would I be safe here? Could the arm reach anywhere? We weren't alone in our cell. An evil tormentor was among us.

Met Pok woke up suddenly and whispered, "Met Aun, are you too warm from the fire?"

"I—I just couldn't get to sleep up there, Met Pok," I said.

I made it through the next few hours with hardly any sleep. Lying on the floor, I held the hand of Met Chan's young daughter as I tried to sleep. My nerves didn't completely recover until the next morning.

"Met Aun, why did you come back down to the floor last night?" whispered Met Chan. When I relayed my spine-chilling experience, she made an admission.

"That's no coincidence. It's exactly what happened to me." I couldn't believe it. The arm was real. She had slept in the bed with Met Pok and had the same suffocating experience. Met Chan confessed that she suggested that I sleep there to see if the same thing happened to me.

Superstitions and ghosts were very real in Cambodian culture. When my mom was a child, she learned a story that was passed down from generations. In ancient times, bamboo thorns were placed around a baby's bed to protect it from danger. It was believed that when a woman gave birth to a child, an evil spirit could be attracted to the house. I know this wasn't the case in prison because the woman, Met Pok, was tormented by the spirit long before the baby was born. She never spoke of it, but frequently asked someone to sleep with her, never wanting to be alone. I never slept up in the bed again, and the woman never asked. She faced her tormentor alone.

SKIRT SLEUTH: NOVEMBER 1978

Poithisat Prison, Pursat Province

Sewing had a way of reminding me I was alive. I got lost in the details of creating a perfect seam with flawless stitching, even if I was patching a boring black skirt or blouse. It took time to reach that level of perfection. On the outside, an observer would see the dull, black stained uniform. Looking closer one would notice the machine-like stitches. They were my pride and joy.

I only owned two skirts in prison. Fashion was not a consideration under the Khmer Rouge. My oldest skirt was worn and thin. I wore it when laboring in the fields. I had just received material for a new skirt in Ou Krabau weeks before I was arrested. I was proud of my new skirt, and when it ripped on a nail I was devastated and mended it the same evening, fixing it perfectly.

A few days later, when I came back from working in the field, my new skirt was gone. Someone had removed it from my bag. I reported this seemingly insignificant incident to the prison guard.

"Please, Met Bong, my skirt is missing. Can you help me find it?"

"Are you sure it's missing? Did you leave it somewhere?" he asked.

"No, Met Bong, I know I left it in my bag."

I have no idea why the guard took notice or cared that my skirt was missing. Not only did I desperately need it, but I was infuriated that someone stole it. I knew it must have been one of my roommates, and I had a suspicion of the guilty party. Days earlier, Met Pok, the woman with the baby, asked me about that very skirt and wanted to make a deal.

"Met Aun, would you trade your new black skirt for two of my skirts?" she asked.

I wanted to say, "No way, are you crazy?" Instead, I politely turned down her offer. That skirt was mine and only mine. My fashion sense was still alive and kicking, and it was the only new item I owned.

I told the guard that my missing skirt had a patched hole and explained exactly where it was. He checked all the prisoners in my cell and found that Met Pok did indeed have my skirt. He was the judge, and I was the plaintiff. He asked both of us questions about where the hole was located and where we got the skirt. Needless to say, I got my skirt back. The patched hole was located exactly where I claimed, and it didn't take a genius to solve the case. The true miracle was the fact that the guard took the time to help me. When the skirt was finally returned to me, it had several holes. I cried in defeat. Met Pok made me pay the price for not trading with her. I never spoke with her again.

BIRD FALLING, NAME CALLING:
DECEMBER 1978

Poithisat, Pursat Province

In prison, we weren't allowed even a morsel more than what was provided. The work camps near Ou Krabau were horrible, but the prison was significantly worse. My face was sunken, and my belly swollen. How could something so empty look so big? I was truly the poster child for starvation. We were given our ration of one small scoop of rice soup to eat at noon and in the evening. Only, there wasn't any rice in the soup, it was just *bâbâ*. I knew that I would die there soon. I would take my place in the ground behind the prison next to my fellow inmates. I harnessed all my strength to get out the door every morning. If I didn't go to work, I wasn't given my meager portion of *bâbâ*.

In Ou Krabau, I ate extra green vegetation and bugs when necessary. All things creepy and crawly had sufficed to get protein under duress. This was not an option in prison. If we were not working, we were locked in our cell. Prisoners were not allowed leisure walks in the jungle.

One day in prison, I learned of a starving boy who died from eating toad eggs. His cell mates begged him not to eat the eggs. The following morning, he was found dead in his cell. The soldiers threw his body in a grave, where his hunger was finally put to rest.

The prisoners waited in long winding lines every day at meal time. Around the prison and among the snaking line of hungry inmates, there were several trees with bird nests. One day, as I was standing in line, a baby bird fell and landed right in front of me. It was so fragile and young, and yet it was still alive. It did not yet have any down on its pink body, and its blue eyes were sealed up. Normally, this would have been considered a gift. Manna from heaven packed with protein. I was at the point where I would have eaten a baby bird raw before allowing someone else to take it from me. I should have hidden it in my scarf to eat later, but something stopped me in my tracks. I was struck by its state of helplessness. I picked up the vulnerable bird very gently. My hands now held its fate.

"Here's your baby. She's safe now." I returned the baby bird to her mother, placing it back in the branch. This was completely out of character and not a smart survival decision. My actions did not go unnoticed. One of the prisoners behind me in line stated the obvious.

"Why would you put that bird away and not eat it? What is wrong with you?"

"Don't you see how panicked that mother bird is?" I defended my actions and the poor animal. "This baby bird has a chance to be with her mother. She can be restored."

At that moment, I knew I did the right thing. I felt such a powerful, unrelenting urge to protect the bird. It didn't make any common sense, but I was obedient. I would think of that bird in the days to come, the bird who was returned to her mother.

⸺•••◆•••⸺

A few weeks later, we were sitting in our cell room and preparing for the night. There was a dark, dim shadow lingering in the air. The Khmer Rouge had recently become obsessed about an impending Vietnamese invasion, and the guards began calling the names of prisoners with a fury. In previous months, prisoners were killed occasionally. Now it was a daily occurrence. They called a few names at a time. With the Khmer Rouge, it was always about efficiency. On this night, it was my friend's turn. We had just finished eating when we heard ominous footsteps, and in a rush our cell door was opened.

"Met Pheap," they said. "Pack your things, and we will take you to your village."

This was code for a death sentence. We weren't allowed to speak, but it wasn't necessary. The unspoken truth was communicated loud and clear. Earlier that day I had borrowed Met Pheap's blouse. I motioned quickly to return it to her, but she spoke with defeated resignation.

"Just keep it, Met Aun." Those would be her last words.

The shirt was a bright royal blue. It was beautiful, and the fabric was well made. She had kept it hidden in her bag and refrained from dyeing it black. She never wore it, except to sleep, and let me borrow it for the first time. I was wearing it that night because I didn't have any other clean clothes. I kept that blouse even years later.

I clearly remember her beautiful face as she walked away. Her features are forever burned in my brain. She looked over her shoulder as she exited the cell for the final time. Soon her footsteps faded from the hallway, a decrescendo with each step. Next the jingle of the key turned slowly in the lock at the front door. When it was safe, the prisoners and I looked out the window sill. All of her belongings were scattered haphazard along the ground. I touched her blouse letting the silk gently run through my fingers and said a prayer. *Leahaey*, I breathed. I didn't dare say it aloud. Met Pheap was my dear friend. I didn't sleep that night. In the morning, we looked outside, and all of her belongings had vanished. We absorbed the harsh reality. Her final resting place was not far from where we slept.

I placed my hands through the handles. Open, close. Open, close. I kept the blades sharp and ready. They never left my side and were always on my mind. I kept them in my bag at all times. When they took my best friend, Met Pheap, I thought about my scissors and often rehearsed plans to kill myself. Would I summon the nerve to slice my wrist? Would it be a slow and painful death? If I had access to pills, it would have been an easy way to go. In the end, I didn't have the nerve to kill myself. I made a conscious decision to hold on to the possibility of escape and a future free of the Khmer Rouge. I thought about Ko Pho, Sourn Leng, Koann, Te, Loan, and Nary. What would my precious brothers and sisters think of what had become of me? Thoughts of my mother and my previous life spurred me to hold on for another day.

SCISSORS AND CEREMONIES: 1969

Eap Khut High School,
Battambang, Battambang Province

When I started high school, Eap Khut had just completed a brand-new building, and my class was fortunate to enjoy the new facilities. The school council selected three students to take part in a ribbon cutting ceremony for an open house to showcase the new building, and I was one of the three lucky girls.

"I can't believe we get to meet him," said a tall girl as she checked her makeup in the mirror.

"Me either," said another girl.

"You look great today," I added, "and I love your hair."

"*Arkoun*," said the tall girl. "But who will hold the scissors?

"Siv Eng will hold the scissors on a tray," announced the Neakru as she entered the room. The teacher wanted to make sure everything looked perfect. We were dressed up in the traditional orange and white *sampot chang kben*.[32] The top was white, and the bottoms resembled bright blousy orange pants with lots of flowing material. The *sampot chang kben* was only worn for special occasions. We were ready to play our part in the ribbon cutting ceremony. Everyone in the student body would be

---

[32]   Traditional, ceremonial Cambodian clothing.

watching, along with several members of the community.

Finally, the honored guest arrived, and my stomach did a flip. He was surrounded by his tight security detail and several government officials. They escorted him everywhere, carrying an umbrella for shade.

"Here he comes," I whispered.

"Stand tall," said the girl on my right.

He was wearing a European business suit and was not dressed in the traditional Cambodian style. I stood in the middle with the two girls on either side. Prince Sihanouk approached us and gestured toward the silk ribbon. With hands slightly shaking, I held up the shiny silver tray displaying the official scissors. The Prince took the scissors and made the ceremonial cut. As the ribbons fell, the girls and I bowed down on our knees to show proper honor to the Prince of Cambodia. Our hands and head were also lowered in *sampeah*.[33] Prince Sihanouk reached out and gently touched our hands in respect. It was a moment I will never forget. The Prince of Cambodia had just touched my hands. Looking back, it's intriguing that I was the one who was chosen to hold the scissors.

Cambodian history and politics are very complicated. Technically Prince Sihanouk had previously been King Norodom Sihanouk from 1941 until he abdicated his throne to his father in 1955 and was given the title of Prince. After his father, King Norodom Suramarit, died in 1960, the National Assembly of the Royal Government of Cambodia voted to adopt a new amendment that made Prince Norodom Sihanouk the Chief of State. No matter the title, the day of the ribbon ceremony, we all thought of him as our King.

---

[33] A formal, Cambodian bow used in greeting.

THE CHILDREN'S CRIES: JANUARY 1979

Poithisat Prison, Pursat Province

tuk min châmnénh, dâ:k chénh kâ: min kha:t
("No gain in keeping, no loss in weeding out.")
– Khmer Rouge saying

After they killed my friend, Met Pheap, I knew they would continue the murders with an increased pace. Every evening they called more prisoners to "take to their village." We never heard gunshots because we were told we weren't worth the ammunition. They were saving their bullets for the Vietnamese Army.

I had hoped that I would be spared, but one day my name was called. The footsteps came closer and closer to my room.

"Met Aun. Met Aun, step forward and come with me."

I froze. The unfamiliar guard continued down to another cell nearby. He kept calling my name. Something told me to wait.

"Met Aun, step forward now."

My heart was thumping at incredible speed. I can't believe it didn't propel my feet in motion. The guard kept walking and continued to call, "Met Aun. Met Aun, step forward."

That night, another Met Aun stepped forward to her death. It was a common name. She was "taken to her village" that evening. It could have easily been me. That same night, they also called another prisoner I knew from working in the fields. Again, I did not sleep soundly. I had just lost two fellow prisoners and had a close brush with my own death.

A few days later, we heard what sounded like young children crying.

"*Ott tay, ott tay*. No, no, please, no." The cries were eerie and sounded desperate.

We didn't know what prison building the children were from, but when we looked outside, there were eight young children tied together, right in front of our building. These poor, terrified children were ages five to eleven. We assumed they were the children of the prisoners with political ties. When the Khmer Rouge killed a husband, they often killed the wife and children as well so that they would not have a chance at revenge. They were killed right outside our cell. We lost all hope. The Khmer Rouge soldiers had now sunk to the lowest level of evil.

At that moment, the prisoners in my cell all embraced each other and cried. Those helpless, beautiful children. How was this possible? If they would kill innocent, defenseless children, we were nothing. My fellow inmates had become my family over the span of the four months I lived at Poithisat Prison. We were next. At that moment, I knew I needed to call out to God. My time to meet my Maker was fast approaching.

A PRAYER: JANUARY 1979

Poithisat Prison, Pursat Province

"Even while you sleep among the sheep pens,
the wings of my dove are sheathed with silver,
its feathers with shining gold."

Psalm 68:13 (NIV)

My mother and father raised our family as Buddhists like most Cambodians. She occasionally bought a cage of birds at the market. As a child, I remember watching as she anointed the birds with perfumed powder to represent our blessings. We followed her up to the high balcony of our building to release the birds and bring good karma. We watched the birds fly away—our blessings taking flight.

Growing up, I occasionally prayed to the Highest Power. I followed the traditional practices of Buddhism and I knew that every people group had their own god. I learned about Hinduism, Buddhism, Islam, and Catholicism in school, but I knew nothing of the Holy Spirit or Christianity.

In Cambodia, a mother was considered next to God. When faced with any loss, a Cambodian Buddhist called out to Buddha and to their mother because it is believed that a mother possesses the most precious and pure love. A follower called to his mother whether she was living or dead. I continued to look to the moon and send messages to my beloved mother. Since I was confused about my personal religion, I decided to recognize God as the Highest Power of the Universe regardless of any particular religion.

In the middle of the night, I thought of those precious children. With their voices echoing in my mind, I got down on my knees on the prison floor and cried out to God. It was a simple prayer.

"God of the Most High Universe, if you can hear me, please spare my life. Creator God, I'm here. If I have to die, please take me now."

That's when a presence entered the room. I saw a young girl who was standing on an upper-level balcony next to a railing. Could it be? The girl was me, and I was looking at myself. She was looking up to the sky, and a golden ray was illuminating her face from above. Soaring beside the golden ray was a bird. It was gliding down toward the girl on the balcony. Everything was golden in color, the light, the rays, and wings of the dove. It was a true gold, even more pure than any priceless ring in Mom's shop. The feathers were flaxen as they reflected the rays of light. This was like no bird I had ever seen.

There was a warmth to the light, and I felt an undeniable, powerful presence in the room. I experienced the bird as if I was the young girl and also as an observer. I was filled with peace and warmth from my head to my toes. It was as if the Highest Power in the Universe breathed, "I hear you, and I am here with you." Then, as suddenly as it appeared, I was jolted back to, reality sitting on the floor of my dark, dingy cell. There was no doubt that it was real—a physical and spiritual meeting. I felt different, changed in some way. I had just witnessed an encounter with the Highest Power of the Universe, and it was good.

If God's presence came to me as a person in a white robe, I would have thought it was an angel or my mother. The bird in my dream made me think of those birds in the cage awaiting freedom. Was I the bird in the cage? Was I going to be set free? No matter the interpretation, I received unspeakable peace from the Holy Presence in my room. Whether I lived or died, I had met my Maker.

I also thought of the bird that I returned to the nest days earlier. That same night, I made a promise to myself and to God. I vowed that if I ever escaped, I would shave my head and tell my story. I promised to shave my head because it was considered a celebration to sacrifice one's beauty in gratitude. In Cambodia, if you make a promise, you keep it. I felt strongly that the Golden Dove would be watching over me. Maybe it was there, unseen from the very beginning.

FUGITIVES: JANUARY 1979

Poithisat Prison, Pursat Province

"May God arise, may his enemies be scattered;
may his foes flee before him.
May you blow them away like smoke—
as wax melts before the fire,
may the wicked perish before God."
Psalm 68:1-2 (NIV)

One fateful night, days following my dream, the Vietnamese invaded a village near the prison in Pursat. That was the night that a switch was flipped. The Khmer Rouge guards abandoned their posts, fled the prison, and escaped. It was they who became the hunted and feared for their lives. They jumped on a train and left us alone. It was a paradigm shift of epic proportions, and at once the prison became eerily quiet. We heard the explosions in the distance. Lights, searing whistles, and explosions came one after another creating a rhythm of war. Mortar and artillery shells came from Vietnamese ground forces, and red rockets were heard flying over our building. The prison was an obvious target. The front was moving closer and closer to our building.

Two inmates in another cell had been in prison for two years before my arrival. They were separated from their wives. The head Khmer Rouge prison guards trusted these two men because they proved to be hard-working, honest, and dependable captives. They weren't locked in a cell like the rest of us, but helped the guards with job assignments, developing a sort of "friendship" with their captors.

Before the prison guards ran away, they gave the keys to these two men.

"Met Chhom and Met Larch, you are now in charge," they said.

These two men, our fellow prisoners, began unlocking the cell doors. In the midst of incoming artillery fire, the prisoners were set free from their cages. It didn't seem real when Met Chhom came to our cell. The jingling keys were the sound of freedom. I joined the released prisoners as we gathered in the hall around our two new leaders. It was dark outside; the only light was from the bombardment overhead. It was after midnight and unceasing explosions continued to rock the earth, making it impossible to hear with the deafening blasts.

The gathering was small in numbers. There were approximately thirty of us altogether. It was void of ceremony or recognition of the momentous occasion. We were free, and our captors had run away, but only a few of us were left in the prison that night. The guards had killed everyone else in our building during the previous days. Just hours before, several of my fellow cellmates were killed. Murdered to be exact. If the Khmer Rouge weren't chased away by the Vietnamese soldiers, they would have continued to murder us all. One more day could have made the difference for me.

Met Chhom took charge and decisions were made in seconds.

"We will split up and lead two groups. I will go west and Met Larch will go to the east. Go where you choose. It is not safe for you to be alone."

It was not a difficult choice for me. I chose to follow the group leader who was heading west toward Battambang and Ou Krabau. Me, a female pharmacy student, had just broken out of prison and was now a fugitive on the run. Several years before, I would have never believed it.

I never knew if the other group of prisoners heading to the east made it to safety. When my prison family said *leahaey* under the rocket filled sky, it was our last. I was now free and headed away from the prison, but new unknown threats lie ahead. There were about twelve of us. As we fled from the prison, we ran across a bridge with blasts landing on either side. Did I survive starvation, disease, and prison just to be killed by the Vietnamese?

In the last weeks of captivity, I made friends with another girl my age. She wasn't my prison roommate but worked with me during the day with the young teenage girls. Her name was Met Sawi, but we called her Met Wi for short. The Khmer Rouge shortened everyone's names when possible; efficiency in its simplest form.

"Take my hand," she said. "Let's stick together." Met Wi ran by my side that night, and I held tightly to her hand like a lifeline.

After months of captivity, it was time to run a marathon. We were relieved and terrified. The evening we escaped, I was terribly skinny. I never had a mirror, but I saw my reflection in the faces of my fellow inmates. My strength came from my liberty, a pure adrenaline rush. Momentum was building with each step.

We safely crossed the bridge and from there followed along the road. Every few minutes a racing comet whizzed over our heads. We passed villages here and there. They were ghost towns. There had been a mass exodus of all villages in the area.

"Down! Hurry, *chap, chap*!"

We hit the ground and threw ourselves along the road in an instant, our faces flat against the earth. The shaking and vibrations pulsated. We knew the Vietnamese were attacking the Khmer Rouge troops, but we did not know that they were attempting to set us free. When the incoming rounds ceased, we got up and ran. It was more like a series of short sprinting races than a marathon.

"Here they come!" yelled Met Wi as I heard the piercing telltale sound.

"Drop now!" I shouted. We repeatedly threw ourselves down and then got up and ran over and over again. Through it all, I never let go of Met Wi's hand.

"I think it's safe to walk now," I said.

It was so black between the earsplitting whistles and explosions that we called out to hear each other so we didn't get separated from the group. At this point we were more afraid of the Vietnamese Army than the Khmer Rouge soldiers.

"I can't make it. I'm so tired," I cried. I had hit a wall and become delirious with exhaustion.

"Met Aun, we have to stay with the group," shouted Met Wi.

Soon we came to another highway, and our leader chose to follow the road, so we wouldn't get lost in the jungle. Met Wi and I were always the last two in line. Run. Hit the ground. Stand. Run. Repeat. Our bare footprints were left along the road. Not just any road, but the road to freedom.

"Another one!" cried Met Wi. We dropped like pancakes flat on the ground. This time when I stood up, attempting to regain my balance, I felt something. Was it a hand? A little girl was standing next to me. Who was this tiny creature, and where did she come from?

"Who are you?" I asked. A tiny hand gripped mine, tugging at my arm. The young child was crying, and her voice pierced the darkness, competing with the blasts.

"Take me with you. Please, don't leave me." She held on tightly and would not let go. Her determination kept her with us. The sky was falling, yet we picked ourselves up off the ground.

Through the noise, I barely heard Met Wi yelling, "Met Aun, Met Aun, let's go, *chap laeng*. Hurry!"

As we ran along, I tried to calm the child.

"Where did you come from?" I yelled. She was probably five years old. I no longer held Met Wi's hand for courage. My hand was now the lifeline. What little strength I had, I willed to her.

"My mom had a baby, and I had a little sister. They killed my Uncle." She never mentioned her father. "They killed my family. I have no one."

I never got her full story or caught her name; my mind was hardly able to think. In the midst of running for my life, a little girl was following in my footsteps. My friend, Met Wi, called out again.

"Met Aun," scolded Wi. "You have to let that girl go. If they leave us, we are on our own." When the little girl heard Met Wi's words, she tightened her grip like a vice. I knew we were in the middle of nowhere. I wouldn't let the little girl go for the world.

If something would have happened to us, no one would have known. The little girl and I were far behind the group. I practically had to drag her along. She was delicate and slight. My steps were small, yet hers were much smaller. Finally, we caught up with Met Wi and the team. Met Chhom counted every one of us. He was an excellent leader and looked out for us.

When we reached a road, the breeze blew the foul scent of death. We were unknowingly smelling the stench of the mass graves nearby. It was a chilling realization. Our group continued on through the night. Met Wi, myself, and the little girl were always at the very end of the line. At one point, I had to stop to relieve myself. We were still following the highway, and I couldn't waste any time. I peed right there in the street with the little girl holding tight to my hand. She would not let go, a little puppy at my side.

As we walked west, the explosions subsided, but we never stopped moving. I planned to go as far as Ou Krabau. Pho encompassed my purpose for living.

PALM SUGAR MEN: JANUARY 1979

Unknown Village in Pursat Province

Later that night, we stumbled into a village. The little girl still held my hand, always by my side. She was the sweetest, loneliest child. Met Chhom learned that the village had recently been emptied. The all-knowing Angkar removed the villagers to keep them "safe" from their Vietnamese attackers. The Khmer Rouge only left two people. These men, the Palm Sugar Men, stayed in the village to keep up their duty to the Angkar. Their job was to make sugar for the collective, regardless of invasions and evacuations. The only people who could partake of the sugar were the high-level officials and upper crust of the Mulethan people.

Sugar was the most precious resource, and the Palm Sugar Men had a thick, deep, round wall near their hut for the purpose of cooking the palm juice. Multiple bamboo containers filled with juice were stacked up ready for cooking. The men boiled the palm juice, stirring consistently until it foamed and became like a dense syrup. When finished, the brown gloppy paste was preserved and used for cooking. It was a painstaking process, but worth it in the end. The men were generous and supplied us with sugar. The fresh sugar paste was the color of toast and tasted blissful, unlike anything bought in a store. We hadn't had any sweetness in years.

Every hut in the village was void of people, but many possessions were left behind. Bowls, spoons, shirts, blankets, and sleeping mats littered the huts, untouched. It reminded me of my apartment in Phnom Penh that was deserted many years ago. The village had an ominous feeling, but tall, friendly palm trees were abundant. The two Palm Sugar Men were helpful to us and our plight. They had no choice but to stay and work because the soldiers randomly checked in on them. When the soldiers arrived, the Palm Sugar Men told them we were from another village and were looking for shelter with the Khmer Rouge. We didn't dare tell anyone that we escaped from prison.

An open shelter was provided for us girls to sleep. We didn't account for the fact that our stomachs were not used to processing sugar. I was hardly able to savor the sweetness and soon became ill. A lot of us paid the price as the diarrhea set in within hours.

"Can you believe we made it here?" I whispered to my friend.

"No, it doesn't seem real. How did we make it past all of the blasts?" asked Met Wi.

I had my own theory and remembered the Golden Dove. "It was a miracle," I suggested.

All night long the precious little girl stayed by my side like a little loyal puppy. She was happily snoring and occasionally stirred. She didn't suffer like me.

The fatigue was overwhelming, yet I hardly slept that night with diarrhea. Sleep took forever to visit and then was abruptly interrupted. Around four in the morning, the Khmer Rouge returned to the village with guns and orders. They spoke to our leader, Met Chhom.

"Get your people up and move out immediately. The Vietnamese are headed this way. You need our protection."

They truly believed we were communists from a nearby village. In their defense, we were dressed like the Mulethan people; everyone in the country was dressed the same. We had no choice but to leave.

Met Chhom burst into our shelter to wake us from our slumber.

"Girls, we need to leave now. Get up and be prepared. The Khmer Rouge are here in the village." The girls scrambled to wake up and get moving. I had been unable to sleep and was weak from the journey and nonstop diarrhea. I didn't move a muscle. Met Wi was awake, but she wasn't sick like me.

"Met Aun," she said. "Did you hear? We must leave right away. You must get up. *Kraok laeng.*" I turned over, and saw the little girl snoring comfortably by my side. She looked so peaceful.

"I can't go. I'm too weak and will slow everyone down. Go on without me, Met Wi, and save yourself." By that time, I was ready to look death in the eye. The power of weariness was overwhelming.

"You will not stay here alone. I will not allow it," insisted Met Wi. She ran from the hut in search of Met Chhom.

Met Wi tattled on me, and soon after, Met Chhom was there in person.

"Met Aun, we've already escaped the prison camp. You didn't die there, and you're not going to die here. You don't have to carry anything, just bring yourself. We didn't come this far to give up now."

His voice was a formidable force. It refueled my mind and re-energized my body. His words reminded me of my brother, Pho. I had to leave.

I shook the little bundle by my side. "Little girl, *kmouy*,[34] wake up. We must leave now. The Vietnamese are coming." I gently touched her head. "Hurry, *chap, chap*. Get up and walk with us," I pleaded.

"Leave me alone," said a grumpy voice. "*Ott tay*. I'm not moving." The girl became angry, responding under the trance of exhaustion. I could relate. I wanted so badly to cuddle up next to her.

"Sweetie, *kmouy*, you can't stay here. You will be safe with us. Come now!" I shook her with vigor.

The little girl defiantly turned over, and the snoring resumed. I had no choice, I had to leave her there that night, my sweet little tag along. I said a prayer that God would have mercy on her and watch over her. The little girl I left behind has her own story.

---

34 A term of endearment that means "little niece."

INTO THE WOODS: JANUARY 1979

Pursat Province

Whether I left with the detested Khmer Rouge or stayed to face the feared Vietnamese Army, my choice was daunting. The twelve of us walked out of the village together with the Khmer Rouge soldiers following us down the road with their guns. They said they were protecting us, but we didn't feel safe. Suddenly, out of nowhere, a new group of Khmer Rouge soldiers advanced toward us from the west.

"Where are you going?" they warned. "Don't go west. The Vietnamese are shooting from the west." At first, we didn't change our course. We continued walking along the road until we saw a Vietnamese tank headed our way in the distance. There was shouting, and Met Wi grabbed my hand. We fled the scene as the tank shot at our company.

The Khmer Rouge, who kicked us out of the sugar village, were not shielding us from danger, but rather using us as a barrier from the Vietnamese. We unknowingly served as their bullet wall and assisted them in their escape. The Khmer Rouge were wise to use our deep-seated fear of the Vietnamese soldiers, and we played into their trap.

As we ran away, we scrambled off the highway heading into the trees. Luckily, in the chaos, the twelve of us all ran to the same side of the road and took shelter in the jungle. Again, Met Chhom took a head count to make sure no one was missing. Everyone was accounted for, except my little companion from the night before.

We weren't the only fugitives in the jungle. There were several groups who had been evacuated from their villages or had escaped the Khmer Rouge like us. Some of the people were Mulethan who had deserted the army and others were April 17 people. It was impossible to tell the difference.

It no longer mattered if you supported the Khmer Rouge or not. Pandemonium ruled with no true direction. Our team leader asked questions of the people and learned that many had been hiding in the woods for several weeks to avoid the fighting in surrounding villages. The highly organized communist villages had become random groups of scavengers working together to survive one day at a time.

When I escaped from prison in Pursat, many people across Cambodia were already free from the Khmer Rouge, but we had no way of communicating with others from across the country. The soldiers, Chhlop, and Mulethan were all fleeing from the impending Vietnamese takeover. Our only defense was to react to the fighting that was at our front door. My group was in the part of the country where the Khmer Rouge still had pockets of control. The despised and feared Vietnamese soldiers were in process of liberating the villages in our area one at a time. If only we had moved toward the armed Vietnamese tanks rather than away.

Once we were settled, our team leader met a family who was living under a large tree in the jungle. They were part of a larger group who were sticking together. There was a husband, wife, and eight-year-old son. This tree family, like most of the people in our country, was missing its daughters. We were all separated from our families. Everyone had the same story. A mother, brother, sister, father, or cousin was missing or had died.

Met Chhom chose to make camp near the tree family, and we were stuck hiding out in the jungle for several weeks. Our leader went exploring during the day. The deeper he went into the jungle, the more groups of people he observed. Met Chhom trusted the tree family, and we made a pact to look out for each other. To obtain food, he and the tree man travelled to surrounding empty villages. They were strong leaders and shared the food with everyone collectively.

There was so much chaos in the forest. Did the Khmer Rouge leave the area? Was the Vietnamese Army still nearby? Could we leave the jungle? No one had solid answers. Our prison family stuck together because we didn't have anyone else. Our team leader tried desperately to find news of his family. He had been separated from his wife and children for two years while in prison. In the jungle, everyone was asking the same questions.

"Do you know my brother? Have you seen my sister? What village did you live in?" The citizens of Cambodia were trying to put the puzzle of their family back together one piece at a time. Finding family was an endless, formidable task, and any morsel of information was valued the same as gold. One day, Met Chhom won the lottery and learned that his family was evacuated to a village to the east. They were far away, but together and alive.

SPILL THE MASTER'S TEA: 1964

Battambang, Battambang Province

prâ:yat a: khmang yuen jo:k kba:l khmaé dam taé ong tiet
("Beware of the enemy from Vietnam who takes Khmer heads
as trophies and ingredients
for the giant pot in which he boils water for the master's tea.")
– Angkar Saying

Several Vietnamese people lived in our community and attended our schools. They were our friends and customers and part of the fabric of our culture, yet we were taught to fear the Vietnamese Army from a young age. As soon as Cambodian children learned to speak and understand the Khmer language, we were taught stories about the violent history of the Vietnamese Army in school and at home.

As a child, I repeatedly heard the story of *kampop tae ong* (spill the master's tea). It's not clear whether this is a traditional tale, a rumor, or a myth.

The message was passed on from the older generation to the young. "Listen children, in pre-colonial days when Vietnam controlled Cambodia, those who did not complete work details were arrested and buried to their necks in the sand. Then the Vietnamese started a fire in the center of them, and a large pot filled with water was placed on top of their heads to boil the master's tea. When the buried Cambodians moved their heads away from the fire, the soldiers would taunt them, 'Don't spill the master's tea.'"

When cooking outside, Cambodian people traditionally placed their cooking pot over a base of three stones with a fire in the middle. This was something we could relate to. The chilling picture was seared into our minds.

The Khmer Rouge reminded us about another popular story involving the pdow vine. "Listen up, for your safety, always run from the Vietnamese. When they take you prisoner, they will put a pdow vine through your ears and lead you around like a chain of animals."

I was probably five when I heard these gory tales the first time. Why we were taught these warnings as young children remains a mystery to me, but I was terrified of Vietnamese soldiers.

The Vietnamese Army and the Khmer Rouge were considered two sides of an evil coin. We didn't trust the Vietnamese Army, and we certainly weren't safe with the Khmer Rouge. Our fear had grown roots and stopped us in our tracks.

When the Vietnamese Army invaded Cambodia in January 1979, it meant freedom from the Khmer Rouge. When they saw soldiers with guns, they asked no questions and took aim as the Khmer Rouge fled for their lives. The Vietnamese Army knew that the civilians were unarmed. When they were unsure if a group of people were innocent villagers, they often shot their guns in the air, sending people in the direction of safety. It helped when someone spoke Vietnamese and was able to communicate effectively. Our group was not aware that they were there to help.

A FIELD TRIP: 1970

Phnom Sampeau, Battambang Province

When we moved to Battambang, I didn't get a chance to get out much between my home responsibilities and school work. I had a close friend group who participated in study groups together. We took our education very seriously and hired a private tutor to help boost our grade point averages. We were economical, splitting the cost of tutoring across the group. We were fiercely competitive, yet we helped each other at every opportunity. I worked hard to achieve good grades in school.

I looked forward to going out with my group of friends. The downtime was much needed after the dedication of studying for exams. My favorite days were the outings to the mountains. It always felt like an adventure. We went to a temple on the occasional weekend for a picnic and fresh air. It was tradition. We enjoyed our independence and each other's company.

"Let's go to Phnom Sampeau this weekend," said Tekhourt.

"Yeah, sounds good to me," said Sovann. We had just finished class and were leaving the building.

"Is Saturday afternoon a good day?" asked Limhourt. "I have an extra bike if someone needs one."

"I can bring some food." Sopeap was carrying a towering stack of books under her arm.

"Sourn Leng and I will make some desserts too," I added. "We all deserve a break this weekend."

A road trip gave me something to look forward to. After finishing exams, our group of twelve teenagers rode our bikes along the highway for about eight miles southwest of Battambang to Phnom Sampeau. The highway was flat on the way to the mountain. It was a two-way road with light traffic, leading to a small village. When the traffic was slim, we took up both lanes, daring the cars to pass us.

"Great day for a bike ride," said my best friend Chhiv Lee, "but now I'm hungry."

When we arrived at the *phnom*[35] we found a place to spread out a blanket for a picnic. The monks lived in small huts near the temple. They were dedicated to the work of Buddha, living away from their families and receiving daily alms as was custom. The women who lived at the temple did the cooking, cleaning, and sewing for the monks. They too committed their lives to the temple and shaved their heads. They left their beauty and their family behind for service to Buddha.

Many families encouraged their sons to serve as a monk for a short time in their life. Some monks chose to serve for their entire lives. The temple was also a popular place for young lovers and friends to enjoy a pristine setting among the beauty of the mountain. Many travelled there to receive blessings from the monks.

Phnom Sampeau had a picturesque area near the temple for meditation. It was very quiet with trees blowing in the wind, a peaceful setting.

"Let's turn on the music while we eat," I suggested. We always brought along our cassette tapes. Teenagers needed their music.

We ate our lunch with Cambodian love songs playing in the background. Our friend, Yut, imitated the sounds of monkeys in the nearby trees. We had to stifle our laughs because it was necessary to be

---

[35]   Mountain.

quiet and respectful of the area. The company, the food, and the scenery provided a break from the everyday grind.

"Let's go to the cave," said Sourn Leng.

We left the picnic area to walk through the huge mouth of a cave and into the open cavern. The natural skylight above the cave allowed the sun rays and light to trickle in. We played with the echoes in the cave, letting our words bounce around. If we stood in the right place, a nice breeze blew over our faces. Our group could easily fit in the large cavernous space at the same time.

"Let's take a picture!" said Sopaep. We all grouped together in the cave, a rush of smiles and laughter.

"One, two, three. Smile, *nhnhum*,"[36] we said in unison.

We wandered around the space, looking at the enormous golden Buddha statue reclining in the cave. He looked so relaxed. Not a care in the world. This was a symbol of the last life that he lived because his mission was complete. Who knew this same Buddha would soon bear witness to heinous crimes of humanity? We were standing in a future crypt. My friends and I dropped our lotus flowers at the statue of Buddha. A lotus flower forms in dark waters and rises to the light to bloom. It represents overcoming.

⋯•◦●◦●◦•⋯

Many years later I returned to Cambodia with my family. I visited this same temple and cave where I had spent many lazy afternoons with my friends. I was shocked to find out what had transpired there.

The Khmer Rouge turned the peaceful temple into a prison and the caves into a mass grave. The soldiers took the monks and prisoners out behind the temple in small groups. There, they brutally stabbed and bludgeoned them to death. Their bodies were tossed from the opening at the top of the cave and fell lifelessly to the bottom. These actions forever

---

[36] Smile.

changed the name of the temple to "The Killing Caves." This place of peace and meditation, where my friends and I enjoyed picnics in the grass, became the scene of mass murders.

A museum was created and there were stairs built to walk down to the place where the bodies were thrown. The same skeletons lie there today to remind us of their story. Their bones lie near the reclining Golden Buddha who was a witness to their fall. That day, I chose to honor the dead and to remember my friends from long ago. Many of them did not survive.

A WEDDING AND A
GRADUATION: 1974

Battambang, Battambang Province

When I was still in high school in 1973, Pho married his beautiful fiancé, Sok Yann. She was younger than my brother and looked up to him. They had been high school sweethearts and fell quickly in love. They were married in Battambang in a two-day, joyful celebration at our home and were blessed by the monks. A long tent was extended in front of our home and into our street to make room for all of our family and friends for the reception.

My generation did not typically have arranged marriages. Our culture was changing with the tides of western civilization. We were given more liberal freedoms compared to our parents. Girls could not yet publicly express their love for a boy, but a young man could pursue a girl's hand in marriage. Parents still gave their permission or granted their blessing. I was proud of my brother. I had no doubt that he would make a fine husband and a loving father. The new bride and groom left for Phnom Penh immediately following their marriage. Pho was starting a new job as an electrical engineer, and Sok Yann was completing her degree in business.

More than a year later in 1974, Sourn Leng and I finished our Class de *Terminale*[37] and prepared for our final exams. There was no

---

37   The last grade level before graduation from high school.

turning of a tassel or throwing of hats, as Cambodian schools did not complete traditional graduation ceremonies. Not all students passed high school finals. Exams lasted three long, grueling days. The classes were demanding, and we worked all year long for the opportunity to sit for our final assessment. It was a great honor to pass. If a student did not pass the first time, they were allowed to take the exam a second time three months later. If unable to pass on the second try, classes were taken again for another full year. At the completion of that repeated school year, a student could take the final exams a third and fourth time. Suicides were rare but did happen on occasion due to the high stakes and stress of passing exams. The pressure was immense, and school was all-consuming.

THE TREE FAMILY: FEBRUARY 1979

A Jungle Near a Road, Pursat Province

After living in the jungle with the tree family for one month, we were left in total confusion. No one was where they were supposed to be. The country of Cambodia was dispersed and displaced. Met Chhom, though, was filled with hope upon learning his family was alive. One night, an announcement was made.

"I have found that my wife and daughter are living in a village far from here. I need to search for them before they move again. I will leave tomorrow morning. Whether I find them or not, I will come back for you. Please stay here, and I will return."

Before he left, Met Chhom made an arrangement with the man who lived under the tree. "Please treat my group like family," he asked. The tree family agreed.

We waved as he walked away, but we never saw him again.

The next day felt empty without our fearless leader. We lost a protector and a familiar face. He had become like a father to our group of escapees. We were now on our own. One by one, my fellow prisoners left to go their own way in the strange new world that was on the brink of liberty. I could not leave because I was still very sick. The succession of illnesses, the malaria, the boil, and the diarrhea had a shattering effect on my body. I was left a fragile shadow of my former self. Eventually, I was the only one left from our group of twelve. Even Met Wi chose to leave and do her best to find her family.

"I hope you find them, Met Wi. You have been a good friend to me. I will never forget you. Be safe," I said, "and don't travel alone."

"I will miss you, Met Aun." Her words crossed through a river of tears. "You have been my only family for the last several months."

The embrace was fleeting, and she didn't look back. "*Leahaey,*" I whispered, as she walked away.

The tree family had names. The husband's name was Met Chhay, and his wife was Met Neang. Their young son lived with them, but their other children were away at separate work camps at the time of the Vietnamese invasion. It was time to go back into negotiation mode and take charge of my destiny. I approached Met Chhay with an obvious question.

"I have no one and was hoping to live with your family. I can help you with whatever you need."

"Yes, Met Aun, you can stay with us. I made a promise. You are the only one left."

It was decided. I had a family, just like that.

Met Chhay and Met Neang offered me a safe shelter. I began to address them as Pouk Chhay and Mai Neang to show respect for their age and to speak to them as foster parents. As a young girl in a war-torn country, being alone was dangerous on so many levels. At least I had someone I could call on, and they protected me from the threat of violence. They didn't choose me, and they probably didn't want me. Circumstances brought us together.

There was a large group of people in the jungle who had the advantage of maintaining communal living with their Chief and Mulethan leaders. Many of them were deserters. They were not a threat to us, but my new family no longer had the resources of a group.

Being with Mai Neang really made me miss my own mother, especially when I was sick. I had been yearning for her all these years, and now that I had a mother figure in the flesh and blood, the realization burned with intensity. I constantly thought about my mother.

I witnessed so many people being killed in prison and hadn't had time to process. We were all dealing with heavy burdens. My new unofficial foster family never asked about my family. They never asked, and I never told. I never mentioned the fact that I was a prisoner. They didn't have time to be curious. We were all too busy surviving.

One day I tried to walk to a nearby pond to bathe in the water. I had to walk very slowly and kept stopping to rest. We benefited from the resources in the jungle, but I was still weak. My fear and anxiety were worse than the physical symptoms. When I made it to the pond for a bath, two women walked up beside me. They were bent over washing their clothes in the water without soap. The women began talking about me as if I was invisible.

"Look at that girl. She obviously has no family. What a pitiful child."

They may have felt sorry for me, but they showed no mercy. I felt as bad on the inside as I appeared on the outside. The bath couldn't wash away the pain, with or without soap.

TO CROSS A LAKE: FEBRUARY 1979

An Unknown Village, Pursat Province

During the time when we were hiding from the Vietnamese in the jungle, the Khmer Rouge never completely disappeared. Some days we were called to work; other days we stayed in the jungle and were left alone. We lived like refugees without tents under the trees of the jungle and slept on the ground. Sometimes we were moved to a village for a few weeks at a time.

The Khmer Rouge soldiers showed up in our village and instructed the strong men to dig large holes. The women were separated and told to carry rice from the fields to storage. Wherever we lived, the soldiers continued to show up and instruct us to do the same tasks. We were told that the large holes were created to store the rice and promised that a celebration was going to take place near the new year. The Khmer Rouge announced that everyone would get to eat the coveted *num banh chok trayong chek*, a Khmer dish of noodles with banana buds which was considered a delicacy. This was something to look forward to. At first, we believed them, but as time passed Met Chhay learned the chilling truth.

Some of the Khmer soldiers who were defectors warned Chhay about the celebration.

"We know what is going on. This is a sick joke they are playing on you. The *trayong chek* is actually referring to the banana bomb grenade.

236

Instead of a celebration, they are planning to draw everyone together in order to kill us."

The men of the village listened in disbelief. The holes that they were digging were meant to be their own mass graves. We knew that the Khmer Rouge were savage, but this was a shock.

---•••◆••••---

We were eventually moved to yet another nearby village, and soon after Chhay and Neang's little boy was sent away to a child work camp. Just like that, their eight-year-old was gone. The pain was raw and fresh. Pouk Chhay was soon sent away for an assignment outside of the village, and I was left alone in the hut with Mai Neang during the day. I was too weak to work, and Mai Neang was pregnant. She was lighter skinned, similar to me in facial features, and may have been part Vietnamese or Chinese. We were newcomers in a new village. Of all the communist experiences I had, I received the best care in this village. For the first time, we had enough food and vegetables to eat. Mai Neang and I helped in the garden with a few elderly people. I began to build some strength and started to gain a few pounds. Our team leader in the village was a lady from the garden named Bong Jak. She was a Mulethan village woman who was bossy in nature, but for some reason she looked out for me.

In the days before medical care, there was fifty-fifty chance of surviving childbirth. In Khmer language, giving birth is called *chhlong tonle*. It refers to crossing a dangerous lake. In Cambodian culture, it is customary for the husband to clean up the bedding after birth. The new mother is to be like a servant in the next life to the person who cleans her afterbirth clothes.

Babies never choose a convenient time to be born. They arrive when they arrive. Instead of a baby, Mai Neang had a miscarriage. Her husband was away, and I stepped in to help my new mother. I had no previous experience, and this was completely foreign to me. There was so much blood. It was everywhere on the blankets and on the floor. I never saw a baby, and there were no cries. I did my best to care for Mai Neang. She was weak from losing so much blood. There were so few babies born during the Khmer Rouge years. If they survived childbirth, they had a slim chance of surviving childhood.

I took her soaked clothes and bedding to wash in the pond. They were no longer the Khmer Rouge black, but were a vibrant, defiant red. I gently dipped the clothes and blankets in the murky water. The water in the pond was almost gone. It was so muddy, and I did my best to stomp on the soiled clothes to clean them. Washing away the red. Washing away the life. The leeches were like ants around the blood. By that time, I started to cry. I paused there in the blood soaked muddy water. I stood alone and thought about my life.

What should have been a joyful day brought more pain than I could bear. Because I cleaned her birth clothes, Mai Neang felt that she owed me everything. I didn't purposefully make her feel that way, it was our culture. Chhay had been gone for weeks and didn't know about the miscarriage. An exhausted Mai Neang worked in the garden the next day. Bong Jak, our team leader, was there watching over our labor. She saw the weakness in my foster mother and the worry in my eyes.

A few days later, Neang came back from a meeting, looking white as a sheet.

"Met Aun, I have to leave the village in the morning. I am being sent to a work camp in the east." Her husband was gone, her daughters were missing, and her son had been taken away. She had just lost a baby.

"I am going with you," I announced.

"You need to stay here, Met Aun. You weren't assigned to go."

With a surge of adrenaline, I implored, "No, Mai Neang, you are my family now. I'm going with you."

"But Met Aun," she said, "they are feeding you here. You are being taken care of here. They are sending me to the front line for hard labor, and you are in no shape to handle it."

"Mai Neang, if I die, I die with you." I wouldn't take no for an answer, refusing to be left alone.

I went straight to the village Chief, recognizing the presence of the Highest Power of the Universe accompanying me. Common sense said that I shouldn't leave this place. I had shelter and nourishment, but my strong sense of family overpowered my sense of security. I wanted to be with Mai Neang, even if I followed her to another hell, because she was my new family.

I addressed the Chief to plead my case, "*Pouk*, please listen. I have to go with my foster mother. She is my family now, and Mai Neang is all I have."

"Why do you want to go? You are still sick and recovering. You know you can't handle hard labor. We have food and will take care of you here," said the Chief.

"I'm so sorry to cause trouble. Please let me go. I need to be with my mother." The village Chief was upset and confused about my motives.

"Okay, Met Aun, you will get exactly what you asked for," he said.

When Bong Jak, our Mulethan garden leader, heard that I was leaving, she was annoyed.

"Why are you doing this?" she demanded. "You will never survive there."

My loyalty was loud and clear. "Bong Jak, I've already made my decision."

Despite the warnings, I placed my belongings on my head to begin the walk to the labor camp. We walked on for hours, stepping through fields and crossing roads. As we moved along under the scorching sun, I began to get chills and knew it was a fever. We were about halfway there when I could no longer walk.

"There's no way you can make it to our destination. We have miles to go," said Neang. "I know an older couple who lives not far from here. You can stay with them," she said.

As we passed a nearby village, Mai Neang hastily dropped me off at a hut with an elderly man and woman. She barely had time to explain the situation. *I* was the situation.

"Please take care of Met Aun. I will come back for her when I can." With those words she walked away and promised to return for me.

LOST AND FOUND: FEBRUARY 1979

Battambang, Battambang Province

YoKuy and her children, Te, Loan, and Nary, lived through the Khmer Rouge regime in Phum Thmei in the Banteay Meanchey Province. They survived together with YoKuy's parents, her two teenage sisters, and the family of Bun Tek. In January 1979, the Khmer Rouge promptly removed the children and teenagers from their work camps and returned them to their assigned village with their parents. They planned to kill everyone in the villages and wanted to keep them together to maintain efficiency. This was the Khmer Rouge way. The Vietnamese Army invasion halted the Khmer Rouge's plans, and the timing was providential for Yokuy's village. Many others weren't so fortunate. When the Khmer Rouge fled the village of Thmei, YoKuy and her relatives took the opportunity to escape together in search of a safe place.

They headed to Grandma and Grandpa's hometown of Mongkol Borei and managed to avoid running into the Khmer Rouge soldiers on their way. When the family reached Mongkol Borei, it was a hurry up and wait situation to find out which relatives survived. YoKuy hadn't heard from her three missing children since they left for college in 1974. She also had no news from her sister, Chhiv Hong, or her brother, Kee, and his family. She was thankful to reunite with Grandma Ma Huoy and her sister-in-law, Kim Eung, YoKuy's brother, Be, and his family also returned to the village of Mongkol Borei. One by one, her family was reunited.

All Cambodians across the country headed back to their hometowns to meet up with their loved ones. It was their only option to wait for news. Even though most of the country was free of the Khmer Rouge, many city dwellers continued to reside in the country where they had access to gardens, rice fields, and fresh water. It was nearly impossible to sustain life in the cities.

It seemed like an eternity since young Te and his mother had hidden all of their jewelry in the pawn shop. In reality, it had been almost four years. A month passed before it was decided that Te and Grandpa would return to the house to look for valuables.

"We can't wait any longer. We need to get back to the house in Battambang to see if any of our jewelry was left untouched," said YoKuy. "Every jewel we find will be useful in the coming days."

The pressure was on Te to remember all the hiding places. Te and Grandpa travelled several hours by bicycle from Mongkol Borei to Battambang. There it stood. The row house was there, waiting for them in expectation. Did the walls still hold secrets? What had happened here over the last four years?

"Well, our home is still standing," Te said to Grandpa.

He stopped near The Lady with the Rice Stack statue, who stood unmoved and untouched. Was she unaware of the horrors the country endured? They stepped inside without a key as the house was left unlocked. It was surreal for Te to enter his home again. He was lucky that there were no squatters or looters in his home, but the once fully stocked pawn shop now stood naked, baring empty shelves and exposing a red-checkered floor void of furniture. Bikes, clocks, and radios had vanished. The Khmer Rouge left their bloody footprints all over the country.

Te went into retrieval mode.

"I remember a place on the roof."

He climbed up to the top right-hand corner of the roof and discovered some gold that was spared. Te discreetly put the valuables in his bag. Next, he went straight to the back of the house to find the obscure bottle that he left in the muddy water. So much had happened since that bottle was buried. The mud was now completely dry, but the bottle top was visible, waiting patiently to be unearthed. A stroke of luck.

As Te headed back to dig up the bottle, he noticed a group of men watching him from a distance. He didn't want to draw any unneeded attention to himself. The weeks following the war were extremely dangerous. People everywhere were looking for items they could steal and trade, and no one was to be trusted. It would be useless for Te to find all the valuables only to be robbed. Young Te wisely meandered around, walking away from the bottle until the suspicious group of men left the area. When the coast was clear, he ran back and subtly dug it up. Not much was left after the initial looting, but Te found a bounty of gold and jewelry undisturbed in the bottom of the bottle. It was a time capsule. Every bit of gold and jewelry would help them to survive in the new economy.

Looters had systematically torn the kitchen apart. Te remembered all the hiding places that he and his mother had created. Several of the secret places stood the test of time, but others were discovered. The thought of strangers tearing up the house was disconcerting. Everything valuable in the expansive jewelry display case was gone. Cleaned out. When Te climbed up to the gap above the large wooden display case, he was relieved to see the bag of gold and jewels covered in dust. More gold was waiting for its true owner below in the secret gap between the floor and the base of the cabinet. Te and Grandpa took bags of gold and jewelry with them when they left the home in Battambang. The family would now have enough for a new start.

Grandpa waited as Te took one last look at his home. He soaked up the empty stillness of what used to be a bustling pawn shop. He considered the long nights of homework, trips to school on motorcycles, the many customers in the shop, and the evenings spent watching TV together as a family. He recalled his beloved father and his missing siblings. Would he ever see them again? So many memories were created between those walls. They were two book ends with a far-off fairytale in between. Now it was time to head to Grandpa's house and find his hidden jewels. They had to be careful that they didn't get robbed on the way back to Mongkol Borei. Thieves were everywhere, and the country was in chaos.

•••••••●••••••

Bun Tek had his own jewels to find. Shortly after the overthrow of the Khmer Rouge, he visited his friend in the country village near Battambang. Bun Tek planned to retrieve his priceless bicycle filled with gold. He found his friend in the village.

"Don't worry, Bun Tek. I buried the gold in the mountains somewhere far away, but it's safe. When the country is peaceful, I will return your gold."

This man was no friend. He made it clear that he wanted his son to marry young Koann. The man was keeping the gold as collateral, never intending to return it to its rightful owner.

"Later on, when we are a family, you will see your gold," he smirked. Bun Tek walked away from his gold with no regrets. He would never let this man or his son near his beloved daughter.

•••••••●••••••

There were many stories of squatters taking residence in people's homes. YoKuy's cousin returned to her home to find several groups living there. She had managed to save jewels and gold from the Khmer Rouge and was determined to buy her house back. She started by squatting in one small corner of her very own house. One by one, the squatters eventually fled to the countryside where food was more abundant. This woman wisely waited out the remaining squatters and bartered to claim her space.

Eventually there was only one family left living on the top floor. They were holding out for a large payment in order to leave the home. The woman knew that she was being taken advantage of when, suddenly, the upstairs family began complaining about a haunting in the house. They heard unexplained noises and groaning and became terrified of the ghost upstairs.

The woman's husband had died in the house years before, and she firmly believed that it was his ghost. She soon became the proud owner of a haunted house, but it was her very own haunted house.

ONE GUEST, TEN HEADS: FEBRUARY – MARCH 1979

Unknown Villages, Pursat Province

I was unable to go with Mai Neang to her work camp. My fever and chills stopped me in my tracks. I was now a package delivered to the front door of two elderly strangers who happened to be the parents of my group leader, Bong Jak. I was worried about my foster mother. I figured the Khmer Rouge were planning to kill all the people in the camp where she was headed.

It was painfully obvious that I was an unwanted guest. The elderly couple expected me to work when I was trembling with fever. They ate alone, never sharing their fish with me. I didn't blame them. Food was a precious commodity, and they had no connection to me. I was literally dumped at their doorstep. I realized then how different my family was from most other families. My mother would have gladly helped a poor orphan.

The older couple arranged for me to sleep under their hut. My presence disturbed their comfort. I saw the fish bones that they threw in their trash down below. Their diet was no secret. I was sad, but that's how it was. I had a new perspective on life. Though lonely, I was glad to have rice and a place to sleep. I lived there a month. The conditions weren't the worst I'd ever experienced, yet every day seemed like an eternity. My fear of abandonment was growing with each sunset.

One day, my garden work leader, Bong Jak, showed up.

"Why are you staying at my parents' hut?" she demanded. Her blatant shock was unmasked. "You should have stayed with me in the village."

"Mai Neang brought me here because I got sick on the way to her camp," I explained. "I don't even know if she is alive."

I longed every night for any information about my foster family and continued to live there under the hut for two more weeks. Bong Jak slept above with her parents. One day, seemingly out of the blue, my foster father, Pouk Chhay came back for me as promised. I packed up my sparse personal items in a *krâma*, and Chhay tied it on the end of a stick.

As we left the hut of Bong Jak's family, I was now the little puppy following along. It was hard for me to walk because my leg was bothering me.

"Pouk Chhay, thank you. *Arkoun*. You came for me," I said, my heart filled with gratitude.

"You would have been fine staying with Met Jak's family," he snapped. "My wife made me come and get you." We walked on in silence until we arrived at Pouk Chhay's village. I swallowed the lump in my throat. Mai Neang kept her promise, and this gave me a gleam of hope.

The people of the village saw how skinny and malnourished I was.

"Met Chhay," they said, "where did you find this little girl, *kmeng touch*?"[38] I soon learned that Chhay had located his wife, his missing son, and his two teenage daughters from other villages. They were now all together as a family unit. I lived with the Chhay family and their three children for one week in an area that was still guarded and controlled by the Khmer Rouge. Chhay was savvy and kept his eye on the situation. He was a leader and collected insider information from the villagers.

I remember the evening when my foster father stepped into our hut,

---

[38] Little one.

his face looking pale as a ghost. He was sick to his stomach and doubted no more.

"It's time to take our chances with the Vietnamese Army," he announced. "We can't stay here any longer."

Earlier that day, Chhay was called to help with a special job. The soldiers had taken a large group of people into the woods to kill them. The people panicked when they realized that it was a death walk. When they ran away, they were shot in the back. Every single one. Chhay and a few other men of the village were assigned to collect the bodies and bury them in a shallow mass grave. The smell was unbearable, a horrific nightmare. Chhay reported that among the victims were young children, pregnant women, and elderly. It was a profoundly disturbing scene, and not one was spared. Chhay knew it would be our turn soon. It was only a matter of time.

A few days later, during the night, a woman in our village left her hut to relieve herself and overheard a private council of the Khmer Rouge leaders.

"Can you take care of *dopp kbal?*"[39] asked the leader. "We've got to do this quickly. The villagers are becoming a burden and slowing us down."

"We can't afford to leave any witnesses," said another leader.

The lady rushed quietly to our hut and spoke to my foster father as he had become the leader of our newly formed coup.

"Listen, Met Chhay. They will kill all of us. Ten heads each, *dopp kbal*. I heard it with my very own ears," said the woman.

Chhay snuck out in the night to secretly meet the other villagers whom he trusted. They planned for an emergency exit. We had to wait for the perfect timing. One of the Mulethan leaders supported our plan and made a point of learning the time of the premeditated murder. He feared for his own life and chose to leave with us. Approximately thirty of us set out just after midnight the next day. We could have been shot at any time. Instead of a mass murder, there was a mass exodus.

---

[39]   Ten heads.

MA MOUY: MARCH 1979

Lake Tonle Sap

I headed east for Lake Tonle Sap with Pouk Chhay, Mai Neang, and their three children. Tonle Sap was the largest lake in Cambodia. Chhay learned that the region around the Lake was liberated. The night we escaped the village, my leg had swollen double its size. I was dragging a water filled log attached to my hip. On the way to Lake Tonle Sap, our group stopped by a village where Chhay's family had previously lived. My foster family and I stayed overnight in the hut of their older trusted neighbor, Ma Mouy. Ma Mouy fed us generously as Chhay explained about the ten heads and the plan to go east to Lake Tonle Sap. The food Ma Mouy prepared tasted delicious. It was the first time I ate hot rice and fresh, salty fish in years.

Ma Mouy was a small but mighty woman who was missing most of her teeth. She kept a little knife with her and told us that she would stab whoever laid a hand on her. She smiled a toothless smile when she said, "I may not be able to kill an attacker, but I can at least do some damage." She was an impressively gutsy woman.

The next morning, she joined with our group of villagers on the journey to Lake Tonle Sap. Ma Mouy had three children of her own, but they were all being held at separate child labor camps. During the journey, my mind was consumed with thoughts of my missing family, and Ma Mouy was thinking of hers. We were two lost souls.

"Met Chhay, who is that young girl?" asked Ma Mouy. She glanced at me expectantly.

"She's an orphan."

"I have no idea where my three children are either," sighed Ma Mouy. "They are like orphans now."

After several miles of walking, we finally arrived along the west shore of Lake Tonle Sap, and the first order of business was to find a boat. Unfortunately, most of the boats were ruined. They eventually rotted, filled up with water, and sank to the bottom of the shallows. It appeared as if no one had been allowed on the shore of Tonle Sap since the takeover. People were seen resurrecting the sad boats from their watery graves. We kept walking along the shore until we happened upon a fishing village. Chhay and some men worked together to lift boats from the bottom.

We stayed the night on an open platform above the water with several other families. The fish were overpopulated in Lake Tonle Sap. It seemed like no one had the opportunity to fish there during the Khmer Rouge reign. The nearest communist village was miles away.

"Look, you can catch them by hand," I said.

A smile formed on my face—a splash of hope. There were posts in the water along the shore. Plants and algae grew around the posts, and the fish swarmed there to feed in large schools. I stepped into the water up to my waist, dipped my hand around the pole, and scooped the plentiful fish into a bucket. We kept some of the fish to dry and save for later. The multitude of fish made a racket flopping around; our dinner was dancing. The buckets were full, and soon after so were our bellies.

After the second day, Ma Mouy made a request.

"Met Chhay, you have three children, why don't you give Met Aun to me? I will gladly take care of her. I miss my children dearly and would love her company." I listened intently and thought of my younger sister Koann, who was adopted by Uncle Bun Tek and Aunt Kim Ly at a young age. Now someone wanted to adopt me. Ma Mouy wanted to take me with her to look for her children.

"I want to look for my family too," I said.

We shared the same purpose, but I wondered, how could a widow feed me? She was an elderly woman. That night, Ma Mouy showed me a bag of jewelry and gold necklaces. She sensed my doubts and wanted me to know that she wasn't empty handed. It reminded me of my mom, always the prudent business woman and entrepreneur.

"Sweetie, you won't starve with me," assured Ma Mouy. She winked when she said, "Met Aun, this gold is for both of us." She was a stranger but took me in, making her intentions clear.

"Okay," I hesitated. "I will leave with you, Ma Mouy." I was torn because of my relationship with Mai Neang, but Pouk Chhay didn't seem to want me around. Once he was reunited with his own children, his feelings of duty and responsibility toward me waned.

Tonle Sap was an enormous and dangerous lake. It had a history of casualties. Pouk Chhay bartered for a small older boat in disrepair. We waited for both the repairs and the weather. Forecasts weren't an option, but Chhay could read the wind and clouds. It seemed like we waited forever, but it was probably only a few weeks. One day while waiting, Ma Mouy heard that some members of her family were headed our way. She wanted to reach dry land to meet them.

"Met Aun, please promise to wait for me here. Even if the Chhay family is leaving tonight, stay here and wait for me. I will get the news of my family and will purchase a boat for us. I will come back for you, Met Aun. I promise."

"Okay, Ma Mouy," I said. She worried that I would leave without her, but I had my own fears. Could I face another abandonment?

"I will come back in the morning for you," said Ma Mouy. "I promise."

I continued fishing every day and appreciated the fresh meals. I waited and hoped. I waited for Ma Mouy to return and hoped that the Chhay family wouldn't leave. Finally, the weather seemed to be cooperating, and

Pouk Chhay was ready to go. Two or three boats planned to disembark at the same time.

Pouk Chhay and Mai Neang asked me the question I dreaded the most.

"What did you decide? It's your choice, Met Aun."

I was faced with a life changing decision. I had already been separated from my prison leader, Met Chhom, and he never returned as promised. If I chose to wait for Ma Mouy, who would look after me? Would I be safe?

The Chhay family didn't offer me any rice if I stayed and waited for Ma Mouy. I didn't dare to ask. I thought often about the Golden Dove, and my vision in prison. Was the God of the Most High Universe watching? Was I still under the wings?

The only two families with whom I had any connection were soon to be separated. The Chhay family took me in when no one else would, yet I also felt an unexplainable soul connection to Ma Mouy. Ultimately, the fear of being alone and abandoned drove my decision, and I left with the Chhay family.

I later learned that Ma Mouy arrived the next day, wanting to know where I was.

A FORTUNE TOLD:
EARLY MARCH 1979

Mongkol Borei, Banteay Meanchey Province

Now that Te and Grandpa had retrieved the hidden jewels from her home, YoKuy planned to stay in Cambodia and make a living with farming. This was a far cry from running a pawn shop in Battambang. YoKuy used some of her remaining gold to trade for two cows, a bicycle, and an ox cart. She and her family stored up rice, sugar, salt, and anything that could be preserved. There was an ever-present fear that the Khmer Rouge could come back to power in the future.

During the confusing time, while she was waiting on her three children to return, YoKuy learned a shocking truth. She was stunned to see her two younger brothers, Kheat and Su, arrive in Mongkol Borei. They should have been safe and living abroad in Europe. She had no way of knowing that they flew back to Cambodia from Italy and France at the deceptive prompting of the Khmer Rouge. They, too, were survivors of the horrors of the Angkar. YoKuy hardly recognized her own brothers. Kheat and Su looked old and were nothing but skin and bones. No one in the country of Cambodia looked the same. The before and after images of both survivors and the landscape were strikingly altered.

After a short time in Mongkol Borei, Kheat and Su decided to leave for France with their families and offered to take YoKuy with them. YoKuy was distraught. She had made arrangements to stay in Cambodia and make a living by farming. She was faced with both an opportunity and a choice. She had an opportunity to leave the dangers and chaos of Cambodia and head to the safety of France. Her young children, Te, Loan and Nary, could have a new start to their lives with a French education. However, this opportunity came at a high price—the cost of leaving her lost children behind. YoKuy learned that her sister, Chhiv Hong, had died, but she was still missing her three oldest children and daughter-in-law. Were they still alive?

YoKuy had on occasion consulted a fortune teller in years past. He was an older man of Chinese descent. Before leaving the country, she visited the fortune teller in Mongkol Borei. He had survived and was willing to help her.

"Please, can you help me find my family?" she asked. "I have three children and a daughter-in-law who are missing. I haven't seen them since 1974."

The two of them sat on the floor of the dark hut as he took her palms in his hands. There was an awkward silence as the old man searched, and a desperate mother waited.

"What do you see?" she asked.

"Please tell me their birthdays and zodiac signs," said the man. YoKuy methodically listed each birthday.

The man paused in a meditative state. "I only see one," he said.

"Who is it?" YoKuy's voice quivered on edge.

"A lady with the fish. She is drying the fish."

"Who is with her?" asked YoKuy. "Do you see anyone else?" He hesitated and continued to hold her hands in his.

The old man shook his head and repeated, "I only see one."

YoKuy's mind was spinning. If this was true, it was a combination of good and bad news. He saw a girl, but even if she was alive, how could a mother go looking, and where would she start? The girl with the drying fish was a needle in a very large, war-torn haystack. The fortune teller never saw a boy. Where was Pho? Why weren't they together? Where were the others? YoKuy's thoughts were concentrated on her missing children. Would she ever see them again?

The best way to find lost family members after the war was to wait in the city or village where they had previously lived. There were no communication lines open in the country. Upon returning from the fortune teller, YoKuy waited. She waited and waited for a few more weeks, hoping that one or all of her children would return to Mongkol Borei. She did not want to leave the country without them. How does a mother choose one child over the other? Her mind was torn, and her heart was in pieces.

Meanwhile, the fighting between the Khmer Rouge and the Vietnamese Army escalated.

"Je Kuy, we need to go. The time is now. We cannot wait any longer," cautioned her brother, Kheat. "Things will not be stable here for years to come."

"I know," said YoKuy with resignation. "If my children return, at least Grandma Ma Huoy and Kim Eung will be here waiting for them." Grandma Ma Huoy was unable to make the treacherous journey and her daughter, Kim Eung, decided to remain with her.

YoKuy's parents, Grandpa and Grandma, also hesitated to leave the country. They wanted to stay but feared for Melaine's and Elisa's safety. There were many Vietnamese troops in the area and very few young women. The family often heard crossfire and hand grenade explosions not far across the Mongkol Borei River. For several nights in a row, the family slept on their backpacks, ready to run at any given minute. It was difficult to sleep with the prolonged screams and cries nearby. YoKuy promised her newly purchased cows, bicycle, ox cart, and food stocks to relatives who chose to remain in the country.

One night, a gas station was burned, creating a huge ball of fire. That was the night the family decided to flee.

YoKuy said a rushed farewell to Koann.

"*Leahaey*," Koann echoed.

YoKuy left her in the care of her parents in Mongkol Borei. They planned to follow later and join YoKuy in France. Bun Tek was leery of crossing the border with his daughter. He feared for Koann's safety and wanted to wait.

A NIGHTMARE, A VOW, AND A
BROKEN HEART: APRIL – SEPT. 1979

Kampong Luong, Tonle Sap, Pursat Province

The moment we began our voyage on Lake Tonle Sap, we were officially liberated from the Khmer Rouge territory. It was a paradigm shift. We were free from the hidden Chhlop, soldiers, rice rations, prisons, and the all-knowing Angkar. The air felt clearer, the sun shone brighter, and the sky revealed colors of blue and purple that had gone unnoticed for years. The people of Cambodia were free and were attempting to re-build their lives from the ashes. We were born again.

We headed down the coast of Tonle Sap to a floating village called Kampong Luong. Once there, Chhay managed to purchase a large sampan boat. It had a small covering for a roof but didn't allow for privacy. I had trouble sleeping at night and often had nightmares. I'm sure I was suffering from post-traumatic stress disorder, along with the entire country.

One night I had the scariest nightmare of my life. I saw an enormous, dark, evil monster with a body covered in thick, curly hair and large penetrating eyes. It chased after me with a large black cloak in its hand. I recognized it to be the same evil spirit that pressed on my chest months ago in prison, attempting to suffocate me. The hairy, black arm reached out again trying to kill me, but this time I saw its massive body and vile, evil face. Its eyes were piercing like daggers. As I ran for my life, it came up from behind, grabbed my hair, and chopped it off with a huge knife. My hair fell to the ground as I tried to escape. I knew it was planning to chop off my head.

It was at that moment I woke up, shaking and painted in a veil of dripping sweat. My heart was pounding with fear. It was pumping so hard it felt as if it would leap from my chest. I could hardly wait for the daylight to arrive, laying still as a statue, afraid to move or breathe. The dream was visceral and powerful. In the wee hours of the morning, I remembered my broken vow. In Poithisat Prison, I vowed two things if I ever escaped: to shave my head in thanks and to tell my story. I could tell my story anytime, but I felt a raw urgency to shave my head immediately.

"Mai Neang, Mai Neang, wake up. You must shave my head this morning."

"Do what?" she asked in a confused daze.

"I had a nightmare and must get rid of my hair immediately," I said.

I hadn't cut my hair for several months, and it was quite long. Mai Neang reluctantly shaved my head to the scalp that day. My long, dark hair covered the ground, and I felt relief covering me. As my hair fell, the chains fell, and I was liberated from the Monster. I fulfilled a vow to honor my escape from prison. I was eternally grateful to Mai Neang for cutting my hair.

I kept my naked head covered with a scarf at all times. When my hair grew back about an inch, I removed the scarf. A lot of people mistook me for a boy. Others thought I was my foster sister's husband. The Monster could no longer catch me by the hair and probably couldn't recognize me either.

Several months later, Chhay bought an actual floating house. It was small and cozy and more suitable for the family. I preferred it to the sampan boat. The floating house had a restroom on the back that emptied into the water. The restroom had walls, but no ceiling. When we stood up, our head popped up over the walls. The living area was the size of a large bedroom, and a mosquito net served as a wall between the separate sleeping quarters. The Chhay family would have had more privacy and space without me, but I helped them with chores and made myself useful. I lived with the Chhay Family in the floating village of Kampong Luong for about five months.

During the first months after the Khmer Rouge was overthrown, individuals were constantly seen walking on the street searching for their families.

"Are you from _____? Have you seen my _____? Do you know anyone from my village in _____?" Everything in Cambodia was still in chaos. There was no established infrastructure, government, education, or healthcare system. Transportation, communication, fuel, and markets were absent. Everyone walked the streets and roads of our country to gather news and barter for supplies. Individuals traded fruits, vegetables, meat, clothing, spices, and wares along the road. Every day was a farmer's market.

There wasn't a day that went by when I didn't think of Ko Pho, Sok Yann, or Sourn Leng. Initially, I couldn't go looking for them because of my health, safety, and the ongoing war. I had no chance of traveling to Battambang because it was too far away. Now that the Khmer Rouge was gone, I was ready to take the plunge. My siblings and I spent a lot of time playing hide and seek as children. I was now the designated seeker searching for any trace of my family.

I told Pouk Chhay and Mai Neang that I wanted to walk the road where I could get the most up-to-date information on my family. They understood my reason for leaving and supported my cause. I assumed I would be safe walking the streets because there were so many people with the same purpose, and I could find safety in numbers.

We said goodbye quickly to lessen the pain, and I realized that this could be the last goodbye. Mai Neang packed some rice for my long journey, and Chhay's daughter walked me up to the dry land where I could start my search on a main road. I brought with me a long tube that I had sewn and filled with rice. It reminded me of the belt that Mom sewed for me long ago. The rice wouldn't even last a week. I didn't have a solid plan or even a pot to boil my rice. It didn't make a difference if they gave me food or not. I made a new vow that I would not stop searching until I found my family.

"Goodbye, *leahaey*," I said to Chhay's daughter when we reached the main road.

"*Leahaey*," she echoed. She turned and began her walk back to the shore.

The crowd was swarming with people and goods, and the chance of seeing someone from my village was slim. Luckily, I didn't have to search long. Right-away I recognized a woman who had lived in Ou Krabau. I ran to her and reached for her arm as if I was reaching for my very own mother.

"Met Sok," I called. "It's me, Met Eng." My mind started reeling. If she was here, maybe Pho wasn't far away? She turned and searched my face. She was astonished, as if she saw a ghost.

"Did my brother Pho come this way too?" I asked.

She pulled me to the side, completely ignoring my question.

"Where have you been, Met Eng? Everyone in the village assumed you were dead," she said.

"Why did you think I was dead?" I tried to keep my focus. "It's a long story, and I don't have time. Please, Met Sok, where are my brother and sister and Sok Yann?" Again, my question was evaded.

"How did you get here, Met Eng?" she asked.

"It doesn't matter. I just need to know about my brother. Where can I find Pho?" She took my hand in hers.

"Met Eng, don't you know? The whole Pho Family was murdered. They were murdered one by one and thrown in the jungle. I assumed you were killed too."

I was shaken to the core. Every cell absorbed the news.

"Met Eng, the Khmer Rouge murdered most everyone in our village of Ou Krabau."

Another shockwave flowed through my heart, and a sharp pain jolted my chest. I turned around and ran away, leaving the woman standing alone in the crowded street without any explanation. I sprinted back toward the shore where I found Chhay's daughter whom I had left minutes before.

"Stop! Wait!" I gasped, trying to catch my breath. "I will come with you. I don't want to go looking for my family anymore. It's over. They are gone."

I never needed any of the rice that was packed for my journey. My trip to find Ko Pho and the others was cut short just the same as when I attempted to rescue my sister. I returned brokenhearted to the floating house. What purpose did I have for living? I was in mourning for weeks, willing myself to get up every day to complete my chores. There was no funeral, no proper burial. Dark days followed, creating a void in my spirit. I no longer feared death but feared living with the knowledge they were gone.

Much later, I realized the significance of the palm leaf letter. If my sister hadn't sent the palm letter from Moung asking for help, and if I didn't follow my heart to rescue her, I would have stayed in Ou Krabau and been killed along with my family. My sister, Sourn Leng, had unknowingly saved my life.

A PATH OF THIEVES: MAY – JUNE 1979

Road to Lumpini Transit Camp, Thailand

YoKuy and her relatives left Mongkol Borei in the middle of the night taking advantage of the chaos from a nearby burning gas station. They fled with their few possessions and walked until they reached the small town of Ou Chrov near the Thai border. They stayed there overnight and waited. That night, YoKuy thought of Koann, whom she left in Mongkol Borei. She hoped that she would be safe and would meet up with the family in France in the near future.

The time to cross the border was near. It was a dangerous mission. Thai robbers were known to search everywhere. Bodies, clothing, bags, and shoes were combed for jewels and valuables. The family knew that the thieves let nothing pass their detailed inspections. Before leaving Ou Chrov, YoKuy was savvy and camouflaged some 24-karat gold jewelry in a sweet rice dessert. "This should do the trick," she said. The gold was the same color as the brown sweet rice.

The large group of relatives were well on their way to freedom when a group of Thai men were seen hiding in the jungle up ahead. A warning gunshot was heard, and the Thai men approached them slowly.

"Stop. We were looking for you. We want to help you find your way," shouted one of the men.

Some Thai people were good Samaritans and did in fact help point refugees in the right direction. YoKuy wanted to believe they were telling the truth, but chances were that they were the evil kind. Loan was very small at the time. Before the robbers were in close range, YoKuy hurriedly shoved 24-karat jewels in Loan's mouth.

"Whatever you do, don't open your mouth or speak," she whispered. "Don't answer any questions, just nod your head."

As they approached, the man who was obviously in charge shouted, "Stand in a line. All of you."

In a matter of seconds, the men were rifling through everything. First, the thieves checked pockets and patted down bodies. When little Loan saw this, he was filled with fear and began shaking. The thieves worked their way methodically down the line of family, inching toward the rightfully scared little boy. One at a time, they stole precious gold, jewels, and watches from their many hiding places. They robbed a start to a new life, a down payment on a house, and a future investment in education. They might not have checked the children, but Loan opened his mouth in fear, spitting out all the gold.

YoKuy's brother, Kheat, had a baby, and the baby's mother was holding an umbrella for shade. Before the men approached, YoKuy hung several gold necklaces in an unlikely place along the top of the umbrella. Somehow, those valuables avoided detection and survived the search. YoKuy's purse was old and tattered. She had smartly hidden jewels in the middle layers. One robber took the purse, shaking it upside down violently. The jewels fell like confetti on the jungle floor, decorating the ground.

The Thai robbers were extremely thorough. They searched everything, and the only valuables that survived were in body cavities, a baby's umbrella, and the sweet rice dessert. Everyone thanked God they didn't take the most precious jewels of all—the children. No one was kidnapped, beaten, or killed, and that made for a successful border crossing.

YoKuy and her family continued walking west through the jungle toward the border with more than one thousand refugees. They slept one night in the jungle, taking turns to stay awake as a lookout. There were dangerous animals, poisonous snakes, and unknown threats in the jungle. Su and Kheat made a fire to keep the animals away, and unfortunately one of the little children got burned. The next day, the family continued through the jungle and cautiously stepped through a dried bamboo field. The sharp stalks sliced through their flesh, yet they continued with bleeding feet.

"I can't walk another step," said YoKuy. She had previously injured her foot, and the infection was spreading rapidly.

"Come here, Je Kuy," said an exhausted Su. YoKuy's younger brother carried her through the fields and jungle the rest of the way.

After a long journey by foot, the family made it to the relative safety of a refugee camp, but as soon as they arrived, they were assaulted by a huge storm. The fourteen family members attempted to sleep on top of a large piece of plastic tablecloth. It was all they had. They used large leaves to wear on their heads in order to keep the rain from their faces. The next day, they made a temporary shelter.

YoKuy's brother, Kheat, got robbed by the Thai soldiers in the camp. He was devastated, but his luck changed later when he met a Thai Special Colonel. The Special Colonel liked Kheat, and the two were able to communicate in English. This was an invaluable resource to the family.

"Do not take your family to France. You should change your application to America. This way you can be expedited and leave the country faster," advised the Special Colonel. Kheat gave the Colonel some gold as a token of thanks.

When it was time to leave the camp, YoKuy had a dream that she was at sea and many boats were sinking around her, but her boat wasn't sinking. She didn't know what it meant, but she discerned that this was a good sign. The next day, as the family prepared to leave the camp, the Special Colonel repeatedly advised, "Kheat, you and your family need to wait and get on the very last truck."

"Okay," said Kheat. "Thank you for your advice and for looking out for our family."

The family waited until the last vehicle arrived. They had no way of knowing if it was truly the last. There were no seats, so they stood on the back with a large group of people. Everyone hoped the truck would take them to the next transit camp. They heard rumors that some of the trucks took people to a mountain called Dang Rek where the Thai soldiers forced families to run down the steep, unforgiving cliff, sending them back to Cambodia.

A passenger on the truck announced that the next intersection would decide their fate.

"If we turn right, we are safe. If we turn to the left, we will be dumped down Dang Rek." Everyone on the truck was terrified and waited in complete silence. As soon as the driver turned the wheel, there was a celebration. Passengers were jumping up and down on the truck, grateful to be born again. The driver could have easily turned the other way, and their fate would have been changed forever.

Approximately forty-five thousand Cambodians were told they were being taken to a camp. Instead, they were loaded on buses, walked through the jungle to the top of a mountain, and forced to run down the side of the steep cliff with their babies, children, and families. If they didn't run down the cliff, they were shot in the back. The top of the mountain was in Thailand, but at the bottom was Cambodian soil. The few who survived being forced down the steep cliff had to manage walking through the mine fields back to their village.

Back in Mongkol Borei, Kim Eung, Grandma Ma Huoy, Bun Tek, Kim Ly, and Koann awaited news from YoKuy. When they learned of the atrocities at Dang Rek mountain, they worried that their family was among the dead.

AN UNEXPECTED GUEST:
SEPTEMBER 1979

Kampong Luong, Tonle Sap, Pursat Province

I lived on the floating house in Kampong Luong for about five months when Ma Mouy showed up unexpectedly. She arrived by boat from several miles across the lake to sell and trade fish and visit with her old neighbors. The Chhay family initially met Ma Mouy during the Khmer Rouge rule, and they became fast friends helping each other on a daily basis. I assumed Ma Mouy never thought about me because she was reunited with her own children. She knew I was being taken care of by the Chhay family ever since I left her months before.

When Ma Mouy arrived at the floating house, I wasn't home. I was fishing on Lake Tonle Sap as I did most days. For five months, I went along on fishing trips with the men. I was sent along with some local girls, and our duty was to clean and dry the fish and cook meals for the fishermen. When we came home from the trip, I saw her sitting on the floor of our floating house. Was it a mirage? I never thought I would see Ma Mouy again, and the tears flowed freely without restraint.

"Don't cry, Met Aun, no need to say anything. I can see it in your eyes," said Ma Mouy. She pulled me aside and spoke life into me. "When I met you the first time, I *needed* you. I had lost all my children. I don't *need* you anymore, Met Aun. I *want* you. Please come to live with me." She didn't want me so that I could help her with chores or fishing, Ma Mouy wanted me because she loved me.

"I don't have a place to live right now and am staying with another family on a boat, but I always have room for you." I listened intently without murmuring a word. "I will be nearby for two or three days to sell my fish. When I return, will you come and live with me and my family?" I nodded my head and searched with my eyes. I had no words for what I was feeling inside.

Pouk Chhay and Mai Neang didn't want me to leave because I had become an asset to their family. On the floating house, I did the cleaning and helped with the cooking responsibilities. I made myself useful on fishing trips to ensure that I earned my keep. The Chhay family gave me a home, food, and shelter, but in essence, I had become their maid. I was never mistreated, but it was apparent that I would never be anything more. Pouk Chhay and Mai Neang expressed their willingness to keep me in their care.

"Why doesn't Met Aun stay with us until you come back another time? We want to get her some new clothes and fabric," said Mai Neang.

Ma Mouy was assertive, stating her agenda clearly.

"You have three days to purchase whatever gifts you would like for Met Aun. When I return, I'm taking her to live with me." No one argued with Ma Mouy. It simply wasn't done.

Mai Neang returned from the market emptyhanded. She mentioned that she couldn't find any suitable material for me. No fabric was purchased as it was never the intention. When the three days passed, Ma Mouy did in fact return.

"Don't worry, Met Aun, I won't let you go naked," she said with her toothless smile. I said my goodbyes to the tree family. I had lived with them through an extremely difficult time. Mai Neang loved me in her own way. She had taken me in when I had no one, and for that I was forever grateful.

A NEW FAMILY: OCTOBER 1979

Chong Khneas, Tonle Sap, Siem Reap Province

"A father to the fatherless, a defender of widows,
is God in his holy dwelling.
God sets the lonely in families,
he leads out the prisoners with singing;
but the rebellious live in a sun-scorched land."
Psalm 68:5-6 (NIV)

Ma Mouy and I left Kampong Luong in a small row boat. We headed for another floating village called Chong Khneas with a fisherman who was a friend of Ma Mouy's.

"It should take several hours to get there," said Ma Mouy. We headed across the lake and up the east coast. It was a bad day for traveling by boat, and we found ourselves caught in a huge storm with high winds. The trip seemed to take forever.

When we arrived in Chong Khneas floating village, Ma Mouy surprised me with brand new sarong. It was the first gift I had received in more than four years. It was a striking, bright red with an intricate floral pattern. I was still wearing the same blue blouse from my friend, Met Pheap, who was killed in prison. The new sarong was very expensive, and Ma Mouy had traded gold for it. After wearing black for so long, I felt like a beautiful queen minus the short, choppy hair. By the time I met

Ma Mouy on the floating house, my hair had grown only a few inches. Every gift is precious, but Ma Mouy was extravagant in her generosity. She had nothing yet gave everything.

Ma Mouy had two daughters and a son named Sok Kong. I now became known as *Aun Thom*, or Big Aun, and Ma Mouy's older daughter was called *Aun Toch*, or Little Aun. It was funny how we shared the same name. Ma Mouy's younger daughter was named Sok Chea. I now had three new siblings and lived with Ma Mouy in the floating village of Chong Khneas located in the Province of Siem Reap on the east coast of Lake Tonle Sap. There were several boats in the Chong Khneas, and huts were also built near the shore. The huts were moved with the shoreline to adjust for the wet and dry seasons.

Ma Mouy's family didn't live alone but shared a sampan boat with her best friend's family. There were already seven people crammed on the small boat, and I made eight, yet I was welcomed with open arms. Ma Mouy had so many friends. People who knew her loved her for her big heart and beautiful, toothless smile. Even my father, lover of perfect teeth, would have appreciated Ma Mouy's smile. When we slept, we lined up like sardines, head to toe. To relieve ourselves at night, we had to crawl over one another. It was such a dreaded task, yet no one complained. The boat was long and narrow with a small cover to protect us from the rain.

Ma Mouy traded gold to purchase supplies to build a shelter. I thought it was interesting that she was a business woman like my own mom. Mom did her business in a pawn shop, while Ma Mouy did her bartering at the market. Ma Mouy became friends with several Vietnamese soldiers, and they eventually built her a hut. She was like a grandmother to all, and everyone she met became a friend. Spices, cigarettes, groceries, salt, and pepper were among the items sold from Ma Mouy's hut. Always involved in business deals, she made things better for her family. I was now part of that family.

One day a familiar looking woman came to our hut.

"Excuse me," I asked. "Where were you originally from?" The woman looked me up and down.

"Battambang," she replied. I asked if she was familiar with So Kuy Huor, the pawn shop.

"I didn't do business with them, but I knew who they were," she said. "Are you part of the family?"

"Yes, *ja,* I am," I said. It felt wonderful to speak with someone who knew of my family, until the woman continued.

"This girl came from the kind of family where the girls never left the home, if you know what I mean," she said to Ma Mouy with a condescending voice. She was insinuating that we were overly protected and strictly raised. "They weren't known as run around girls, but rather the studious kind, always being watched by their mother."

I asked the woman if she knew anything about my family. She knew nothing.

When the woman left, I spoke privately with Ma Mouy.

"Please, Ma Mouy, please understand that we weren't high class people with our noses held high in the air." It bothered me the way this woman spoke to Ma Mouy and referred to my family.

Up until that point, Ma Mouy never asked me about my parents, schooling, or upbringing. She loved me for who I was, a poor sickly orphan without a piece of gold to my name. She knew me only as Met Aun. She never knew Siv Eng or asked about my background. That part of me was still alive, but it had been buried in a shallow grave with my brother and sister.

"Thanks for loving me without knowing who I was," I said. "I don't know how you had so much love for such a skinny, poor, lonely girl."

Ma Mouy took my hands in hers, "Aun Thom, I didn't know your background, but I saw love in your eyes." Ma Mouy was a good Samaritan. She had lost her husband and a daughter at the hands of the Khmer Rouge. I only knew Ma Mouy as a widow, and she only knew me as an orphan.

STORM ON THE LAKE: DECEMBER 1979

Chong Khneas, Lake Tonle Sap, Siem Reap Province

> *"Where can I go from your Spirit?*
> *Where can I flee from your presence?*
> *If I go up to the heavens, you are there;*
> *if I make my bed in the depths, you are there.*
> *If I rise on the wings of the dawn,*
> *if I settle on the far side of the sea,*
> *even there your hand will guide me,*
> *your right hand will hold me fast.*
> *If I say, "Surely the darkness will hide me,*
> *and the light become night around me,"*
> *¹² even the darkness will not be dark to you;*
> *the night will shine like the day,*
> *for darkness is as light to you."*
>
> Psalm 139:7-12 (NIV)

I frequently went on fishing trips and took pride in contributing to the family income. One day I returned from a trip with a neighbor when I was invited to go on a second one with a young girl named Met Rane. I continued to use the word *Met* to address others. Even though we were free from the rule of the Angkar, our language was still held captive out of sheer habit.

As we left across Lake Tonle Sap, the water was calm and the sky was clear. Met Rane was seventeen years old. We followed the larger boat with a man and his two young sons. They were our neighbors and were avid fishermen, familiar with navigating Lake Tonle Sap. Met Rane and I would have never dreamed of crossing the Lake alone, but we trustingly followed after the men. We brought food for five to seven days.

"We need to keep the fish fresh," said Met Rane.

I reached down to pick up the salt. "Don't forget the salt," I added.

We covered the fish with salt as we caught them to preserve our catch. We didn't fish with hooks but stayed close to shore and used nets tied to the bushes. When we were done spreading our long nets, we rowed away to a tree on the edge of the water and slept there in our boat.

After several days of fishing, we stored the cured fish in baskets on the boat.

"They may be small, but there are so many," said Met Rane.

One morning, when we were ready to head home, a sudden unpredicted wind storm came from nowhere. I climbed a tree to get a glimpse across the Lake and saw the waves surging with a powerful force. In the evening, the storm dissipated and blew away.

"Met Aun, it's safe to head home now," the neighbor shouted. "Be careful not to get too far behind." We dipped our oars in the water and began to paddle back across the lake. It was a productive trip, and our baskets were filled with fish. Met Rane and I paddled in sync for several hours. We talked about getting home, sharing a hot meal, and sleeping on land.

When we reached the middle of Lake Tonle Sap, the sky was completely dark and eerily quiet. The fisherman kept shouting at us to row faster, but we didn't understand the urgency. The storm that had died down hours ago decided to come back with a vengeance. In the stillness, a rumbling was heard in the distance. The sound of horses running a race.

A pounding that mimicked the beating of my heart. The wind began its roaring, and the waves grew by the minute. It happened in a matter of seconds. The father and two sons were a distance ahead of us. They had a much greater combined rowing strength compared to two young girls in a smaller boat. The father cupped his hands to his mouth to shout, but his voice was no match for the storm.

We rowed as fast as possible, but the white-capped waves were overpowering. The larger boat didn't want to wait around for us in the middle of Tonle Sap. They made a survival decision, and we were deserted.

"Come back! Come back! Don't leave us here." We waved our arms frantically, but they could no longer hear our cries. We screamed and called out, our voices drowned by the waves and storm.

Sweet young Met Rane was terrified and broke down in tears. It was then that my survival instincts kicked in. I looked in the boat for any supplies we might put to use and cried out once again to the God of the Highest Universe. If my prayer was heard in prison, surely God could hear us now.

"Start scooping. Quick, *chap, chap*!" Met Rane grabbed the buckets. Hours passed. All night long we scooped water out of our boat. We tossed and turned, rising and falling in the swells. My fishing companion was a terrified girl in a state of panic. I knew we were in trouble when she began calling to her mother for help. Her mother had died several years earlier.

"Throw the fish in the lake. Get rid of them," Met Rane yelled over the raging storm.

"Wait!" I shouted. "Calm down. What are you saying?"

I rightfully feared for our lives but managed to think straight after years of living in life or death conditions. This was a storm. It, too, would pass. If I would have listened to Met Rane's advice, we wouldn't have had any fish to show for our troubles.

In the middle of Lake Tonle Sap, I thought about my father and the swimming lessons with floating coconuts. At that moment I would have welcomed a taste of Dad's nasty whale oil if it would have saved us. When the storm was at its worst, I began to contemplate my life. I had no one to leave behind. My family was gone. My only worry at that time was the fear of drowning. I knew how to swim, but could I swim in those waves?

"Please, stop screaming. I can't think straight." I reached out to Met Rane. "I need you to help me keep our boat afloat. We are not going to die here," I said. The shivers made our teeth chatter in the relentless wind. In the back of my mind was the nagging worry of getting lost. If we ended up surviving, how would we find our way home?

We did have some supplies on the boat. We brought several vining plants to hang out our fish like a clothes line. We also had a long, heavy pole and a rope. The pole was about nine feet long. I quickly tied one end of the rope to the top of the pole and tied the other end to our boat.

Miraculously, I had managed to make a makeshift anchor with the rope and pole. At the very least it would slow us down in the waves. Somehow, my anchor held through the night.

When the storm cleared, the moon appeared. I bathed in the moonlight, holding out my arms and thinking of my mother.

"I'm still here, Mom, wherever you are." I could never send enough messages to the moon.

We couldn't see land and had lost our sense of direction. I recalled learning survival skills in a class at school and followed my instincts. I put the moon to my back and hoped that we were headed east. We rowed and rowed into the morning hours, our puny arms were exhausted. Eventually, I saw a little mountain on the shoreline and recognized Phnom Chong Khneas, the mountain of Chong Khneas.

"See, over there," I said. We weren't too far off course.

When the shore came into view it was mid-morning, and Ma Mouy was there waiting for us. I was grateful to see dry land and even more appreciative to see her. I did have something to live for. I had Ma Mouy and my new family.

The other fishing boat had reached the shore sometime in the middle of the night. The man found Ma Mouy and apologized. Ma Mouy was furious. She was waiting and hoping and praying all through the night in a panic. She had already asked the Vietnamese soldiers to search for us in a motorized canoe. Ma Mouy feared the worst and was overjoyed to see us.

"If we didn't come home alive today, it would have probably been a couple days until our bodies floated to shore," I said.

"That's what I feared," admitted Ma Mouy. After that, Ma Mouy broke down in tears.

"No more fishing for you, Aun Thom. You must go home and rest for a few weeks and then come with me to sell goods in the market."

SEWING SEEDS OF BUSINESS:
JANUARY 1980

Chong Khneas, Tonle Sap, Siem Reap Province

Since I was recovering at home, I mentioned to Ma Mouy that I knew how to sew. She welcomed my idea and traded and bartered for new material. She had excellent taste and surprised me with beautiful fabrics.

"I found a neighbor woman who owns a sewing machine," announced Ma Mouy. "Now you can make clothes for our family."

I now had a new daily routine. I left for *Om*[40] Hey's house to sew in the morning, went home for lunch, and returned in the afternoon for more sewing. Om Hey was impressed with my work right from the start. I paid her in rice for the rental of her machine at the end of every week. It was a Singer like my mother's and didn't use electricity. My first project was to make three shirts. One for me and one for each of my two younger sisters.

"I have a machine, but I have no knowledge of sewing," said Om Hey. "Whenever you need it, it's yours. You have talent and an eye for fashion."

"Thanks, Om Hey," I said with a smile. I wasn't used to getting compliments.

---

[40]   An honorific used when addressing a person who is older than you, but younger than your parents.

"You know, Met Aun, we should start a business together," she suggested.

"I enjoy making clothes for my family, but I'm certainly not good enough to design for customers," I said. Om Hey adamantly disagreed and insisted that we start a business without delay.

"What if I ruin the fabric and have to buy more?" I asked.

Om Hey reassured me that no excuse was a good excuse. "I promise to pay for the material if you make a mistake," she said with a wink. Om Hey believed in me. She saw a promising seamstress with a profitable business venture.

My excuses kept rising to the surface.

"I don't know anyone in town. How will I get customers to build a business?"

"You let me worry about that," said Om Hey.

Just like that a business was born. The next day Om Hey's daughter came to my house and announced that I had my first customer. Our business plan was decided; we would split profits fifty-fifty with the customers making the investment of purchasing their own material. Weeks after surviving a storm, I was now terrified of ruining fabric.

When the first customer arrived, I was nervous.

"Did you bring another blouse for a sample pattern?" I asked. She had no blouse and was unsure of her measurements. It was at that moment I realized we did not own a measuring tape. In my high school sewing class, we used patterns. When I made clothing for my little sister, Koann, I always measured from one of her existing blouses. I had no measuring tape, but I did have string. I improvised by devising a method of using different knots to mark shoulders, bust, waist and arms. After many knots and blouses, I became a well-known seamstress in Chong Khneas. It all started with a borrowed sewing machine, an assertive business partner, and a piece of string—not to mention my faithful scissors.

"I trust you, Met Aun, and you can now take the sewing machine to your house. You have lots of work to do, and don't need to waste time going back and forth."

"Thanks, *arkoun*. Thanks for your generosity and trust, Om Hey." I thought of my mother and her mountain of fabric waiting for her customers in our home in Khla Kham Chhkae. If only she could see me now.

Ma Mouy extended a room in her hut for my new sewing venture. I had approximately ten customers every week. I eventually had a waiting line and had to turn down clients. My business grew by word of mouth and referrals only.

Another woman in town was a seamstress, and when she saw my work she proposed that I work with her for an increased pay. I specialized in blouses and men's shirts, and the other seamstress promised to teach me how to make pants. I chose to stay with Om Hey because she believed in me and got me started. She also depended on me for her income. It wasn't a good business decision but was a matter of loyalty. The customers paid for their sewing in rice and often asked for pricing.

"This shirt is worth two cups of rice," I said. "A blouse with ruffles is three cups of rice." Sewing proved to be a valuable source of income. I never really learned how to make pants, which is ridiculous. Anyone who knows anything about sewing knows that pants are much simpler compared to blouses. However, I never regretted staying in business with Om Hey. It was the right thing to do.

A HOLE IN THE WALL, A HOLE IN MY HEART: FEBRUARY 1980

Chong Khneas, Tonle Sap, Siem Reap Province

Ma Mouy's hut by Lake Tonle Sap was crudely made with an unforgiving, rough, bumpy floor. At night, we slept on a large sheet of commercial tin to avoid the harshness of the floor. One morning my foster siblings and I were sitting on the floor eating leftover rice from the day before. In the hut next to us, on the other side of the wall, our neighbors were also eating their breakfast.

"Pass the rice, Je Aun," said my little brother, Sok Kong. He was the only boy among all of us girls. As I bent over to reach for the rice on my left, a bullet flew under my right arm. The air whizzed by, making a whistling sound. The bullet had entered through the wall of our hut, flew under my arm, passed through the neighbor's wall, and hit a little neighbor boy on the side of his face. The little boy was Met Rane's little brother.

"Ouch! Oh. Help me, *jouy phong*." Within seconds everyone in the hut next door was screaming.

Even though we were free of the Khmer Rouge, we still heard gunshots on occasion. My little brother asked for rice at the right moment. The God of the Most High Universe had spared my life again. The boy wasn't killed but was taken to a Red Cross trauma center nearby. I was blessed to be alive.

I thought of my biological family every day. I wanted to travel to Battambang. I fantasized about walking down the street and seeing my little brothers and sisters playing near my old home. My brain couldn't process the fact that six years had also passed for them, and they were grown. I was so discouraged when I learned of the death of Pho, Sourn Leng, and Sok Yann that it squelched my desire to continue the search for my mother. I had no form of transportation and owned nothing but the clothes on my back. Everything I earned by sewing went to Ma Mouy and our family.

I was safe with my foster family. What if I travelled to Battambang, and my family was not there? How would I return to the safety of Chong Khneas? There were horror stories of what happened to young girls with no family. Travel was expensive and dangerous, but greater than the fear of travel and safety was my fear of the truth. How would I handle it if I learned that my mother and siblings didn't survive?

ANGKOR WAT: APRIL 1980

Siem Reap, Siem Reap Province

As a young child and teenager, my family took frequent trips to the famous Temple, Angkor Wat. On one occasion, the day before we left, Aunt Chhiv Hong sent me a note. We didn't have phones, and the note was brought by the maid on a bicycle. The letter inquired about highly important matters.

> *Siv Eng,*
>
> *Should we wear a skirt or pants to Angkor Wat?*
>
> *What color blouse will you wear?*
>
> *How are you doing your hair? Please respond as soon as possible.*
>
> *Chhiv Hong*

I replied to her pertinent questions by the same messenger. We were obsessed with how we looked and presented ourselves. We were typical girls with typical teenage concerns. My mom, however, didn't concern herself with appearance.

Mom frantically rushed into my room.

"Siv Eng, quick. I need some perfume."

I was busy combing my long hair. "Look on the dresser, Mom. It's right there."

As I looked up, I saw my mom rubbing "perfume" on her neck and wrists.

"Mom, that's my fingernail polish remover," I shouted.

"No wonder it burns," she said with a smile. "But it sure smells good to me."

My mom was a beautiful woman with or without perfume. Thoughts of her kept me grounded.

---••◦●◦••---

I couldn't wait any longer. I decided to take the plunge and ask Ma Mouy if we could travel to the ancient temple, Angkor Wat. The temple would be a perfect place to meet people who might know news of my family. Many went to Angkor Wat on holidays because it was a famous tourist attraction. I begged Ma Mouy to go.

"Ma Mouy, I've had a question on my mind. Would you please, please take me to Angkor Wat for the New Year? I have so much hope to find news of my family there."

Ma Mouy understood my desire. She had found her lost children and experienced the joy of a family reunion. Now she wanted to do everything in her power to help me.

"It is time, Aun Thom. We will go together," said Ma Mouy.

Chong Khneas wasn't far from Angkor Wat. Both were in the Siem Reap Province. We didn't have the means to travel to Battambang but could take a remok to the temple.

The day finally arrived, and Ma Mouy and I set off to Angkor Wat. I could hardly contain my excitement. Were my mom and younger siblings on their way to Angkor Wat this very minute? My emotions were a rollercoaster. I imagined my mother standing on the steps of the temple looking for me.

On the way to Angkor Wat, our remok driver asked if we would like to see a mass grave on the way to the Temple. We stopped along the road and walked a short distance on a trail. The stench led the way. Several others were on the same path to view the mass grave and show their respects. I wasn't prepared for the scene. The half-buried bones and remains were a chilling reminder of what we had survived. The smell of rotting flesh was hovering, stagnant in the air. Clothes were scattered here and there. An arm here, a shoe there. I wanted to run away. We returned to the remok and continued our journey with a sobering awareness. The massive structure of the ancient temple was fast approaching, looming larger with every mile.

Ma Mouy was so patient, walking around Angkor Wat with me all day. I looked carefully at the faces, not letting one escape my examining gaze, but not one looked remotely familiar. I remembered going to Angkor Wat as a child on many happy vacations, dressing up with my cousins and sister, and meeting relatives. It brought back a flood of happy memories.

I knew I looked very different from 1974 when I last saw my mother. I began to wonder if anyone would recognize me. Six years had passed since I'd seen my mother, and I was no longer a young college student. The years of forced labor, starvation, and disease had taken their toll on everyone. I combed the faces, searching for a familiar nose, eyes, or high cheekbones. I looked for any feature that I could recognize.

After several hours, I couldn't bring myself to leave and pleaded with Ma Mouy, "Can we please stay one more hour?" She willingly complied, but after the whole day of searching, I only found disappointment. Devastation was settling in, and hopelessness was getting comfortable in a chamber of my heart. This was it. It was over. Finally, it was time to leave.

In front of Angkor Wat, right at the end of the gate, was a beautiful, huge ancient tree. It seemed to be as old as the temple itself. A large concrete space was built around the tree where many people sat enjoying the shade. Ma Mouy and I rested under the shade of the tree waiting for a remok. As I sat between Ma Mouy and a lady selling water, a young couple in their forties pulled up on a motorcycle. The man looked to the woman sitting next to me.

"Can I please buy some water?" he asked. At once I noticed his scar. It registered a memory, and I knew immediately that I had seen this man before.

"Ma Mouy," I whispered. "He looks familiar." I was so afraid to speak, I almost lost my voice.

"Excuse me, did you ever live in Battambang?"

To my utter surprise, he said, "Yes, *bat*,[41] I lived in Battambang."

"Did you know the pawn shop, So Kuy Huor?"

He paused to reflect. "Yes, I know that store well. My aunt and uncle ran that shop."

I couldn't believe it.

"My parents ran the shop," I said. It was a small world after all. He stopped and looked at me closely. This time it was my face that was being meticulously examined.

"Which one are you?" he asked.

"I am Siv Eng," I nodded.

"I hardly recognized you," he admitted. "You've changed so much."

We stood staring at each other transfixed with wonder.

When he told me his name, I remembered exactly who he was, a cousin on my father's side. He had scars on his face from acne when he was younger, and that's what sparked my memory. Sometimes it's the little things. When I knew him he had been a young teenager. At first, I thought maybe he was a customer at the shop, but it was even better. He was family.

A scar was a beautiful thing. A scar had been part of my healing in Ou Krabau, and this man's scarred face was the first step in reuniting me with my family.

We were both unaware that many other travelers had moved in closer around the tree to observe our reunion and absorb our conversation.

---

41   A word for "yes" only used by males.

When we cried, they cried with us. When we laughed, the growing crowd laughed along. All of Cambodia was experiencing joy-filled reunions with long lost family members while simultaneously learning of the tragic deaths of loved ones. Our country was mourning and celebrating together, all in one breath. There under the tree at Angkor Wat, magic was happening before our eyes.

I blurted it out. "Have you been to Battambang? Have you seen my family?" I could hardly spit the words out, my stubborn tongue moving in slow motion.

"Siv Eng, your mother, young siblings, and grandparents are still alive!"

I couldn't believe my ears. At that very moment, I was on a mountain top, but his next words came with a punch to the gut.

"Wait a minute. Your family all left the country. They are in France with your Uncle Su," he reported. "Siv Eng, your mother, YoKuy, believes that you are dead." His words hung heavy as a thick fog.

My mountain top quickly crumbled as I fell down a landslide into a pit. I broke down crying and knew that I would not ever see my family again. My feelings wavered from the joy of their survival to the reality of continued separation. Despair took residence once again. Crossing the border was a life or death journey, and we had no way to contact them from Cambodia. No way to tell them that I was alive. If I shouted from the top of the Temple Angkor Wat, it would bring me no closer. Reunion denied. They were here and yet so far away. I couldn't see them, touch them, or tell them I loved them.

"Siv Eng," he continued. "Your Grandma Ma Huoy was unable to make the journey and is living in Mongkol Borei with your Aunt Kim Eung's family." A blossom of hope was budding.

It was a quiet ride back to Siem Reap on the remok. So many thoughts were brewing in my mind. From the stop at the mass graves and the search through the temple to the news of my family. How will I ever see Mom again if she believes that I'm gone? Does she know about Pho, Sok Yann and Sourn Leng? Will the rest of my life be lived here with Ma Mouy? Can I live with that reality?

I went back to Chong Khneas to resume my sewing business as if nothing happened. I waited and waited, my family constantly on my mind. My cousin from Angkor Wat took the news of my location to Grandma Ma Huoy in the village of Mongkol Borei.

I continued to live with Ma Mouy's family in Chong Khneas. I truly enjoyed being with her children; her two daughters had become like sisters to me. We used to tease each other about who was fattest, myself or Little Aun. Giggles were welcome guests to the hut. We often took turns weighing ourselves from the hanging scales to brag about who was the biggest. It was such a blessing to make fat jokes after starving for so many consecutive years. At the time of the takeover, I was a thin girl of ninety pounds. During the next several years I was easily down to less than seventy-five pounds. Now, with rice being plenty, I had become a fat girl with a full belly. A happy fat girl.

In May 1980, Ma Mouy took me by boat on the Mongkol Borei River to meet my grandmother. Grandma Ma Huoy was in her nineties when I was reunited with her. Her mind was strong, but her legs were weak. She was unable to make the harrowing journey across the border and lived with Aunt Kim Eung's family.

When I look back, it was a beautiful thing. My father was gone and had died many years previously, but it was *his* cousin I met at Angkor Wat who reunited me with *his* mother and *his* only sister, my Aunt Kim Eung. It's like Dad brought us all together. The God of the Most High Universe was watching over us all.

Grandma Ma Huoy and I embraced in a shower of tears. There were no words until the tears gave way.

"Siv Eng, you're alive. How can this be? We missed you so. I would hardly recognize my own granddaughter. You look so different, but I love you just the same."

"I love you, too, Grandma."

Ma Huoy tried to speak through her tears. "First you were fatherless, then you became motherless," she said. "I can't take care of you anymore. I'm too old. What can I do for you?" Just being there in her presence was enough for me. She was like a second mother to me, growing up with her in our home.

I was in the arms of Ma Huoy, my grandma who helped raise me, and beside me stood Ma Mouy, the mother who chose me and took me into her family when I had nothing. Grandma Ma Huoy never knew me as Met Aun, and Ma Mouy never knew me as Siv Eng. It was a blessed moment. The line between two identities and two lives was blurring and fading into one.

After a shared cup of tea and a delicious meal, Grandma Ma Huoy handed me a letter with a picture. There in the picture was my mother and her younger sister, Aunt Elisa, smiling back at me. I was overcome with emotion. My mother was alive. I flipped the photo over and saw an address. I blinked and looked again.

"Grandma, this address is South Bend, Indiana. That's the United States. They aren't in France!"

Grandma Ma Huoy was unable to read English and assumed the photo was from France because that is where they planned to go. She was as shocked as me. This news was another kick in the gut. My family was even farther than I realized, across the vast ocean in the land of America. Over the next few days, Aunt Kim Eung took me around in Mongkol Borei to visit my relatives and to show them that I was indeed alive. It was as if I came back from the dead, a resurrected girl.

FAT GIRL ON A BIKE: JULY 1980

The Road to Mongkol Borei, Banteay Meanchey

Grandma Ma Huoy and Aunt Kim Eung assumed that I was there to stay, but Ma Mouy wanted to bring me back to Chong Khneas to finish all the sewing projects that were in process. I agreed to return with her and close up my business. I stayed with Ma Mouy for another six weeks of sewing.

One day, we had a surprise visitor. Aunt Kim Eung hired a young cousin to travel to Chong Khneas by bicycle. It was such a long journey for my young cousin, Logn. He rode a single bicycle with an extra seat on the front—not exactly a bicycle built for two. I was shocked when he revealed his promise to bring me back to Ma Huoy's home in Mongkol Borei.

How do you say goodbye to your mother not knowing if you will return? I embraced Ma Mouy and told her how much I loved her and appreciated her.

"I found my family, Aun Thom. Now you go and find yours." Her words were those of sacrifice and love. I had become a true daughter to her. Ma Mouy never treated me like a foster child but lavished me with her generosity.

"*Leahaey*," I said as I rode away.

I assumed I would be back to visit someday soon. My younger sister,

Little Aun, happened to be visiting Chhay and Mai Neang at the floating house. I never had a chance to say goodbye to her.

My young cousin, Logn, who had just completed a marathon journey by bike, was preparing to turn around to make the return trip. A bike had always been there for the important moments in my life.

I was excited to see my Grandmother again, but I also felt guilty about my poor second cousin pulling my weight. It took him twice as long on the return trip because he had to stop and rest several times. I was no longer emaciated or starved, and I wasn't skinny either. My cousin had no idea what he signed up for.

I now had three families in Cambodia: the Chhay family, Ma Mouy's family, and my Grandma Ma Huoy and Aunt Kim Eung. I also had a family across the ocean who had no idea I was alive. Sitting on the bicycle on my way to Mongkol Borei, I had a feeling that things would work out in the end. I was determined to connect with my family overseas.

When we finally arrived in Mongkol Borei, the gate to the city was closed for security. Crime was a widespread problem.

"Where should we go?" asked Logn. Our safety was now in jeopardy.

"We can knock on doors and ask for a place to sleep," I suggested. It took courage for us to beg. We took a chance and stopped at one of the first houses in the village. The door opened slowly.

"Excuse me, can you please help us?" I asked. A kind woman opened the door and offered her outside patio providing us with pillows and a mat.

"You must know, I can't sleep out here with him," I said. "He is not my husband."

She had mistakenly assumed we were husband and wife. I had no place to sleep, yet I was concerned about propriety. This kind woman let me sleep in the house with her daughter—another stranger who showed me kindness without reward. My brave cousin, who was trekking me across the country on a bike, was sleeping on the outside patio while I slept comfortably in the house. In the early morning when the gates were opened, Logn delivered me as promised to Grandma Ma Huoy's doorstep.

Aunt Kim Eung, Grandma Ma Huoy, and my cousin, Sophal, were there waiting for me. Sophal was a few years younger than me. Over a meal of rice soup and fish, I learned the news that my younger sister, Koann, was not only alive but living across the Thailand border in the Khao I Dang refugee camp. She was there with her adopted parents. My flesh and blood sister was not far away in distance, but she was an eternity away in reality.

"Why didn't she cross the border with my family?" I asked.

"Bun Tek and Kim Ly were worried about Koann's safety. They waited to cross the border, thinking that the situation might improve. Now they have been stuck at Khao I Dang camp for two years and have been unable to get the necessary paperwork to be released," explained Aunt Kim Eung.

"I must go to Khao I Dang," I said. "I need to be with my sister."

Grandma Ma Huoy knew it wasn't so simple.

"You can't go straight to Khao I Dang. It's across the Thai border," said Grandma Ma Huoy. "You have to go to Nong Chan Camp first. It's a refugee camp on the Cambodian/Thailand border. People travel there by ox cart to get rice from the Red Cross. You could go with them."

"I will go with you," said a young and brave Sophal.

When the day arrived, we left in a rush.

"Here, Siv Eng, I want you to have this. If you never come back, please keep this to always remember me."

Grandma Ma Huoy handed me a beautiful scarf with one last embrace, and we left with a large group of people in an ox cart, headed to Nong Chan camp. Another *leahaey*. We looked to the group for safety in numbers. Robbers and thieves were plentiful along the road, and it was extremely dangerous to travel alone, especially for young girls. Sophal stayed with me in Nong Chan for a few weeks to make sure I was settled in. Even a refugee camp wasn't safe for a young girl.

Once again, it was as if my dad was looking out for me. It just so happened that a friend of my father was in charge of the orphanage in Nong Chan. He remembered me and allowed me to stay in the orphanage at night. I was safe there and given rice and one sardine every day for sustenance. I looked young enough to be a teenager. As I slept among the orphans, I again looked to the moon and thought of my mother.

JEWELRY DREAMS: JULY 1980

South Bend, Indiana, United States of America

Soon after arriving in Fort Wayne, Indiana, YoKuy and her family were moved to South Bend. One morning, YoKuy woke up from a vivid dream. She sat up in bed, blinking her eyes awake. It was so real. In the dream, even though she wasn't searching, she found her long-lost jewelry. It was lost long ago, but she hadn't forgotten it. She found it under the bed in a box. Had it been there all along? In the dream, she was overjoyed to find her precious jewelry.

She got up, thinking of all she had to accomplish that day. She watered her plants, ate some rice and fish for a quick breakfast, had a cup of hot tea, and left for work. YoKuy was a seamstress for the furrier at Mr. Leonard's Fur Shop. It was a far cry from her Singer in Khla Kham Chhkae. As she sat at her sewing machine working on a mink coat, YoKuy shared her dream with a co-worker.

"I had such a vivid dream last night, I found my long-lost jewelry that I'd been missing for years. It seemed so real."

Her co-worker was intrigued with the dream.

"YoKuy, maybe you will find something missing in real life. Dreams are funny things, you never know."

What could this mean? Surely it was something good. In Cambodian culture, when you have a dream about finding something lost, it is a sign of good luck.

A LETTER AND A PICTURE: AUGUST 1980

Nong Chan Camp, Cambodian/Thailand Border

At the Nong Chan Cambodian Refugee Camp, I had but one purpose. I went to the post office daily to find someone who was willing to take a letter across the Thailand border to my sister, Koann. I spoke with the Cambodian workers at every opportunity and entreated with anyone who would listen. I became the squeaky wheel.

"I am looking for a way to communicate with my sister in Khao I Dang Camp. Please help me. I have to let my sister know that I am alive," I pleaded. I explained my situation like a broken record over and over again. "I'm staying at the Nong Chan Orphanage. Please find me if you hear of anyone who can help."

I left my name with the workers at the post office day after day. There were thousands of refugees in the camp, and it would have been very difficult for them to find me. I was one desperate voice of thousands of misplaced persons asking for help. I made sure that my voice was the squeakiest one of all. The Khmer Rouge had succeeded in separating families, and I was equally determined to succeed in connecting with my sister.

Sophal was a young girl, yet she travelled back and forth from Nong

Chan to Mongkol Borei to share news with Grandma Ma Huoy. She was quite the entrepreneur, buying goods from Thai smugglers and then selling them in Mongkol Borei to turn a solid profit. Sophal was my lifeline, post office, cousin, and friend.

Exactly fifteen days after arriving in Nong Chan, a messenger showed up at the orphanage claiming he knew of a translator who could help me. This translator was planning to cross the Thailand border to the Khao I Dang Refugee Camp and then head to America. My heart began racing, my blood flowing in overdrive. This was perfect. I ran all the way to the post office kicking up the dust and stepping inside out of breath.

"I am…Siv Eng," I said, catching my breath. "I hope you can help me." The American had a kind face.

"Yes, I believe I can," he said. "I will take anything over the Thai border except for you." He offered to take my belongings, letters, anything I wished, but he wisely refused to smuggle refugees for fear of losing his life and the lives of those he helped.

"I want to send a letter to my mom in the United States and to my sister in the Khao I Dang camp."

With a reassuring smile he said, "I'd be glad to help. Where are the letters?"

After all the waiting and harassing people at the post office for fifteen days, I hadn't prepared ahead by writing the letters. This was a huge oversight. Now, I had to write them in a hurry.

"Let's take photos, Siv Eng, so your sister and Mother can have another form of identification."

"Good idea," I said, smiling the biggest warmest smile possible.

I could hardly wait for Koann to read the letter, see the picture, and learn that her sister was alive and well. We were in such a hurry that I never even saw the pictures. The translator had a kind heart. He was a volunteer at the camp with the sole purpose of helping refugees. He was able to cross the border easily without being arrested because he was American and possessed the magic immigration papers. What I wouldn't give for those papers.

He promised to deliver one photo and letter to the Khao I Dang Camp, and another photo and letter to my mom, YoKuy, in South Bend, Indiana. Because he took the items in person, I knew that they would be delivered. The Post Office system in Cambodia was rudimentary. The country was in such turmoil that mail delivery was not considered an essential.

KHAO I DANG CAMP: AUGUST 1980

Prachinburi Province, Thailand

The next day, the translator crossed the border and personally brought the letter and photo to the immigration office at Khao I Dang Refugee Camp.

"I need help finding a family," he said. "I have a letter and a photo from a girl in the Nong Chan Camp. She is trying to locate the daughter of Bun Tek."

"We know where to find him," they said. The immigration office sent a boy after Bun Tek, who arrived at the immigration office in a rush.

"Who is in this picture?" asked the immigration worker. Bun Tek looked carefully at the image.

"I'm not sure," admitted Bun Tek.

"This is Siv Eng, your relative," said the worker.

"I haven't seen my niece for years," said Bun Tek.

He didn't recognize Siv Eng in the picture but didn't dare to admit it to the immigration workers. Bun Tek was unsure of the situation and thought someone was trying to take advantage of him by getting money to cross the border.

"I must find her sister, Koann, and show her the picture," Bun Tek said. "She will know if this is truly Siv Eng."

At that moment, Koann was sitting in her English class at Khao

I Dang. Koann was an eighteen-year-old who had just endured the roughest years of her life. She desperately wanted to go to the U.S. to join the rest of her family. Every day for a year she begged and begged her parents to leave for the States. When the decision was finally made that it was safe to leave, they were stopped in their tracks at Khao I Dang. The authorities vetted all refugees, asking a barrage of questions over and over again. Koann's mother, Kim Ly, was nervous and kept failing the frustratingly elaborate tests. She messed up the names of relatives, birthdates, and how exactly they were related. When this happened, she had to wait for a period of time before attempting the test again.

Bun Tek went immediately to the room where Koann was attending English and called his daughter out of class. She was alarmed. Her father had never barged into her classroom before.

"What's wrong? What is going on?" she asked. Koann followed her father to the immigration office.

"Koann, please identify the person in this photo," said the immigration worker. Her eyes strained as she gazed unknowingly at the picture.

"Who is this?" thought Koann. She held the letter and the picture in her hand. The letter appeared to be Siv Eng's handwriting, but she did not recognize the person in the photo.

Sitting and waiting impatiently in Nong Chan, I pictured my sister's joyful reaction when she saw my picture and learned I was alive. She was probably celebrating this very minute and writing a letter in return. Little did I know that my own uncle and sister didn't recognize me. I looked more like an overweight boy with short hair, but I was simply a lost girl. A family reunion couldn't happen soon enough for me.

My young cousin, Sophal, continued traveling back and forth from Mongkol Borei to Nong Chan. When she returned, she brought news that there was threat of a Khmer Rouge attack near the camp.

"Ma Huoy wants you to come home to Mongkol Borei right away," said Sophal. I refused to leave. Nothing could stop me. I was too close to my sister to give up now. Sophal was torn. She was worried about my safety, but she understood I was not going to change my mind. I never returned to the comfort of my Grandmother's home for fear of missing a letter or news from my sister.

"Goodbye Sophal, *leahaey,*" I said as she was preparing to leave.

We both knew. This could be the last.

In Khao I Dang Camp, Koann didn't know for sure the identity of the person in the picture, but she was curious. The letter arrived out of the blue without any warning. How does one mentally process a letter from a sister who was believed to be dead? Koann was afraid to admit she couldn't identify the person in the photo. She knew it wasn't Siv Eng, but she still wanted to meet this person. What if her sister had survived? Residual hope was gaining momentum. Koann told a little white lie. It was time for her to meet this impersonator, whomever she may be.

"*Ja*, yes, this is my sister," she said with confidence while holding in her hand the picture of a stranger.

INTERVIEW WITH A SMUGGLER:
SEPTEMBER 1980

Nong Chan Refugee Camp, Cambodian/Thailand Border

Uncle Bun Tek wanted to ensure that I would be safely smuggled over the border. Even if it wasn't me, he didn't want the guilt of paying for someone to be killed crossing the border. Many crooked smugglers took their payment and then disappeared. Not just any smuggler would do. There were stories of refugees being deserted, robbed, killed, raped, or sold into slavery. Most people crossed with their families, but I was completely alone.

Aunt Kim Ly and Uncle Bun Tek vetted and interviewed a well-known smuggler. The man travelled all the way from Khao I Dang, Thailand to Mongkol Borei, Cambodia only to be denied by Aunt Kim Eung. She simply didn't trust him. The smuggler was sent back across the dangerous border to Uncle Bun Tek empty handed.

Back at Khao I Dang, the smuggler hastily explained the situation to Uncle Bun, "It is indeed your niece at Nong Chan, but Kim Eung refused to let me bring her back with me." Uncle Bun Tek had to pay the smuggler a fee even though I was left behind. The man was angry because he didn't get his full payment.

Uncle Bun Tek trusted the smuggler and re-hired him a second time, but this time it wasn't satisfactory to only have one smuggler. Bun Tek hired an additional sixty-year-old man to accompany me. This way, there would be a witness of the border crossing. Both smugglers had children and grandchildren living in Khao I Dang, and Bun Tek was confident they would return to their families. This time, they were sent straight to Nong Chan to meet me in person.

Not only had Uncle Bun Tek hired two smugglers from Khao I Dang, but Aunt Kim Eung also hired a young boy named Heng from Mongkol Borei. Heng arrived at Nong Chan and stayed with me for a few weeks. He explained that he was there to cross the border with me when the smugglers arrived. Heng posed as my brother at the orphanage. It was ironic that he played the part of an orphan because in real life he lost both his parents to the Khmer Rouge. Young Heng was given an immense task. He was to cross the dangerous border, witness the meeting between Koann and myself, and then return to Mongkol Borei to report to Ma Huoy and Aunt Kim Eung of my safe arrival. When the two smugglers arrived at camp, I knew it was safe to follow them. Koann had written a letter, and I instantly recognized her handwriting.

SPECIAL DELIVERY:
SEPTEMBER 1980

South Bend, Indiana, United States of America

When the letter arrived at YoKuy's home in South Bend, she was at work. Te grabbed the mail and opened the envelope as he was walking into the house. Could this be real? The enclosed picture didn't look like his sister, and he wasn't sure about the handwriting. Was it really Siv Eng? Te rode his bicycle to Uncle Su's house.

"Uncle Su, you must see this letter right away. It's signed, Siv Eng. Do you think she is alive?"

Uncle Su read and re-read the letter three times making sure he was processing correctly.

"This is unbelievable," he said as he grabbed the telephone.

He quickly dialed the number to Leonard's Fur Shop. YoKuy was there working at her electric sewing machine. It was unusual for her to be called to the phone at work.

"Je Kuy, I hope you are sitting down," said her brother, Su. "You're not going to believe this. I may have proof that Siv Eng is alive."

"Please let this be true. Please let this be true," she cried. A very strong woman lost all sense of herself and broke down in tears.

August 27, 1980

Nong Chan Camp, Thailand/Cambodia Border

Dear Mother,

I've been in Nong Chan Camp (near Khao I Dang) 15 days trying to find the way to cross the border to Khao I Dang and meet Uncle Bun Tek, Aunt Kim Ly, and Koann. They will try hard to find a way to get me safely out from Nong Chan Camp.

The situation right now is very dangerous to cross the border because Thai guards seriously control and watch the cross-border traffic. There is also the fear of robbery and kidnapping. I don't have the ability to get out of this place on my own. Hopefully, from there you can find the way to get me out of this camp soon as possible because it is not a safe place to be.

Goodbye Mother. Khnohm leahaey. I have so much to tell you, but there is not time now. I'm in a hurry to have this letter ready to send out to you.

Love from Your Long-Lost Daughter,

Siv Eng

P.S. All my love to our family there.

Looking forward to seeing everyone!

GOOD HEARTS, GOOD NEWS: SEPTEMBER 1980

LaGrange, Indiana, United States of America

They were sitting on their side porch rocking back and forth on the white swing and enjoying the Indiana Sunday sunshine. The two of them had a heart to help people in need. Grandpa Willis and Grandma Vera lived in the middle of corn fields on a dairy farm in LaGrange, Indiana. Willis and Vera made a habit of helping refugee families. When Willis read in the local newspaper that a family of Cambodians was living nearby, Vera immediately made some pie.

"Don't even think about tasting those pies, Grandpa," said Vera with a smile.

"Just a taste?" asked Grandpa.

"Not one bite, but I'll get you some ice cream," said Grandma as she stood up from the porch swing. Grandma was always serving people.

Willis and Vera faithfully brought the pies, fresh bread, vegetables, and berries from the garden to the family of YoKuy. It wasn't just about helping refugees. Visiting people in need was a part of their culture.

Kheat lived with YoKuy and her family and spoke English fluently. After the first meeting, the two families became fast friends. Two completely different cultures came together with the purpose of celebrating life and family. Willis was a pastor at Plato Mennonite Church in LaGrange, Indiana. When they learned of YoKuy's three missing children and family members, Willis and Vera prayed fervently for them daily.

Two prayer warriors across the ocean were praying for people they had never met. It was a joyous occasion when YoKuy shared the news that one of her daughters was alive.

ROAD TO KHAO I DANG: SEPTEMBER 1980

Prachinburi Province, Thailand

The two smugglers found me at the orphanage with Heng in Nong Chan. They had been vetted by Uncle Bun and now were being vetted by me. "This is from your sister," the younger man said.

> *Je Eng,*
>
> *September 14, 1980*
>
> *This is your destiny. You must come to Khao I Dang with these men right away. If you don't leave now, there is no one coming for you, and we may never see you again. We are hoping to leave camp in the coming week. I hope for your safety and to see you soon. Whatever you decide, I want you to know that our family is waiting here to reunite with you.*
>
> *Your Sister,*
>
> *Koann*

I read the words over and over again. I didn't have time to second guess a decision or check with my Aunt Kim Eung. I had nothing: no papers for identification, no gold or jewelry to trade. I only had a few clothing items and not one, not two, but three smugglers ready to start a perilous journey. I was dressed like a boy, wearing a shirt and pants. I also had the scarf my Grandmother Ma Huoy gave me when we said our last goodbye. The younger man was the designated leader and explained the seriousness of our situation.

"You should know that we could be killed at any time. You must listen to all instructions carefully and immediately. I can't guarantee your safety," he said. "Keep your eyes open. If I run, you run. Just aim to survive. I will lead you through, but if something happens, you are at your own risk."

It was an understatement to say that getting into Thailand was difficult and dangerous. Everyone in the western part of Cambodia wanted to reach Khao I Dang. It was the door to citizenship in several other countries.

Before we left, the older smuggler looked me over. "How are you going to make it across the border?" he balked. "You are too white." My skin hadn't seen the sun due to the endless hours of sewing indoors.

"Here, rub this mud on your face and cover your head with the scarf." I took Grandma's scarf and did as instructed.

I exhaled a silent prayer before we left.

"God of the Most High Universe, you've brought me this far. Please watch every step of our journey. I am under your wings."

The distance to Khao I Dang wasn't far, but we were taking the round-about way and zig zagging to avoid robbers and thieves. The smugglers knew the checkpoints and areas to avoid. My eye never left the leader's shirt tail for the entire journey. I planned to grab it, so I could follow him if he ran from thieves. Fear was ever-present, always a few steps ahead on the winding path.

My feet screamed in agony as we walked across a burned bamboo field. The stalks were like dull, pointy knives, slicing fragments of my foot with every step. Bits and pieces of my DNA were left in that field. My feet were cut to shreds, but I was more fearful of the robbers who were known to kidnap young girls.

From out of nowhere, it started pouring. The God of the Most High Universe sent a heavy rain; therefore, no one was patrolling due to the awful weather. Next, we crossed a rice field dam. It was like keeping your footing on a slippery balance beam. The rain that provided protection also blurred our vision. The four of us kept falling to one side or the other as we walked across the dam. At one point, a farmer spoke in Thai to my smuggler leader, and they smiled when they saw me. I understood their meaning to be, "Good for you." I later learned that the smuggler told the Thai man I was his wife and would be reunited with my children soon.

When we approached a river, a pool of fresh blood soiled the ground at our feet. A witness to recent violence. The dark stain was a sobering reminder of the ruthlessness of the robbers. Our head smuggler stopped our group, holding up his hand for silence. No one moved a muscle, and I was afraid to breathe.

He quietly whispered, "They like to wait at the river to make their move. It is to their advantage to take us by surprise. We have to cross quickly."

The water wasn't deep or wide but possessed a strong current. The sound of the river masked my fear and trembling. I was thankful that I was a strong swimmer. I didn't need coconuts to make it across. My father had taught me well. The boy Heng and I swam behind the men.

When we were within miles of Khao I Dang, we stayed at a camp where our smuggler had family. We had made it to relative safety for the night. I stayed in the tent of the smuggler's sister, and she showed me to a mat on the floor.

"I wish you and your sister the very best. You should be with her soon," she said. I could hardly sleep that night absorbing the nearness of Koann.

The next morning, I could see the mountain where the camp was, but once again we had to walk around in a circle, avoiding the direct route. It was evening when we arrived at Khao I Dang. Our lead smuggler began casually picking up pieces of wood for a disguise.

"Do as I do," he instructed. He knew how to speak Thai. We followed him as he walked up to the guard with his pile of firewood and made small talk. From there, we walked right through the gates of Khao I Dang. As soon as our leader signaled we were safe, we dropped the logs. My feet were blistered, my legs were exhausted, and my heart was pumping adrenalin with full speed. I was alive.

The men led me straight to Koann. We hugged and cried, and she looked me over.

"I can't believe it," said Koann. "My sister is alive and here with me."

I could hardly speak through my tears. I had dreamed of this moment for years. I was now together with Uncle Bun Tek, Aunt Kim Ly, and my long-lost sister. My poor Aunt Kim Ly hadn't slept all night because she was worried about me getting kidnapped. There was a sense of relief, yet we had a long way to go to get to the U.S. The next day, Heng, the young boy, returned to Mongkol Borei by bus to tell Grandma Ma Huoy and Aunt Kim Eung the news of my safe arrival. The two smugglers were paid in full by my uncle Bun Tek and remained in Thailand with their families.

At Khao I Dang, I was taken directly to the immigration office to get registered. Koann told them my story before I arrived so that they would be aware of my situation, and my information could be processed with their paperwork. We wanted to ensure we could leave the country together. Koann was relentless when she spoke with the authorities.

"I promise she is my sister. Please check our DNA if you don't believe us."

Koann and her parents had lived in Khao I Dang for two long years waiting for the proper paperwork. Years earlier, the officials wanted to fly Koann back to the U.S. to be with her biological family, but she refused to leave her adopted parents. She stood by them faithfully.

⸻⸻

When Koann and I had time to catch up, I shared with her the devastating news of the deaths of Aunt Chhiv Hong, Sok Yann, Pho, and Sourn Leng. I also explained how I hadn't heard from Uncle Kee or Aunt La Nee for several years. It was a sobering exchange.

Over the next few days, I relayed my experience of crossing the border, and Koann told me about hers. When Koann crossed the border to Khao I Dang with Bun Tek and Kim Ly, she emptied a bag of candy and wrapped the small jewelry pieces in the wrappers. Bun Tek was thinking ahead of the thieves. He had all the gold he possessed melted down into thin strips. He then wrapped the strips around a kettle handle and covered it with black. The kettle was openly carried across the border. It was solid gold. He also cut into his rubber shoe base and inserted more gold strips there. He even smartly concealed some along the seams of skirts and shirts. The flat strips were stuck everywhere.

SEPTEMBER – DECEMBER 1980

Chonburi Refugee Camp, Thailand

Four days after I arrived at Khao I Dang, the Bun Tek Family were unexpectedly approved to move to Chonburi Camp. It was the next camp on the way to freedom. If I didn't get to Khao I Dang in time, they would have had no choice but to leave without me. The timing was providential.

We stayed in Chonburi for three and a half months waiting to be shuffled to the next camp. Chonburi Camp was more sanitary than the Khao I Dang Camp, and the sleeping arrangements were a step up, but it was still a camp. I could have slept anywhere as long as I was near my sister.

At Chonburi, Koann and I volunteered to work with the Mennonite Central Committee organization or MCC. I had never heard of Mennonites before, but quickly learned that they were a kind, caring people on a humanitarian mission. The MCC tents were a ray of light at the end of a dark tunnel for many refugees. I assisted in feeding the sweet little children daily. The cook made a huge pot of soup and the multitudes of children lined up like little, wiggly ducklings. They were so cute and had such joy on their faces, making jokes and being silly, as children should. It was fulfilling to have a purpose, get involved, and make a difference. Serving the children was like a balm to my open wounds. Healing happened in Chonburi, and I made good friends. I was paid in full with the smiles and laughter of children.

----••◦●◦••----

After a few days in Chonburi, I happened to meet a woman who lived in Ou Krabau in the last days before the takeover.

"Siv Eng, I have news of the Pho family," she said. Although it was a painful revelation, any information was welcomed. I learned that not long after I left the village, Pho got official permission from the Chief to move Sourn Leng back to Ou Krabau. Soon after she arrived, the murderous killing frenzy began.

The woman continued her story, "In the last days of Ou Krabau, if someone was perceived to be happy about the Vietnamese invasion, they were killed without question. Pho was taken first. They killed him because he had been chosen by the people and acted as their leader. A few days later they came for his young wife, Sok Yann. The young couple were both buried in the jungle near Ou Krabau, their bodies were identified later in a shallow grave."

My tears flowed freely, a strong salty current released from a dam. The woman continued.

"Siv Eng, I saw a man who was wearing Pho's clothes, and the man's wife had Sok Yann's ring."

"What about Sourn Leng?" I asked, choking on my tears. "She was left all alone knowing her fate?" A ball of grief was forming in my throat.

"Yes," said the woman. "She was alone. A week later, she and all the villagers were taken away from Ou Krabau to avoid the Vietnamese invasion. She was killed after they left the village. Two soldiers came for your sister and the others in the middle of the night. All of her belongings were left in her hut, and her body was never found. At the very end, the Khmer Rouge took people by ox cart load to be killed. They planned to leave no witnesses to their brutal atrocities."

I absorbed this information, thinking of their last moments. Ko Pho, Sok Yann, and Sourn Leng were my whole world for the years living in captivity. I knew they were gone, but every bit of information was precious to me. According to the timeline, Pho, Sok Yann and Sourn Leng were killed around the same time that I was escaping from prison.

I had no time to process because we were preparing to leave Chonburi and I was kept busy with the children. I tucked this news in my heart. I was still alive and had more journeys to take.

⸺•••●•••⸺

One by one my newly made friends began to leave Chonburi and start a new life. Many went to Australia, Canada, France, and America. We tried to exchange addresses when possible, but some friends left so quickly we never said goodbye. The workers at MCC had become like another family to me. Koann continued to work by my side, and we made twenty-five American cents every day. I wasn't going to return to America empty handed. The change jingling in my pocket made a cheerful sound. Many people under the Khmer Rouge used money as toilet paper. It felt much better to earn it and keep it in my pocket.

LUMPINI CAMP: JANUARY 1981

Bangkok, Thailand

Finally, the immigration office called our names. For so many years we feared hearing our names called out, but today, we rejoiced. We left with approximately one hundred other refugees the same day. When the buses pulled away, I looked back and waved goodbye to my friends in Chonburi.

Lumpini was a nasty, smelly camp and appeared to be an empty market place. There was no safe place to sleep, so we made our beds on the ground. We slept by the sewer like so many others. Three women and one man. Uncle Bun Tek was consumed with worry for our safety. It was such a disgusting place, but we were only there for three days. Lumpini was a literal revolving door with groups of refugees entering the camp while others headed to the airport. We were finally taken by bus to the airport in Bangkok. When we boarded the jet, the fuselage smelled like the refugees who slept next to the sewer. It smelled like us.

Before communism, my family occasionally flew on a small commuter plane, but this was our first experience being on a large jet.

"This is unreal," said Koann. "We are as high as the clouds."

"And headed far away from our country," I said.

We both looked out the window. A note of sadness was hanging in the air. Goodbye Ma Huoy and Ma Mouy. Goodbye Sophal and Aunt Kim Eung. *Khnohm leahaey*. Memories were playing in my head like slow motion movie clips.

COMING TO AMERICA:
JANUARY 1981

San Francisco, California Refugee Camp

When the plane landed at the San Francisco airport, we were transported to yet another Refugee Camp. Koann and I carried all the possessions because Bun Tek and Kim Ly were older. Their bags were heavy with several random items that Uncle Bun Tek brought with him to America. Our assigned room at the camp was like a posh hotel. First, we all took very long showers, attempting to wash away the memories of the Khmer Rouge. We rinsed off our fear. We scrubbed off the dirt, grime, and smells of the sewer. I was careful not to wash away the treasured memories of my father or my heart for Cambodia. If only my brother and sister could be with me in America, given a fresh, clean start. I would have given anything to have them by my side.

The camp in San Francisco was exquisite. Everything we experienced was a culture shock. After showers, Koann and I celebrated our arrival by jumping on the mattresses like giddy school girls and falling asleep with exhaustion. We had beds and cots and actual pillows. The food was mouth-watering and consisted of huge dumplings with sausage. We savored every bite. We were all given winter coats as a welcoming gift. We were supposed to leave the next day and head to South Bend but were delayed once again.

On the third day there was a knock at our door.

"Who could it be?" I asked. Koann and I exchanged mutual looks of confusion.

"Is that someone crying?" she asked.

One of our relatives who lived in San Francisco had learned we were at the camp. He had been in San Francisco on a student visa at the time of the Khmer Rouge takeover. It was a happy reunion with tears of joy. Cousin Hourt took us out of the camp that night and brought us to his home.

He was so happy to see us that he delayed our flight for three more days. I wanted so badly to see my mom and siblings I hardly soaked up beauty of San Francisco. Back in South Bend, the sponsor church had planned a welcome party for us. We never made it to our own party.

"You really should stay here and make a living in San Francisco," he begged. "It is the place to be. The weather in South Bend at this time of year is very cold. It's like nothing you've ever experienced in Cambodia. You will be needing those winter coats if you stay in Indiana."

I did not come to America to enjoy the weather. I came to see my family.

A WHITE LANDING:
JANUARY 21, 1981

South Bend, Indiana, United States of America

Doubt crept in as we landed in Indiana. What was wrong with this place? Why did they have so many dead trees? My eyes were accustomed to the colors of Cambodia—varying shades of green, colorful skies, vibrant flowers, vivid blue water, and red dirt. Flying over Indiana, everything was white with patches of brown. The trees were brown, the ground was white, and the sky was a soupy grey. Was this strange place to be my new home? I now spoke very little English in a country where very few spoke Khmer. The town was small, and the dead trees were everywhere. The only cities I associated with America were New York and Los Angeles. Indiana was nothing like my idea of America. However, the destination was planned by God, and it held a purpose for me—it held my family.

As I stepped off the plane, I took each step with hope. I hadn't seen my family in almost seven years. The last time was in our home in Battambang as I left for university in 1974. Not only was I returning from the dead, I felt as if I were being born again. The seven years of separation were filled with a series of goodbyes, but today was a day for hello.

Walking down the gate to the terminal, I was overcome with emotion knowing I was about to see them, touch them, and hear their familiar voices. I first saw my family standing in the middle of the South Bend Airport. They were all there: my mom, my younger siblings, both grandparents, Uncle Be, Uncle Su, and Uncle Kheat with their families. There were eighteen of my family members in all. It was a beautiful moment. I hardly noticed the flashes of the camera from the local newspaper. Onlookers watched as we stopped and stared for a moment. Just a moment. It was an attempt to stop time.

In a flash, we ran to each other. There were no words, and the silence was wet with tears. Our embraces spoke volumes. My family had already heard through a relative that Sourn Leng and Pho were gone. We felt the weight of their absence and equally sensed their presence. I couldn't hug my siblings enough and kept going back for more. It was a privilege to look into their eyes and an honor to share the same space. I embraced my mother. I thought of all the nights I looked to the moon to send messages to her. Here she was in the present, in the now. I gazed, soaking up my mother's face like a thirsty sponge. There were many conversations waiting to be had, many heartaches longing to be heard, and many meals to be shared.

Te, Loan, and Nary weren't so young anymore. The last time I saw little Nary, she was throwing a temper tantrum on the floor before I left for college. Now she was a beautiful young lady. My brothers were both taller than me in size, but my heart had grown larger than ever. It was filled with an unspeakable peace and joy at seeing their smiling faces.

I longed to sit and be alone with my family, but from the airport, we were taken straight away to the South Bend Church. A welcoming party was being held in our honor to celebrate our return. We were served a strange food. It was flat, dry, stringy, and red, and it had no taste. Spaghetti, they told me—it didn't impress me at all.

My first meal with my long-lost family was anti-climactic and was shared in the company of thirty church sponsors. Among the spaghetti-filled Styrofoam plates, plastic table cloths, and folding chairs occupied by strangers, I attempted to share the sobering stories about

Ko Pho and Sourn Leng. Seven years of history could not possibly fit into a spaghetti dinner.

I could only communicate with my family in Khmer. My mother, YoKuy, was now fluent in English and served as my translator to speak with the English sponsors.

⋯⋯•••●•••⋯⋯

I cannot put into words how I felt in those first few weeks living at home with my family. I thought of Aunt Chhiv Hong; I had treasured her companionship and friendship through the years. I remembered my sister-in-law, Sok Yann. She had become like a true sister to me, a young bride who had loved Pho with all her heart from the beginning to the very end. My brother, Ko Pho, and my sister, Sourn Leng, were unable to attend our reunion in person, but I believe they knew I made it to snowy, white Indiana. I left them in Cambodia, but they did not leave my memory. They were the reason I was alive. The selfless care of my older, wiser brother nursed me back from the brink of death on several occasions. The palm leaf letter from my dear, missing sister spurred me to leave Ou Krabau and ultimately saved my life.

Now that I was safe in America with my family, far away from the Khmer Rouge, I no longer needed to climb to the tree canopy among the birds for fresh air. My escape, my memories, now took me to a very different place. I returned to our dingy hut in Ou Krabau to remember the true love demonstrated by Aunt Chhiv Hong, Sok Yann, Sourn Leng, and Pho when our worlds were falling apart. Memories forever cherished.

PSALM 68 NIV

May God arise, may his enemies be scattered;
may his foes flee before him.

2 May you blow them away like smoke—
as wax melts before the fire,
may the wicked perish before God.

3 But may the righteous be glad
and rejoice before God;
may they be happy and joyful.

4 Sing to God, sing in praise of his name,
extol him who rides on the clouds;
rejoice before him—his name is the LORD.

5 A father to the fatherless, a defender of widows,
is God in his holy dwelling.

6 God sets the lonely in families,
he leads out the prisoners with singing;
but the rebellious live in a sun-scorched land.

7 When you, God, went out before your people,
when you marched through the wilderness,

⁸ the earth shook, the heavens poured down rain,
before God, the One of Sinai,
before God, the God of Israel.

⁹ You gave abundant showers, O God;
you refreshed your weary inheritance.

¹⁰ Your people settled in it,
and from your bounty, God, you provided for the poor.

¹¹ The Lord announces the word,
and the women who proclaim it are a mighty throng:

¹² "Kings and armies flee in haste;
the women at home divide the plunder.

¹³ Even while you sleep among the sheep pens,
the wings of my dove are sheathed with silver,
its feathers with shining gold."

¹⁴ When the Almighty scattered the kings in the land,
it was like snow fallen on Mount Zalmon.

¹⁵ Mount Bashan, majestic mountain,
Mount Bashan, rugged mountain,

¹⁶ why gaze in envy, you rugged mountain,
at the mountain where God chooses to reign,
where the Lord himself will dwell forever?

¹⁷ The chariots of God are tens of thousands
and thousands of thousands;
the Lord has come from Sinai into his sanctuary.

¹⁸ When you ascended on high,
you took many captives;
you received gifts from people,
even from the rebellious—
that you, Lord God, might dwell there.

¹⁹ Praise be to the Lord, to God our Savior,
who daily bears our burdens.

²⁰ Our God is a God who saves;
from the Sovereign Lord comes escape from death.

Praise be to God!

EPILOGUE

Not long after living in South Bend, I was driving with my sponsor around town when I saw a blue church sign with the shadow of a dove.

I learned that the symbol of the dove stood for the Holy Spirit of the Christian Church. The sign spurred my curiosity, and I was drawn in. I now have a personal relationship with Jesus Christ and am forever thankful that God met me in my darkest hour on the floor of that prison. I did not discover Psalm 68 or the reference to the golden dove until the writing of this story.

I married the son of the praying grandparents, Willis and Vera, who reached out to my family and many other refugees. I am forever thankful for their legacy of servanthood. I now live in California with my husband, Willis Junior, and my mother, YoKuy.

Of the thirteen of us who left the apartment on April 19, 1975, only three survived: myself and two of Aunt La Nee and Uncle Kee's children. Of the six other relatives who left Phnom Penh with us, only one survived. I have travelled back to Cambodia on two occasions. I visited the village of Khla Kham Chhkae, the city of Phnom Penh, and my home in Battambang. I saw Phnom Sampeau with the golden Buddha in the cave and the prison in Pursat where I was held. I took pictures with Ma Mouy and travelled to Angkor Wat. My mother and I sat on the very bench under the same tree where I learned that my family was still alive.

I remember so that I don't forget.

ACKNOWLEDGMENTS

I want to give a special thanks to Koann, Te, and Melaine for sharing the private pieces of your lives and trusting me to tell your story. To Sonny, your military expertise and hours of discussion about Khmer culture were invaluable. To Mom, for being my very first editor, proofreader, traveling companion, and recording assistant. To Dad, for being my number one fan and history expert. To Laurie, Holly, Carrie H, Aunt Leona, Ron, Carolyn, Jen and Cassie, I've treasured your enthusiasm and patience with reading the many versions of my manuscript. Kudos to Jill R and Mandie J. Your last minute read through was a lifesaver. To Carrie R., wine + take out sushi = savory metaphors. Barclay, Liv, Em and Harry—thanks for supporting this endeavor and my many trips to California. To Ma Mouy, I've never met you, yet I will never forget you. To YoKuy, every time I eat mi cala, I will think of you. To Uncle Junior, a gracious host, chauffer, and the provider of 2:00 a.m. snacks. To Aunt Siv Eng, I will never forget the precious moments we shared. May your life story of family bonds and faith live forever.

Heather

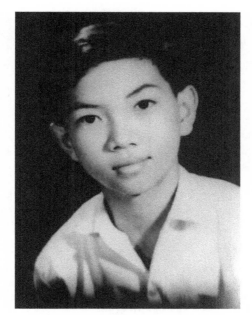

Pho

Siv Eng

Sourn Leng

Bun Huor

Aunt Chhiv Hong (YoKuy's sister)

The Funeral of Bun Huor at the Buddhist Temple in 1967
From left to right: YoKuy holding Nary, Pho, Siv Eng, Sourn Leng,
Koann, Te, and Loan

Grandma Lap So and Grandpa Bun Suy (YoKuy's parents)

The Wedding Reception for Pho and Sok Yann at the city Swimming Pool
Reception Center in Battambang, 1973
Back Row: YoKuy's cousin in-law, Grandpa Bun Suy (YoKuy's father), Uncle
Kee (married to La Nee), YoKuy's cousin, YoKuy's nephew, YoKuy's nephew
and YoKuy's cousin.
Front Row: Grandma Lap So (YoKuy's mother), YoKuy, Sok Yann's cousin, Siv
Eng, Sok Yann, Pho, YoKuy's cousin, Sourn Leng, Chhiv Lee (a cousin and
best friend of Siv Eng)

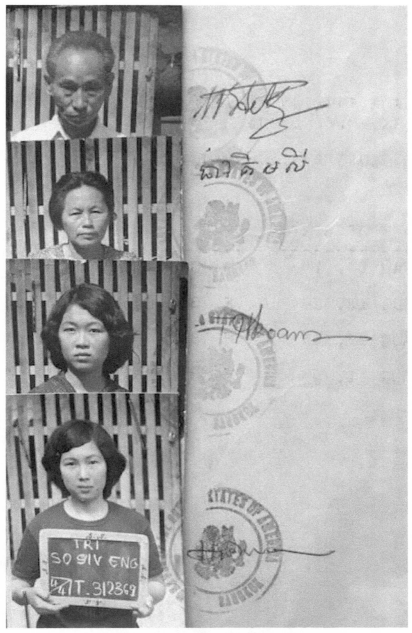

Official pictures taken at Chonburi Refugee Camp in
Thailand in December 1980.
From top: Bun Tek, Kim Ly (YoKuy's cousin), Koann, and Siv Eng

The special tree at Angkor Wat – a return trip to Cambodia 2002.
Seated in the center: YoKuy (left) and Siv Eng (right)

YoKuy (left) visiting Ma Mouy (right)
on a return trip to Cambodia – 2002.

Our Home in Battambang near the Lady with the Rice Stack – a return trip
to Cambodia 2017.
From the left: YoKuy, Siv Eng, Willis Junior
(Siv Eng's husband), and Jenna (Siv Eng's daughter).

YoKuy's 80th Birthday Celebration.
Back Row, from the left: Loan, Nary, Koann, Siv Eng, and Te
Seated Front Row: YoKuy

GLOSSARY

Arkoun – Thank you.

Bâbâ – A very thin soup made of rice and water with barely any rice in it.

Bat – A word for "yes" only used by males.

Chap laeng – Let's go.

Chap, chap – Hurry.

Class de Terminale – The last grade level before graduation from high school.

Coining – A healing practice also known as *gua sha*.

Dopp kbal – Ten heads.

Hea – A Chinese honorific that means "older brother."

Ja – A word for "yes" only used by females.

Je – An honorific used when addressing an older sister.

Jouy phong – Help.

Khnhom strektuk – I am thirsty.

Kmeng touch – Little one.

Kmouy – A term of endearment that means "little niece."

Ko – An honorific used when addressing an older brother.

Krâma – A versatile scarf.

Kraok laeng – Wake up.

Leahaey – Goodbye.

Lokru – Male teacher.

Mai Om – Mother Aunt.

Majuer – Head student of the class.

Met – a new form of address used under the Khmer Rouge regime.

Met Bong – a form of address used by civilians to refer to Khmer Rouge soldiers and Mulethan.

Met Neary – A female form of address used by the Khmer Rouge.

Ming – An honorific used when addressing an older woman who is not a relative.

Mreas prov leaf – Holy basil.

Neak – An honorific used when addressing an older woman.

Neakru – A female teacher.

Nhnhum – Smile.

Om – An honorific used when addressing a person who is older than you, but younger than your parents.

Ongkrong – Red ants that live in the trees.

Ott tay – No.

Paa Hum – A special Cambodian blanket.

Phnom – Mountain.

Phum – Village.

Pouk – Khmer word for father.

Prâhok – Fermented fish paste.

Remok – A bike with a carriage that pulls passenger from behind.

Riel – Currency used in Cambodia.

Sampeah – A formal, Cambodian bow used in greeting.

Sampot chang kben – Traditional, ceremonial Cambodian clothing.

Ses – Students.

BIBLIOGRAPHY

Locard, Henri. *Pol Pot's Little Red Book: The Sayings of Angkar*. Chiang Mai, Thailand: Silkworm Books, 2004.

Maps of Cambodia. Creative commons on wikipedia

CPSIA information can be obtained
at www.ICGtesting.com
Printed in the USA
LVHW030348110121
676155LV00006B/1153